National Income and Nature: Externalities, Growth and Steady State

Economy & Environment

VOLUME 5

The titles published in this series are listed at the end of this volume.

National Income and Nature: Externalities, Growth and Steady State

edited by

J. J. Krabbe

and

W. J. M. Heijman

Wageningen Agricultural University, Wageningen, The Netherlands

SPRINGER SCIENCE+BUSINESS MEDIA, B.V.

Library of Congress Cataloging-in-Publication Data

National income and nature : externalities, growth, and steady state / edited by J.J. Krabbe and W.J.M. Heijman.
p. cm. -- (Economy and environment ; v. 5)
Includes index.
ISBN 978-94-010-5143-9 ISBN 978-94-011-2590-1 (eBook)
DOI 10.1007/978-94-011-2590-1
1. Economic development--Environmental aspects. 2. National income. 3. Externalities (Economics) I. Krabbe, J. J. (Jacob Jan), 1928- . II. Heijman, Willem. III. Series: Economy & environment ; 5.
HD75.6.N38 1991
333.7--dc20 91-38236
CIP

ISBN 978-94-010-5143-9

Originally published by Kluwer Academic Publishers in 1992

ACKNOWLEDGEMENTS

The International Society for Intercommunication of New Ideas arranged a congress at the *Université de Paris Sorbonne* in August 1990. The convention was organized by Anghel N. Rugina, Emeritus Professor at Northeastern University, Boston, and President of the Society. At this congress a series of papers in the field of environmental and resource economics was presented, which served as the basis of this collection of essays on national income and nature. The collection was further developed and some studies were added.

We would like to thank Henk Folmer, Professor of Economics at Wageningen Agricultural University for his support in outlining the collection. Roel Jongeneel, Lecturer at the Department of General Economics, Wageningen Agricultural University, should also be mentioned for his substantial help in editing the book. We would also like to thank Mrs. M.C. Rigg-Lyall BA and Mrs. A. Kooijman-Timmers for their valuable linguistic suggestions.

The editors

ACKNOWLEDGEMENT

CONTENTS

INTRODUCTION

Since the 'environmental revolution' began in the late 1960s, economists have done a lot of work in the field of economic theory-building on the preservation of nature. Meanwhile, environmental economic literature has swelled to a large stream of articles in journals of different signature. As a result, a coherent economic view of the phenomenon of environmental degradation has emerged. Several kinds of 'green' public policies and their impacts on both nature and the performance of the economy have been analysed. The feasibility of specific types of policy has also been discussed. The aim of the book is to provide an insight into the ways economists analyse the problems of environmental pollution and the depletion of natural resource. To this purpose a number of articles have been selected. Some of them have a fundamental character, others an applied nature and are foremost, practically oriented. The presentation of the collection emphasizes our belief that economists are able to deliver an essential contribution to the design of policies to protect nature. It is clear that 'nature' and 'environment' may no longer be regarded as 'free gifts' to society. Rather, they have to be seen as scarce resources, and environmental disruption and resource depletion as allocation problems. If a natural resource is scarce, a price must be charged in accordance with the degree of scarcity since otherwise society will be confronted with misallocations.

In this connection there are two topics which are of particular interest to economists. The first is the role environmental externalities play in the system of 'economy and nature'; the second, the relationship between resource depletion and environmental degradation, and economic growth. These topics form the themes of this collection of essays. The book offers a variety of economic approaches to the problems mentioned and describes a number of different policy issues aimed at incorporating nature in economic decision making. National income functions as a main indicator of a country's economic performance. A direct relationship exists between social production and GNP, as is reflected in detail in the system of national accounts. There is also a link between economic policy and GNP-growth. Growth of GNP is commonly regarded as the main condition for the continuation of the Western welfare state and a rising consumption level in developing countries. However, the GNP indicator has some real flaws, of which the unsatisfactory reflection of the utilization of nature is not the least important. On the one hand, nature can be regarded as a supplier of a big variety of means of production. On the other hand, it serves as a public consumption good and as a receptacle of wastes. It is these competing and conflicting functions of nature which raises severe problems of a fundamental and practical nature. Traditional approaches have not always dealt with this arbitrary character of GNP in a satisfactory and theoretically consistent way. In this volume, there are a number of contributions which aim at solving these problems and avoiding inconsistencies.

This volume is divided into two parts. Part One is devoted to environmental externalities. Here attention is focused on character, valuation and accounting of such external effects. Part Two deals with the relation between nature and economic growth. It provides an investigation into the dynamics of this relationship. The impact of economic growth on environment and resource availability is analysed. In this context, attention is also paid to the implication of technological change and to the concept of steady state. Methodological aspects of the way problems are approached are eludicated as well.

Part One begins with a reflection by Krabbe on the significance of Pigouvian welfare economics for environmental economics. Pigou's approach to welfare is tied to his concept of national income, incorporating the idea of externalities. When applied to the environmental problem, not only the volume of the national product counts, but also its composition. A direct link with the system of national accounts is established.

In the second chapter, Hueting focuses on the valuation problem of nature in the absence of markets. Shadow prices should be computed on the basis of 'artificial' supply and demand curves, taking into account sustainability standards for the components of nature concerned. These computed prices have to be used to correct national income for environmental losses.

In Chapter Three, den Butter chooses a different approach from, for example, Hueting. Instead of arguing for a correction of GNP, he proposes the construction of an explicit environmental quality index. Using different methodologies, such as average and geometric means, CES aggregator functions and principal components, indexes are developed which summarize all available (time series) data on the state of pollution and environmental damage.

Adger and Whitby in the subsequent chapter analyse how the existence of land use externalities can be incorporated into the system of national accounts. They illustrate their methodology by a case study on Great Britain's agriculture and forestry and show the high informational requirements necessary to correct the traditional accounts.

A related chapter is provided by Thijssen and Laan. Using a model of the Dutch intensive livestock sector, they evaluate two policy scenarios aimed at reducing the sector's ammonia emissions by 75% of the 1986 level by the year 2000. The first scenario comprises abatement measures and involves reducing the number of animals, while the second scenario focuses on levying taxes on the agricultural output price and on the subsidization of farm incomes.

The international aspect of pollution abatement is dealt with by Bergman, Cesar and Klaassen in Chapter Six. They show how the ex-ante costs of additional emission control for individual countries can be significantly reduced by using a relatively simple cost-sharing scheme. They demonstrate a mode of operation for such a scheme, which could be established by introducing a supra-national institution, such as a 'European environmental protection fund'. Several game theoretical implications are also discussed.

Part Two of this volume begins with a chapter by Nentjes and Wiersma on the relation between economic growth, technological progress and environment. The authors provide a survey of the literature on the economic growth debate. Moreover they analyse the relation between environmental pollution and economic growth within a macroeconomic framework of reference. Attention is also paid to ways of stimulating innovations in pollution control at a micro level.

In Chapter Eight Heijman analyses the relation between population growth and the possibility of a steady state economy. Beginning with an elaboration on steady state concepts, he then looks at the role of abatement of environmental damage, the importance of renewable resources, the development of the ecosystem and the impact of nature-conserving technical change, using a number of models.

The two last chapters have a somewhat philosophical character. In Chapter Nine Karsten explains the evolution of economic theory, drawing on the first and second law of thermodynamics and on Hegel's dialectics. The entropy law forms the major link which connects economics to the larger physical and social system of which it is a part. Karsten argues that this linkage of economics with the rest of reality is of essential importance to the understanding of the evolution of economic paradigms. The role of the economist as impartial spectator is also questioned.

Finally, in Chapter Ten Jongeneel describes the methodological differences between the neo-classical and the steady state approach to environmental economics. Drawing on the philosophy of science literature, he discusses the problem of how non-economic aspects within economics can be approached.

Part One

EXTERNALITIES

Chapter 1

NATURE IN PIGOUVIAN ORIENTED ECONOMICS

Jacob Krabbe*

The figure expressing the volume of national production or national income gives an indication of the prosperity of a community. However, nowadays eyes have been opened to the fact that the process of production and consumption is a burden on the environment. Certain capacities of nature are being threatened or are even declining, and it is recognized that this is hampering prosperity. Therefore there is a wish to relativize the national income figure; to do justice to the environmental effects of economic process. This chapter deals with attempts to do so. In it the train of thought moves from environmental welfare economics, via 'Pigouvian' economics and the system of national accounts to preservation policy. Attention is given to indices of nature quality and to institutional matters, since political considerations oriented towards national accounts should be complemented with standards and instruments of preservation policy.

1. Nature in general welfare economics

In this context, general environmental welfare economics is conceived of as the most complete and detailed presentation of welfare theory, oriented on the utilization of the production factor nature. So, in this type of theory, the question of the optimum distribution of income is discussed and there is room for all kinds of welfare functions and production functions. Other basic features of the general model are its dynamics (so that the phenomena of degeneration of nature as well as exhaustion of natural resources can be represented), the substitutability of the production factors under consideration, and the impact of induced technology on the capabilities of

* J.J. Krabbe is Associate Professor of Economics, Wageningen Agricultural University.

nature and the quantities of natural stocks. This section also examines characteristics of this general theory model in the context of the idea of nature preservation.

Degeneration and production of nature

The functioning of nature in the economic process has many facets. Therefore, in environmental welfare economics, the factor nature must be represented as a multifarious factor of production and consumption, at least in principle. The model must be capable of reflecting that, in the economic process, components of nature are utilized in various ways. It must also reflect the fact that certain components are favoured by nature preservation measures. Thus, nature must be seen as a complex means of production and direct consumption and also as subject to production.

The welfare theory model must reflect substitution processes, also within the sphere of nature. In this way it elucidates the implications of substituting certain components of nature that have grown comparatively expensive with cheaper ones, within or beyond the category nature. Therefore, in the context of utilization of nature, one can speak of internal and external compensation (Krabbe, 1983). Thus the specification of the category nature must also be tuned to the problem of compensation for losses in specific qualities of nature by gains in other welfare-determining factors, as far as such compensations make sense from a political point of view.

Further it is useful for the data of the model to correspond with a system of environmental quality indicators of a natural science origin. This set of quality indicators should include indices of the quantities of the natural stocks available. Since environmental problems have a spatial dimension, it should be possible to regionalize the model.

Nature as an organistic entity is affected by pollution. The two main aspects of this phenomenon should be expressed in the model. First, there is the function of nature as the environment of life on earth, as far as nature functions beyond the sphere of production with the help of scarce means. In this context, attention is focused on the direct appraisal of nature by man. Second, nature functions as a production factor, *e.g.* in agriculture. As such, its capacities are also under pressure. Therefore, the model should include a detailed representation of the production factor nature. Furthermore, the model should contain not-aggregated production functions in physical terms, as well as prices and deductively determined shadow prices of the products and means concerned.

It appears to be no easy task to decide on actual social preferences on the basis of the set of data provided by the microscopic picture of general welfare economics. Heertje (1990) coped with this problem by introducing a social aims function into the detailed theoretical structure. Preferences of future generations were inserted on the basis of the postulate of identification of such desires by the present generation.

Quality indices of nature

Quality indicators of components of nature form an essential element in environmental economics. Such indicators may have a natural science character. The insertion of these quality indicators in welfare economics brings some difficulties with it. The problems are comparatively easy to overcome on a micro level. On a macro level, however, one is confronted with the problem of the aggregation of basic indicators. Georgescu-Roegen posited (1976, p.9) the solution as being in the idea of entropy. According to him, "the Law of Entropy is the taproot of economic scarcity". He believed that the concept of entropy has an anthropoid character. In this vision, the idea of entropy forms the link between the social and the natural sciences. From a general scientific point of view this idea is valuable. However, it is not yet clear how it can be operationalized in economic theory and in policy based on it.

A topical idea in the sphere of quality indicators of nature is the concept of 'sustainability' of the socio-economic process, in cohesion with the capacities of nature. Pearce and Turner (1990, p.24) maintained that a policy of sustainability implies the rules:

> Utilise renewable resources at rates less than or equal to the natural rate at which they can regenerate.
> Optimise the efficiency with which non-renewable resources are used, subject to substitutability between resources and technological progress.

One is looking for holistic indices that indicate whether, and to what degree, economic activity violates sustainability. This index must be based on actual values of a number of indicators. Yet, it is no easy task to find a complete set of data in the complicated picture of cause and effect in the world of affection and exhaustion of nature.

A specific problem is that various types of welfare consideration must be introduced into the aggregated sustainability index. The first type of consideration concerns the determination of what the ideal state of nature is that the actual situation is related to. The second type of welfare consideration is the determination of the weights in the aggregation process assigned to the basic indicators. The third type is the valuation of the gap between the actual and the ideal situation. What must be avoided is that the same welfare consideration of nature is reflected twice in one model. The various welfare considerations must be complementary to one another, shaping the unique picture of social preference.

In the theoretical context of social oriented welfare economics it is not so difficult to formulate quality indices of nature (Krabbe, 1989, Ch.9). Yet, a nearly insoluble practical problem is how the various social welfare considerations can be quantified beyond the sphere of prices and shadow prices.

Extension of the pricing system

Welfare theory representing events directly oriented towards the market only is not broad enough to elucidate the optimal utilization of nature. This is bound up with the fact that a government has specific responsibilities for the quality of the environment of life and for the preservation of natural resources. Thus, on a hypothetical basis, the basic image of the pricing mechanism has to be extended.

The additional hypothetical market segment may reflect situations in which government is considered to be the supplier of components of nature and, moreover, to represent the users of it. An example of this is a recreational area freely used by the public. Shadow prices must be determined on the basis of social opportunity costs on the one hand and demand functions on the other, the latter either on an empirical basis or derived from individual utility functions or a social utility function. The additional market segment may also refer to situations in which rights to utilize some components of nature are offered by the government at a certain price, and demanded by private individuals. An example of such tradeable property rights to nature is a market where pollution permits are negotiated such as unused emission permits granted on a historical basis, known as 'grandfathering'. Howe (1991), referring to Freeman, Tietenberg and Portney, noted that tradeable discharge systems are recommended on the grounds that:

(1) such systems can, under some conditions, reach the specified ambient standards at costs approaching a minimum; (2) the system motivates polluting parties to seek their own minimum cost solution; (3) it stimulates the search for better technologies because of the market value of the permits held; and (4) it can accommodate changing demands for pollution emission resulting from changes in industry and population.

The situation in which a government levies pollution fees can also be considered as a market for nature. In this case tariffs function as prices.

It should be noted that if the supply and demand of property rights to nature is entirely in the private sphere, then a government, in order to make prices justifiable from a social point of view, may have reason to intervene in the market through specific taxes and subsidies. There are two principle arguments for this. The 'prisoner's dilemma' would frustrate rational choice in the utilization of nature. The individual producer or consumer could wonder what the effect of his nature conservating behaviour would be, if he were to be one of the few to act in this way. In such cases, levies are substituted for voluntary spendings in favour of nature preservation. Another argument for government intervention is the specific responsibility of a government to future generations. The decision horizon of a government lies further in the future than that of individual members of society, or even of big firms. This means that, from a social point of view, the interest rate at which future needs and sources of wealth are discounted may be considerably below the actual interest. The result of economic behaviour oriented towards comparatively high interest rates is a redundant use of nature. The obvious response of government is a fiscal system that is also directed towards nature preservation.

It will be clear that environmental welfare economics is based in price determining institutions.

2. The Pigouvian approach

Approaching welfare in the tradition of Pigou forms the link between general welfare theory and the system of national accounts. In his *Economics of welfare*, Pigou (1932, p. 31) stated:

Just as economic welfare is that part of total welfare which can be brought directly or indirectly into relation with a money measure, so the national dividend is that part of the objective income of the community, including, of course, income derived from abroad,

> which can be measured in money. The two concepts, economic welfare and the national dividend, are thus co-ordinate, in such wise that any description of the content of one of them implies a corresponding description of the content of the other.

Pigou's 'national dividend' can be interpreted as the present day's concept of net national income, indicated by the symbol Y, where external effects are included. Pigou gave an extra dimension to the symbol Y, that has the double meaning of production and the aggregate of incomes. It can also be said that Pigou threw light on a specific characteristic of the income aspect of the concept Y.

Pigou's welfare idea may be seen as a specific interpretation of the general welfare idea. To this end, a number of restrictions ought to be placed on the general idea. The homogeneous welfare function should be conceived of as linear (Krabbe, 1974, p.60). Optimizing utility, the Lagrange multiplier should be unity. Further, all production functions must be homogeneous to the first degree. In this context, Mäler (1990) mentioned the linear support of the Hamiltonian to the social welfare function.

The distribution of income was recognised by Pigou as a complicating factor. Only if this distribution is considered to be optimal is there no problem. In other cases Pigou believed that the national dividend, in its property as welfare indicator, is subject to correction.

In Pigou's theory the idea of externalities serve as a basis for correcting the national dividend. Speaking about the divergence he noticed between private and social national product, Pigou (1952, p. 192) stated:

> It is plain that divergences between private and social net product of the kinds we have so far been considering cannot, like divergences due to tenancy laws, be mitigated by a modification of the contractual relation between any two contracting parties, because the divergence arises out of a service or disservice rendered to persons other than the contracting parties. It is, however, possible for the State, if it so chooses, to remove the divergence in any field by 'extraordinary encouragements' or 'extraordinary restraints' upon investments in that field. The most obvious forms which these encouragements and restraints may assume are, of course, those of bounties and taxes.

Applied to environmental problems, the Pigouvian approach implies the principle that the polluter pays, by way of internalizing environmental effects.

Yet, Nentjes (1990) remarked that direct government prescriptions in the sphere of nature preservation are also in accordance with the polluter pays principle. In this connection, Nentjes talked of the centrally guided economy of the environment.

Sustainability

In the Netherlands, a group of scientists from various disciplines together with policy makers were trying to construct a 'sustainability index' to reflect to what degree the exploitation and burdening of natural reserves deviates from a durable or sustainable level of exploitation and burdening (Kuik and Verbruggen, 1990). It appears that, in order to obtain an aggregated figure, the various basic indicators have to be weighted according to 'social valuations' of these figures. Thus, welfare theory considerations function as a tool in the process of aggregation. A further step might be to transform this aggregated index into an index that is comparable with the figure of national income. The function expressing this transformation is a kind of Pigouvian welfare function, bringing quality of nature under the 'measuring rod of money'. Besides the problem of social valuation, there are several technical problems in selecting and measuring the basic indicators.

Next to this pragmatic approach, Mäler's typically theoretical approach should be mentioned. Mäler (1990) defined sustainable development as a development in which net national income never decreases. However, his concept of national income is a specific one. It comprises production in households, including measures in the private sphere for improving the environment of life. Further, the purity of the environment and the current value of the stock of natural resources are included, both valued at household's marginal valuation. The value of the change in this stock is also in the concept, at prices reflecting its future value.

Mäler came to the remarkable conclusion that, if national income is conceived of as a measure of welfare, wages should not be included in the national income. Yet, for the sake of macroeconomic analysis, he did not object passing over this aspect, following the custom of including the income from labour in national income.

In Mäler's model, the change in natural stocks is conceived of as a form of saving, or dissaving, which it usually is. So net national income is determined by the value of production, minus degradation of flow capacities of nature at household's valuation, plus savings in which depreciation of natural stocks are taken into account.

Opschoor (1990) suggested estimating the depreciation of 'environmental capital'. He first proposed a holistic indicator tuned to the set of macroeconomic data for use in economic policy. He then proposed a system of 'resource accounts', functioning as 'satellites' of the conventional system of national accounts. Opschoor's approach may also be seen as being oriented towards the Pigouvian world of ideas.

Lost paradise: new scarcity

The question arises as to how far environmental degradation is subject to subtraction of the figure expressing national income. In Paradise there are no prices and thus the value of national income is zero. This truth illustrates that national income is also an index of scarcity. Even the Classics in economics were aware of the phenomenon of the existence of 'new scarcity' in economic development. Therefore, as far as degeneration of nature affects production and leads to high prices, it cannot be excluded from national income. This does not alter the fact it would be of great use to reflect this effect in the system of national accounts.

Yet, if consumer's valuation is under discussion, as far as it is effectuated outside the sphere of the market, there is ground for subtracting degradation of nature under the influence of the economic process. Mäler's appraisal of the degree of purity of the environment and that of the volume of natural stocks can serve as an example. Both Mäler's and Opschoor's valuations of the current decline in the stock of natural resources are based on a broadening of the current idea of disinvestment. It requires proper assumptions about the economic situation in the future.

Price determining institutions

Relating total degradation of nature, valuated in terms of money, to the national income is not the only nor even the most important aspect of Pigouvian welfare economics. This comparison may be of some political significance but offers no insight into the process itself. Noting the various aspects of the degradation process reflected in the system of national accounts is more informative. In this way, the structure of the national production, including its environmental effects, is elucidated.

This production structure is conditioned by indirect and direct price determining institutions. Examples of the latter include abatement fees, royalties, subsidies and specific turnover taxes. Further, environmental technology is induced by the price structure, with its institutional dimension (see the appendix to this chapter). Thus an institutional analysis is part of environmental welfare economics. In this context Nijkamp and Verbruggen

(1990) spoke of 'sustainability incentives'. Direct price determining institutions, already mentioned by Pigou, form a part of the structure of institutional incentives.

3. Preservation policy oriented towards national accounts

The significance of welfare economics to preservation policy depends upon whether and to what degree the points of departure of welfare theory are adopted in policy. The implications of actual welfare theory axiomas to the system of national accounts are subject to comparison with current figures. The next step is to design a system of measures which will bring the facts into accordance with aims.

Policy of nature preservation is implemented along various lines. One line of policy lies in determining the government budget directly, since government expenditures and subsidies to protect the environment can vary in magnitude. Another line is directed towards institutional constellation. Actors in socio-economic intercourse are forced or induced to act in certain ways. This has an impact on receipts and expenditures both in the private and the public sphere. The effects of both lines of policy are reflected in the system of national accounts.

Interpreting national accounts

Nature preservation should be considered as a form of production. In national accounts, this kind of production is reflected at various places. First there is the abatement sector. Nature 'produced' in this sector can be considered either as a welfare increase (given a certain production situation) or as a necessary additional production effort (given a certain environmental situation). Further, in the accounts of the government sector, funds are granted for a number of other activities to preserve nature. Just as in the case of other government activities, it is assumed that the value of the productive activity is equal to expenses made for this purpose. Yet, it makes sense to be critical on this point.

The above data are subject to judgement in the context of comparative analyses. Comparison may be intertemporal, but it may also involve various economies. Figures should not to be related to the volume of the national income only. The volume of the abatement activities should especially be seen in proportion to the polluting components of the national production.

Consideration of complementary data

Preservation policy is also oriented towards data that are nowadays not included in the system of national accounts. Such a complementary figure may be a sustainability index in which welfare considerations serve for aggregation purposes only. Judging this index in the way of welfare theory, it is a fundamental question whether it has a 'non-lexicographic' character or not. The axiom of non-lexicographically was introduced into welfare economics by Debreu (1954). It states that the component of welfare is supposed to be substitutable with other welfare components. If the political conviction is that no sustainability of nature must be sacrificed at all, then for the sake of production, sustainability is supposed to be ordered *lexicographically* (with a fixed ordering towards other welfare components as letters in the alphabet are). If the quality index is expressed in the Pigouvian way, this implicates the axiom of *non-lexicographically*.

The sustainability index can be based on various ideas. Some authors propose estimating the costs of hypothetical preservation projects for this purpose.

Another fundamental political problem arises if sustainability figures of the Mäler type are taken into consideration. In Mäler's conception the appraisal of nature is based partly on household valuations outside the market mechanism. Yet, it is questionable whether the degree of perspective declination of future needs in this valuation is in accordance with the view of policy makers. Policy makers who consider nature as a 'merit good' give more weight to nature when valuating future needs.

Implications of pricing

Direct price determining institutional measures will change the picture of national accounts. A price change, by definition, implicates a change in volume as it is the product of price and quantity. However, the picture of national accounts is also affected by all kinds of substitution processes.

In order to economize on nature, this production factor should not be too cheap, as environmental oriented technology is induced by comparatively high prices for this factor. A shift of taxes from the factor labour to the factor nature would serve preservation policy (Krabbe,1990).

4. Conclusions

Internalization of nature in welfare economics appears to be a rather complicated matter, especially if the theory has to have practical significance. Via Pigouvian welfare economics and the system of national accounts, a fruitful link can be laid between general environmental welfare theory and preservation policy. It is useful to complement the latter system by specific quality indices of nature, reflecting the purity of the environment of life and the quantities of natural stocks that are currently used up as well as those that are still available.

Appendix: The technology - price ratio factor

In this appendix attention is focused on the problem of the impact of the price ratio of production factors on the use of these factors. Two production factors are mentioned: nature and labour. Yet these can be replaced by, for example, two components of nature: a very scarce one and one that is comparatively abundantly available. The approach is such that room is made for various substitution elasticities.

The basic model

The basic model, with a restricted number of magnitudes in which technology is considered to be given, has the following form. Production (Y) is an increasing function of the amount of nature (N), the amount of labour (L) and the amount of capital (K); the price of a product is supposed to be unity. Thus:

$$Y = Y(N, L, K)$$

In this model K is considered to be exogenous[1]. Production factors are supposed to be rewarded according their prices. The price of nature (P_N) is

1 In a long-term analysis the factor capital may be deleted from the production function, since capital is a derived production factor. In this approach, however, mutual substitution between two factors, nature and labour, has a specific character, and the returns to both of these factors are partially capital income.

the sum of the income pro unit of nature (p_N) and an environmental levy (t); the price of labour (P_L) is the wage (p_L) minus a subsidy pro unit of labour (s). So, if Y satisfies linear homogeneity:

$$Y = P_N N + P_L L + P_K K \tag{1}$$

$$P_N = p_N + t, \quad P_L = p_L - s \tag{2}$$

Levy t and subsidy s are set by government policy, which faces the following budget constraint:

$$tN - sL \geq 0 \tag{3}$$

The substitutability between the production factors under the influence of the transfer of income from nature to labour is given by the equation:

$$\frac{L}{N} = \mu \left(\frac{p_N + t}{p_L - s} \right)^{\sigma} \tag{4}$$

In this formula, σ is the substitution elasticity and μ is a positive constant, related to the distribution parameters of the production function.[2]

In the context of the approach of this essay, magnitude μ is of crucial importance. If production factors are available limitless, then μ, multiplied by a factor determined by the price ratio of these factors and by the

2 Assume for example the following CES production function (substitution elasticity being positively defined):

$$Y = \left[\delta N^{\frac{\sigma-1}{\sigma}} + (1-\delta) L^{\frac{\sigma-1}{\sigma}} \right]^{\frac{\sigma}{\sigma-1}}$$

In this form δ represents the distribution parameter, reflecting the relative factor shares in the product $(0 < \delta < 1)$. In this case counts:

$$\mu = \left(\frac{1-\delta}{\delta} \right)^{\sigma}$$

See also Hamberg (1971, p. 161) and Huisman (1983, p. 112).

substitution elasticity concerned, indicates the ratio in which the factors are applied in the economic process. Note that μ reflects the latter ratio if factor prices are defined in such a way that the price ratio concerned is unity.

Assuming that the amount of nature used in the economic process is given by preservation policy, then:

$$N = N^{*} \tag{5}$$

From the above model it can be concluded that, using (3), (4) and (5) and assuming that σ is positive, in a situation of unemployment an increase of t (and thus of s also) leads to an increase of employment (L). If $\sigma = 1$, close to the equilibrium situation the relation will be:

$$L = \frac{(\mu + 1)t + \mu p_N}{p_L} N^{*}$$

provided the supply of labour is fully elastic.

If the supply of labour is an increasing function of wages, the model should be extended by:

$$L = c p_L \quad with \quad c > 0 \tag{6}$$

Then, if $\sigma = 1$, the effect of a small increase of the level of environmental charges (t) on employment (L) is:

$$L = \sqrt{[(\mu + 1)t + \mu p_N] c N^{*}}$$

Thus, in both variants of the model, an increase of income transfer from nature to labour results in more employment. Substituting, *ceteris paribus*, the increased value of L in the production function results in a higher value for Y. For substitution elasticities other than 0 and 1, calculations are more complicated. Yet, it is clear that the higher the value of substitution elasticity is, the stronger the effects are.

Technological change

To investigate the implications of technological change, equation (4) may be replaced by:

$$\frac{E_L}{E_N} = \mu\left(\frac{P_N}{P_L}\right)^{\sigma - 1} \qquad (4a)$$

in which E_L and E_N are production elasticities of labour and nature, respectively (Krabbe, 1989, pp. 6-9). A certain technology is characterized by distinct sets of values of E_L, E_N, σ and μ. Of these four magnitudes, one is determined by the other three, given the prices of the factors concerned. In the above approach, μ is the dependent magnitude, and each technology is characterized by the parameters E_L, E_N and σ. Under the condition of linear homogeneity, as assumed in this context, only two of the three technology indicators can vary independently.

In order to investigate the significance of the three corresponding aspects of technological change, in this case the implications of changes in E_L, E_N and σ for the value of μ, then (4a) can be rewritten as:

$$\mu = \frac{E_L}{E_N}\left(\frac{P_L}{P_N}\right)^{\sigma - 1} \qquad (4b)$$

It appears that, except in cases in which $\sigma = 0$ and $\sigma = 1$, the 'technology - price ratio factor', μ, also depends on the way prices are defined. To overcome the difficulties involved, prices should be defined in such a way that, at the beginning of the analysis the price ratio chosen is unity.

On this basis, the effects of the three aspects of technological change can be quantified by differentiating (4b) partially to E_L, E_N and σ. The effects are of the following nature:

$$\frac{\partial\mu}{\partial E_L} > 0 \quad and \quad \frac{\partial\mu}{\partial E_N} < 0$$

$$\frac{\partial\mu}{\partial\sigma} > 0 \quad if \quad \frac{P_L}{P_N} > 1$$

$$\frac{\partial\mu}{\partial\sigma} < 0 \quad if \quad \frac{P_L}{P_N} < 1$$

To illustrate the practical significance of this, an example is presented. Let the supply of both production factors be fully elastic and σ be positive. If nature's production elasticity (E_N) increases and labour productivity (E_L) remains constant, then μ declines. This means that, according to (4), comparatively more of the factor nature is used.

This process is weakened if the substitution elasticity is simultaneously changed in one of the following ways. *Ad* a: Substitution elasticity increases while price ratio P_L / P_N decreases. *Ad* b: Substitution elasticity decreases while price ratio increases. Thus, from the point of view of nature preservation, a more elastic substitutability is favourable if nature becomes comparatively more expensive. A less elastic substitutability is favourable if nature becomes comparatively less expensive. In the context of protection of nature, a rise in the price of nature (the first case) is the more realistic. The price ratio can be manipulated by way of income transfer, *e.g.* on the basis of equations (2) and (3). In this context an increase of σ supports nature preserving aims. Further, it is clear that preservation of nature is especially served by an increase in production elasticity of labour, supported by elastic substitutability, provided there is a comparative decrease in the price of labour.

Induced technology

The idea of 'induced technology' implies that, to a certain degree, the character of technology is determined by the structure of factor prices and factor shares in production (Kennedy, 1964; Binswanger, 1974; McCain, 1974). This idea includes 'induced institutional change' (Binswanger and Ruttan, 1978).

The concept of 'technology - price ratio factor' can be placed into the idea of induced technological change. The idea that technological change is directed towards an increase in applicating factors that are becoming comparatively cheaper, labour in this model, is reflected by the two following coherent functions:

$$E_L = f_L\left(\frac{P_L}{P_N}\right) \tag{6a}$$

$$E_N = f_N\left(\frac{P_L}{P_N}\right) \tag{6b}$$

Functions f_L and f_N are decreasing (6a) and increasing (6b), respectively. In a situation in which nature becomes more and more scarce, the reaction is stronger if the reaction time is longer.

Thus income transfers from distinctly scarce factors to factors that are less scarce stimulate not only factor substitution within the context of a given technology, but also through induced technology. Yet, for the production factor labour a complicating element is that high wage subsidies may have a disincentive effect on personal willingness to achieve.

Insertion of (6a) and (6b) in equation (4b) gives:

$$\mu = \frac{f_L}{f_N}\left(\frac{P_L}{P_N}\right)^{\sigma-1} \tag{4c}$$

In the above model substitution elasticity is yet determined exogenously. It is a magnitude reflecting the ways technical solutions are found. In general this parameter has a greater value if the reaction time is longer. So, in a properly institutionalized market economy, induced technology forms an additional contribution to efficiency in production, also from an environmental point of view.

References

Binswanger H.P., The measurement of technical change biases with many factors of production. *American Economic Review* Vol. 64 (1974), pp. 964-76.

Binswanger H.P. and V.W. Ruttan (eds), *Induced innovation: technology, institutions and development.* Johns Hopkins University Press, Baltimore, 1978.

Debreu G., *Theory of value: an axiomatic analysis of economic equilibrium.* New York, 1959.

Georgescu-Roegen N., *Energy and economic myths: institutional and analytical economic essays.* Pergamon, New York, 1976.

Hamberg D., *Models of economic growth.* Harper, New York, 1971.

Heertje A., Groei en krimp bij duurzame ontwikkeling: welke kennis is nodig? In: Nijkamp P. and H. Verbruggen (eds), *Het Nederlands milieu in de Europese ruimte.* Stenfert Kroese, Leyden, 1990.

Howe Ch.W., Lessons from the U.S.: environmental policy experience for the single European market and Eastern Europe. Wageningen Agricultural University, Wageningen, 1991.

Huisman S., *Conjunctuur- en stuurtheorie* 2. Wolters-Noordhoff, Groningen, 1983.

Kennedy C., Induced bias in innovation and the theory of distribution. *Economic Journal* Vol. 74 (1964), pp. 541-7.

Krabbe J.J., *Individueel en collectief nut.* Mededelingen Landbouwhogeschool Wageningen Vol. 74-4. Wageningen, 1974.

Krabbe J.J. Milieu-economie, harmonie en conflict. In: van Drunen A.A.P. *et al.* (eds), *Economie en landbouw.* Vuga, The Hague, 1983.
Krabbe J.J., *The idea of environmental welfare economics.* Wageningen Economic Studies, Nr 12, Pudoc, Wageningen, 1989.
Krabbe J.J., Environmental welfare economics: implications for technology, wages and income. *International Journal of Social Economics* Vol. 17 (1990), Nr.1, pp. 49-58.
Kuik O. and H. Verbruggen, Ontwikkeling van nationale duurzaamheidsindicatoren: plan van aanpak. IVM, Free University, Amsterdam, 1990.
Mäler K.G., National accounts and environmental resources. *Environmental and Resource Economics* Vol. 1 (1991), pp. 1-15.
McCain R.A., Induced bias in technical innovation, including product innovation, in a model of economic growth. *Economic Journal* Vol. 84 (1974), pp. 959-66.
Nentjes A., Economische instrumenten in het milieubeleid: financierings- of sturingsmiddel. In: Nijkamp P. and H. Verbruggen (eds), *Het Nederlands milieu in de Europese ruimte.* Stenfert Kroese, Leyden, 1990.
Opschoor J.B., Ecologisch duurzame economische ontwikkeling: een theoretisch idee en een weerbarstige praktijk. In: Nijkamp P. and H. Verbruggen (eds), *Het Nederlands milieu in de Europese ruimte.* Stenfert Kroese, Leyden, 1990.
Pearce D.W. and R.K. Turner, *Economics of natural resources and the environment.* Harvester Wheatsheaf, New York, 1990.
Pigou A.C., *The economics of welfare,* fourth edition. MacMillan, London, 1952.

Chapter 2

CORRECTING NATIONAL INCOME FOR ENVIRONMENTAL LOSSES: a practical solution for a theoretical dilemma

Roefie Hueting*

In economic policy, in the media and, alas, also in some economic literature, the increase in production as measured in national income (or Gross National Product, GNP) is called economic growth, is identified with increase in welfare and is conceived as ***the*** indicator for economic success. Defining production growth as economic growth means defining economics as production. Such a definition excludes, among other things, the scarce environment from economics. Defined in this manner, economic growth obtains the highest priority in the economic policy of all countries[1]. At the same time we see all over the world growth of national income in accordance with the present pattern being accompanied by the destruction of the most fundamental scarce and, consequently, economic good at man's disposal; the environment.

From this simple observation three conclusions can be drawn: 1. society is sailing by a wrong compass, at the expense of the environment; 2. the error is covered up by a wrong use of terms; 3. the belief in ever continuing exponential growth in production, as measured in national income, is the heart of the environmental problem.

---

* R. Hueting is head of the Department for Environmental Statistics, Netherlands Central Bureau of Statistics. An earlier draft of this chapter was prepared as a paper for the Conference on Ecological Economics of Sustainability held in Washington, D.C., May 21-23, 1990.

1 Even though in most countries there are some politicians and bureaucrats who have realized that growth of the current pattern of production and consumption for more and more people (the population growth is, with a timelag, also reflected in GNP) is accompanied by the destruction of the environment, official policy still gives the highest priority to increase of production.

1. The interaction between environment and production: the urgency of correction

The current terminology for growth and welfare expresses the strong belief that things go well, economically speaking, only when the production, as measured in GNP, increases. The notion that production should be increased in order to create scope for financing the conservation of the environment reflects this belief. This notion is widespread and highly popular in official economic and environmental policy. The proposition is disputable, because environmental deterioration is, to a large extent, precisely a *consequence* of production growth. The production growth attained in the North is largely the result of increases in productivity[2], in which the loss of scarce environmental goods has not been taken into account[3]. Few people seem to be aware of the following. A quarter to one third of the activities making up national income (notably state consumption) do not contribute to its growth because, by definition, no increase in productivity can result from them[4]. Other activities result only in slight improvements in productivity. The 3% annual growth (a doubling of production in 23 years) desired by official policy, and also advocated in the Brundtland report (WECD, 1987), must therefore be achieved by a much higher growth among the remaining activities. Unfortunately, these are mainly the activities which, by their use of space, soil and resources or by the pollution they generate, in production or

2 Production growth results from growth in the labour force and increase in labour productivity. The labour force growth in the North has been small over the last decades. Consequently production growth in this area is mainly the result of increase in labour productivity. See also Note 4.

3 Polluting, degrading and depleting environment and resources is free of charge. Preventing this process, by levies or by regulations, means that, given the existing technology, more labour input is required for the production of a given number of goods. This reduces labour productivity and consequently checks production growth. Saving the environment without checking production growth (corrected for double counting, such as treatment plants), is only possible if a technology is invented that is sufficiently clean, reduces the use of space sufficiently, leaves the soil intact, does not deplete energy and resources (*i.e.* energy derived from the sun and recycling) *and* is cheaper (or at least not more expensive) than current technology. This is hardly imaginable for our whole range of current activities.

4 GNP growth results from two factors: increase in productivity and increase in labour volume (LV). In the 15-year period examined (see Note 5), the growth of GNP amounted to 72%, of which 5% was caused by LV increase. In principle, the allocation of this 5% forms an unsolvable allocation problem. But allocating this LV increase to the various sectors in proportion to their value added would first of all hardly change their relative contribution to growth of GNP, and secondly have a negligible influence on this contribution in absolute figures. However, a slight contribution to growth of state consumption and the like would, of course, result.

consumption, most harm the environment. Among these activities are the oil and petrochemical industries, agriculture, public utilities, road building and mining.[5]

A shift in human activities to reduce the burden on environment and resources can be achieved in two ways. First by dictating environment-saving measures for production and consumption and secondly by directly changing the production and consumption patterns.

The first method, *e.g.* applying end-of-line provisions or changing processes, mostly results in higher real prices of the products and thus in a decrease in the growth of national income[6]. (Note that when process changes do not result in higher prices or even result in lower prices, no environmental problem exists; market forces will bring about these changes 'automatically.')[7] Of course, price increases resulting from the environment-saving measures cause a shift towards more environment-friendly activities.

Technical measures often do not really solve the problem, either because the growth of the activity overrides the effect of the measure, or because, owing to the persistent and cumulative character of the burden, the measure only slows down the rate of deterioration. In these cases, in addition to the technical measures, a direct shift in behaviour patterns must ensue, forced by rules and regulations, and levies. Thus it is estimated that to stop its contribution to the acidification of forests and lakes, apart from applying all available technical means, the Netherlands must reduce the number of car miles and its farm livestock by 50%. A direct shift in production and consumption patterns (the second method) will usually also check the growth of GNP, as follows from the above analysis of the National Accounts (the environmentally most burdensome activities contribute most to GNP growth). Bicycling contributes less to GNP growth than the use of private cars does. Saving energy and materials checks growth, insofar as it either anticipates the

---

5 This emerges from an analysis of the basic material for the Dutch National Accounts, of which the sectorial composition does not differ appreciably from that of the UK nor probably from that of most other Northern countries (see Hueting, 1981).

6 A disturbing factor is that provisions made by *others* than private firms are entered in the System of National Accounts (SNA) as final deliveries instead of as intermediate (costs). This is generally considered as double counting. When the text says: growth is checked, it always means: growth, corrected for double counting. The double counting, however, is marginal to the losses, because by far the greatest part is not repaired.

7 Of course the market is not perfect, and it is possible that introduction of processes that are both clean and cheaper is delayed for some time by inertia or lack of knowledge. It is, however, very unlikely that clean processes that are cheaper than the polluting ones are not introduced after some time. As soon as one firm applies such processes, competition forces other firms to follow suit.

rise in prices or pays as a result of price increases. (Again: where this is not the case there is no environmental problem.) However, if we were to value bicycling, more herbivory and the safeguarding of the future higher than traffic jams, extreme carnivory and an increase in the risks of overshoots, such a shift would increase our welfare (satisfaction of wants evoked by dealing with scarce means) and economic growth in the true sense (*viz.* increase in welfare). Unfortunately there is no method which states whether or not this is the case. (See Section 2.)

Two conclusions can be drawn from the above. First, it is unlikely that stimulating GNP increase in industrialized countries will solve the problems of the developing countries. Such increase would most likely be possible only by accelerating encroachment on the limited energy stocks and the limited carrying capacity of the environment, which would be at the expense of developing countries. (If we try to avoid this encroachment, growth would be checked.) Secondly, growth of GNP and safeguarding the environment and resources are two conflicting goals. Sustainable use of the earth's resources requires a shift in priority from the first to the second. This certainly does not mean "Stop production growth", but rather a shift in production and consumer activities in an environmentally acceptable direction in order to arrive at sustainable economic development, and then to wait and see what the increase in production would be. Those who advocate both goals are apparently either blind to present-day reality or are speculating on as yet uninvented technologies while putting at risk the basis of our existence. Such advice will likely do more harm than good to the environment, because it strengthens the forces behind the increase of national income, which are already much stronger than those defending the environment.

The recommended shift in priority in economic policy would avoid both risks and future financial losses. Restoration after the event is usually much, often very much, more expensive than prevention, while a number of environmental losses are irreversible or may lead to overshoot. This shift would also stimulate the search for and application of environment-friendly technologies much more strongly than current policy does.

2. The unsolvable problem of shadow prices for environmental functions

It follows from the above that the environment constantly risks falling victim to the misconceptions of economic growth and welfare, and the resulting one-sided stress of economic policy on the increase of production as measured in national income. Therefore, a correction of national income for environmental losses seems highly recommendable, provided that it is made clear in the presentation of the results that the figures found do not constitute a complete indicator for society's welfare in the course of time (see Section 3). In view of the severe criticism and the pressure for carrying into effect such a correction that has been evident now for decades, one might be surprised why up to now this work has not been completed, or even begun. The main reason for this is that it is impossible to find a theoretically sound solution for one of the two problems involved in such correction.

First of all 'the environment' has to be defined in a manageable way and the link between environment and economics must be made. This problem can be solved with the aid of the concept of environmental functions[8]. Very briefly, the reasoning is as follows.

For an economic approach, the environment can best be interpreted as the physical surroundings of man, on which he is completely dependent in all his activities. Within the environment, a number of possible uses can be distinguished. These are called environmental functions or, for short, functions. When the use of an environmental function by an activity is at the expense of the use of another (or the same) function by another activity, or threatens to be so in the future, loss of function occurs. We call this competition between functions, and make a distinction between qualitative, spatial and quantitative competition.

When competition of functions occurs, the environment acquires an economic aspect. Economics boils down to the problem of choice in the use of scarce alternatively applicable means for the satisfaction of classifiable wants (the subject matter). A good is scarce if the demand for it exceeds its availability, or if something else we would like to have (an alternative) has to be sacrificed to require it, which amounts to the same thing. Environmental functions meet this definition fully as soon as they compete. Competing functions are scarce goods. Losses of function form costs, irrespective of whether or not they are expressed in monetary terms. The terms 'money' and 'market' do not occur in the definition of the subject matter of economics.

---

8 For a detailed description and elaboration of this approach see Hueting (1980), which is based on Hueting (1970).

Qualitative competition occurs when the use of the environmental function 'dumping ground for waste' (or: 'withdrawal or addition of species and matter') is at the expense of other functions. There is, as it were, an intermediate step. An activity introduces or withdraws an agent into or from the environment, as a result of which the quality changes. This may disturb other use or render it impossible. By agent is meant a constituent or amount of energy (in whatsoever form) which may cause loss of functions by its addition or by its withdrawal from the environment by man. An agent could be a chemical, plant, animal, heat, noise, radioactivity, *etc.* In the case of spatial and quantitative competition the amount of space or matter is insufficient to meet the existing wants for it. Note that the use of a function also comprises the passive use of the function 'natural environment' in order to conserve the actual and potential utilities of ecosystems, now and in the future, and to retain the diversity of species of our planet. Competition between functions can take all sort of forms. However, in most cases by far it is a question of the environment being used for current production and consumption activities at the expense of other desired use or (with a certain degree of probability) of future possible uses, including production and consumption. A well-known example of the latter is the loss of top soil resulting from deforestation.[8]

The second problem pertains to the construction of shadow prices. National income is recorded in market terms. For confrontation of environmental losses with this figure it is therefore necessary to construct shadow prices for environmental functions that are directly comparable with market prices. For this a demand curve and a supply curve have to be construed. In the period 1969-1974, the Netherlands Central Bureau of Statistics attempted to do this (CBS, 1972, 1973, 1975; Hueting, 1980), with the following results.

The supply curve can, in principle, always be constructed. It consists of estimates of the costs of measures for various degrees of eliminating the causes of the loss of function, as a result of which the function is partly or wholly restored. The measures will often be a mix of technical provisions, such as add-on technology (treatment plants and the like) and changes in processes, and reducing or halting the burdening activities (which also can be expressed in monetary terms). The supply curve is called elimination cost curve.

Constructing a complete demand curve, however, is mostly not possible. The reason for this is that only in exceptional cases can the intensity of the *individual preferences* for environmental functions be entirely expressed in market behaviour or other behaviour that can be translated into market terms (money).[9] Loss of function can sometimes partly be compensated by provisions which act as a substitute for the original function and in some other cases cause financial damage. When, for instance, water is polluted by chemicals, compensation of the function 'drinking water' or 'water for agriculture' is possible to a certain degree and during a certain period by purifying the intake of the polluted ground water or surface water. In the long run, however, because of the cumulative effect, elimination of the pollution is necessary. An example of financial damage is the damage by floods to crops and properties resulting from loss of the function 'regulator of the water management' of a forest.

Both compensation and financial damage can be interpreted as revealed preferences for a given function. In the case of compensation, this will be immediately clear. After all, provisions are made to replace the function originally present. However, amounts of damage can also be conceived of as revealed preferences, since they are losses suffered as a result of the disappearance of the function. As stated above, preferences can seldom be manifested entirely via the market. It is clear that only a very small proportion of the losses of environmental functions are compensated; they are also not always reflected in financial damage. Often, too, the possibility of compensation does not exist. Thus a compensatory measure like moving to a clean area is feasible only for the happy few. Moreover, it evokes new traffic streams causing new losses of function. Financial damage through noise nuisance and air pollution is very incompletely reflected in the fall in value of the house, as a result of the tightness of the housing market and the immobilization caused by ties to work and the neighbourhood (Jansen and Opschoor, 1972). The construction of new forests and lakes is pointless so long as the process of acidification is not halted by elimination measures. The loss of soil by erosion cannot be compensated. Most important of all, much of the damage caused by losses of function will occur in the future, such as the damage caused by loss of the stability of the climate, by loss of the functions of tropical forests ('gene reserve', 'regulator of the water management',

9 The possibilities for this are limited. An example is the costs of travel involved in visiting a nature area (see Hueting, 1980).

'preventor of erosion', 'supplier of wood', 'buffer for CO_2 and heat', 'regulator of the climate' and the like), and by the disruption of ecosystems resulting from the extinction of species. The risks of future damage and the resulting poor prospects for the future cannot manifest themselves via the market of today.[10] Yet there is obviously a great need for unvitiated nature and a safe future.

Because of the limited possibilities for preferences for environmental functions to be manifested in market behaviour, efforts have been made to trace these preferences by asking people how much they would be prepared to pay to wholly or partially restore functions and to conserve them. At present quite a lot of research is being done on willingness to pay for the environment and willingness to accept environmental losses (an overview of the methods used , including quite a few results, can be found in Johansson, 1987; Kneese, 1984; Pearce *et al.*, 1989). It is questionable, however, whether this method is suitable for arriving at the construction of a complete demand curve, certainly on a macro scale and certainly for functions on which current and future life depends. Insofar as people are directly affected by environmental losses, the approach might be justified. Many environmental losses, however, constitute part of a process which may lead to the disruption of the life-support functions of our planet and endanger the living conditions of generations to come, and therefore cannot be considered separately. In all these cases the approach is pointless. Arguments for this view are listed in Hueting (1989).[11] See also Kapp (1972).

Thus it follows that the construction of shadow prices that are directly comparable with market prices (a prerequisite for a theoretically sound correction of national income) is mostly not possible.

---

10 The unsolvable problem of the level of the discount rate in environmental costs and benefits causes the break down in calculating the net present value (NPV) of future damages, the current extent of which can be established via the market (*e.g.* damage by flooding resulting from loss of the function 'regulator of the water household'), (see Hueting, 1991).

11 To these arguments the following can be added.

- A number of people will probably have their doubts about the participation of others (the prisoner's dilemma from game theory) or prefer to wait and see (the free rider principle from the theory of collective goods). Thus in developing countries (where the tropical forests are) the view is wide-spread that people from the rich countries should pay, because these countries a) have much more money to spend, b) nevertheless are destroying their own environment, *e.g.* what is left of their forests, by acidification, c) contribute considerably to global effects such as the greenhouse effect, d) have a clear interest in saving natural resources in the third world.
- In cases where the whole community is involved the willingness to accept or to pay approach is pointless. For who is then paying whom?

3. What can be done immediately

In Section 4, a practical and defensible proposal is put forward for overcoming the problem of the impossibility of constructing shadow prices for environmental functions, comparable with market prices. However, elaboration of the method proposed will probably take at least three years in a country with a relatively well-developed system of environmental statistics like the Netherlands. For some other countries it might take longer. In expectation of the results, one thing can be done immediately, *viz.* making clear in the publications of the National Accounts what changes in the level of national income do *not* mean, in order to prevent these changes giving wrong signals to society about the economic success of its activities. In addition to this, the costs of compensating, restoring and preventing environmental losses that are wrongly entered as final delivery (see below) can be made visible with relatively little effort.

Proposal for a text to avoid misinterpretation of the national income figures
In order to prevent the wrong use of figures indicating the changes in the level of national income, the following information could be given about their limited significance for welfare and economic success, without, of course, denying their importance.

Economics boils down to the problem of choice in the use of scarce means that can satisfy human wants. Welfare is defined as the satisfaction of wants evoked by dealing with scarce means. So welfare, or satisfaction of wants, is a psychical category, an aspect of one's personal experience. Economic theory assumes that, when dealing with scarce means, we try to maximize our welfare (the opposite is nonsensical). As well as maximization of welfare with given means, the desire to raise the level of satisfaction of wants (welfare) in the course of time is also regarded as a motive of economic action.

It follows from this brief description of the subject matter of economics that economic growth and economic success can mean nothing other than increase in the level of welfare. Our economic actions have scored success when our satisfaction of wants has increased. Since satisfaction of wants is not directly observable 'from the outside' and thus not in itself a cardinal measurable quantity, it seems logical to look at factors that *are* measurable in figures and that can arguably be supposed to determine the level of welfare.

There are a number of objections to using the production of goods and services, as measured in national income, as *the* indicator for welfare, economic success and economic growth in this procedure.

These objections could be classed in three categories, which will be summarized very briefly. The ***first*** category is of a more or less 'technical' nature. It comprises five points.

1. The consumer surplus which relates to the difference between the total utility of a good and the product of price (as the criterion of marginal utility) and quantity is not expressed in the height of national income.
2. In national income the value added by production is calculated at market prices. This means that the (marginal) utility of goods of different subjects is added. This is already unallowable with equal income distribution since it is impossible to compare utilities between individuals: some people attaching greater value to goods than others. With the existing inequality of incomes this is not allowed *a fortiori* on account of the diminishing marginal utility of money as income grows. The impossibility of comparing utilities between individuals further implies that, if part of the population of a country regresses and the rest progresses, no pronouncement can be made on the final result (this situation certainly occurs).
3. The law of diminishing marginal utility applies to individuals. However, the same tendency is noticeable for the whole economy, as has been shown by recent research (van Praag and Spit, 1982). It appears from this research that ever more extra goods are necessary for the attainment of the same increase in welfare as income rises. This relativizes the importance of an ever-growing production for welfare.
4. Real national income is obtained by expressing the income in current prices in constant prices, with the aid of a composite price index. This can only be done correctly for a constant package of goods. Because the package of goods is constantly changing, the calculated value of the price index varies, depending on the solution chosen (Kuznets, 1948; Hicks, 1948; Pigou, 1949). This problem weighs especially heavily over a long period.
5. Not all production takes place in business enterprises or in government agencies. This may not only influence the level of national income but also the changes in it, if, for instance, the work of former housewives is taken over by paid domestic help, crèches, dishwashers and restaurants.

The ***second*** category of objections to identifying increase in national income with economic growth and economic success relates to the intermediate character of some elements of national income. In the calculation of national income in accordance with the present conventions, a number of activities which have a cost character and therefore ought to be entered as intermediate deliveries are designated as final consumption. Kuznets (1947, 1948), who deserves to be mentioned as one of the great theoreticians of the conception of national income, emphasizing this, dividing these activities into three classes.

1. The first class is caused by the fact that in industrial countries the dominant modes of production impose an urban pattern of living, which brings in its wake numerous services whose major purpose is to offset the disadvantages. As examples, Kuznets gave the expenditure necessary for bridging the greater distance between home and work, and the money spent on compensation for the inconveniences entailed in living in dense agglomerations.
2. The second class distinguished by Kuznets relates to expenditure that is inherent in participation in the technically and monetarily complex civilization of industrial countries. Payments to banks, employment agencies, unions, brokerage houses, *etc.*, including such matters as technical education are not, according to Kuznets, payments for final consumer goods. They are activities necessary for eliminating the frictions of a complicated production system and not net contributions to ultimate consumption.
3. The third class is the major part of government activity. The legislative, judicial, administrative, police and military functions of the state, according to Kuznets, are designed in order to create the conditions under which the economy can function. These services do not provide goods to ultimate consumers. It is wrong to count the whole of government activity as a net contribution to national income.

To this, a fourth class can be added.

4. The expenditure on measures that compensate or restore the losses of environmental functions (see Section 2) or prevent losses of environmental functions from occurring. These expenditures are entered as intermediate deliveries if the measures are taken and directly paid for by private firms, but as final consumption if they are paid for by private households or the government and also if they are taken by private firms but financed via levies imposed by the government. All these outlays should be entered as

intermediate when a long time series such as that for national income is composed, since the losses of environmental functions are not entered as costs at the moment they originate. At that moment the environment is excluded from the System of National Accounts (SNA). When these losses are eliminated or compensated the environment is - be it partly - included in the SNA. This is generally considered as double counting. This procedure also makes figures from different years incomparable, at least when they are used as a measure for economic growth and welfare.

The ***third*** category of objections to the identification of increase in national income with economic growth (increase in welfare) relates to the fact that production is only one of the factors that determine the level of welfare. At least seven factors play a role.

1. The package of goods and services produced by man.
2. The scarce environmental goods in the broad sense, *i.e.* including space, energy, natural resources, plant and animal species.
3. (Leisure) time.
4. Income distribution.
5. Working conditions.
6. Employment.
7. The safety of the future insofar as this depends on our behaviour with regard to scarce goods (such as the life-support functions of the environment).

All these seven factors play a part in economic action. They have to be constantly weighed against each other whenever the desired quantity or quality of a given factor is at the expense of one or more other factors. (Note that when this is not the case, no economic aspect is at stake and so no choice has to be made.) Seen from the point of view of those who choose, citizens or politicians, there is thus an unbreakable link between all factors influencing welfare.

From this it follows that no judgement can be given on the development of welfare in the course of time since the factors which influence welfare cannot be brought under a common denominator. To give one example, the effect of an increase in production on our welfare depends on the importance we attach to a greater quantity of produced goods on the one hand, and to the resultant loss of environmental functions on the other. Depending on this weighting, an increase in production may lead, on balance, to economic progress, to a neutral effect or to economic decline (loss of welfare). If the value of the environment is, rated marginally, higher than the value of the amount of goods produced, and government brings in measures relating to production processes and consumption habits, resulting in a reduction in the number of goods and services,[12] the environment will be improved and the overall satisfaction of wants obtained from economic goods is enhanced. In this case, less production leads to greater welfare.

Correcting national income for double counting

A correction for expenditure on compensatory, restoratory and preventive measures would be feasible without theoretical difficulties. This expenditure, which only re-establishes or maintains environmental functions that would remain available without the negative impact of our activities on the environment, is wrongly entered as value added, thus leading to an overestimation of the increase in national income and concealing what is going on in the environment: loss is not written off, restoration is written up. On the one hand, such a correction would be a step forward, as it would partly solve the well-known problem of double counting (see above) and provide more information about the relation between production and environment. Thus it appears from a study by Leipert (1989) that between 1970 and 1985 the defensive outlays in the Federal Republic of Germany increased from 5 percent to nearly 10 percent of GNP, which means that in this period about one fifth of the growth of GNP consisted of an increase in additional costs caused by the same growth.[13] On the other hand, it would express the environmental losses very incompletely and introduce the *pars pro toto* problem: part of the information is conceived as the total environmental effect. For, as is well known, most environmental losses are not restored or compensated.

4. A practical solution

Since the period 1969-1974, during which the Netherlands Bureau of Statistics made an attempt to construct shadow prices for environmental functions with the intention to correct national income, the call for national

---

12 This is very likely to occur, see Section 1.

13 The calculations comprise not only expenditure induced by environmental deterioration caused by man, such as restorative and compensatory outlays, but also defensive expenditure in the fields of traffic, housing, security and health.

income to be corrected to include environmental losses has been steadily growing. In the course of a working visit to Indonesia in 1986, I was provoked by the following remark made by the Indonesian Minister of Population and Environment: "In my policy-making I need an indicator in money terms for losses in environment and resources, as a counterweight to the indicator for production, *viz.* national income. If a theoretically sound indicator is not possible, then think up one that is rather less theoretically sound".

The answer to this is obvious: an estimate based on standards. The setting of standards was also discussed during this period (Hueting, 1980), but the point was not elaborated then because the question "What standards are to be set and by whom?" could not be answered. This situation has now changed. Especially after the publication of the report of the World Commission on Environment and Development *Our common future* (1987) (the so-called Brundtland Report), politicians and organizations across the world have declared themselves in favour of a sustainable development. This can be conceived as a preference voiced by society which opens up the possibility of basing a calculation on standards for a sustainable use of environmental functions, instead of on (unknown) individual preferences.

I proposed (1986 and 1989) the following procedure, the feasibility of which has been being investigated at the Netherlands Central Bureau of Statistics since February 1991. Define physical standards for environmental functions, based on their sustainable use. Formulate the measures necessary to meet these standards. Finally, estimate the amounts of money involved in putting the measures into practice. In technical terms, this means that in the familiar diagram of the supply and demand curve for environmental functions we have to determine a point on the abscissa which represents the standard for sustainability (see Figure 1). A perpendicular on this point intersects the supply curve. The perpendicular replaces the (unknown) demand curve. The point of intersection indicates the volume of activities, measured in terms of money, involved in attaining sustainable use of the function. The volume will often be a mix of necessary technical measures and the necessary reduction in activities (expressed in money terms) which, even after application of the measures, will be required to attain sustainable use of the function.

The reduction of national income (Y) by the volumes found gives a first approximation of the activities level which, in line with the standards applied, is sustainable. We call the sustainable level Y'. The difference between Y and

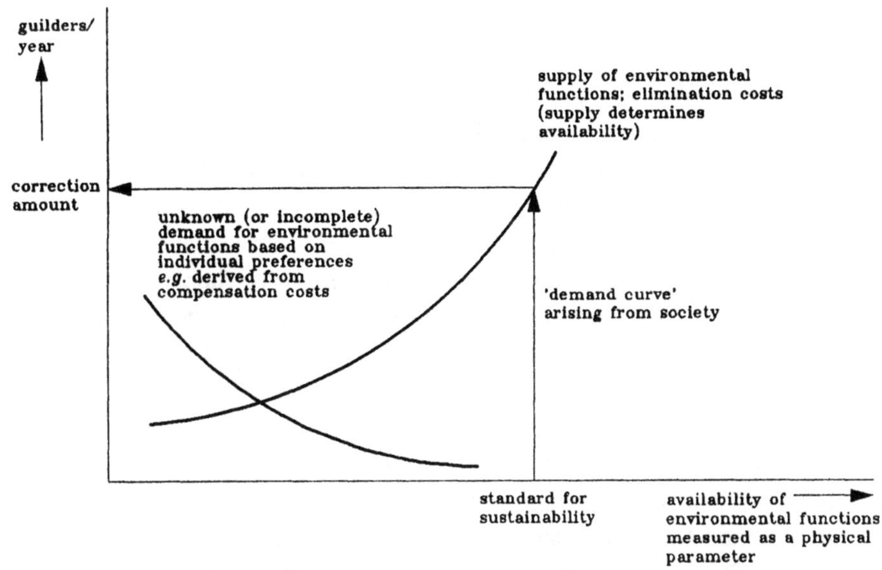

Figure 1: Demand and supply curve of environmental functions.

Y' indicates, in money terms, how far society has drifted away from the desired sustainable development. In other words, this difference indicates the sacrifice involved in attaining the desired sustainable use of the environment.

To be absolutely clear, it should be pointed out that this is a partial equilibrium and static approach. Effects on other sectors of the economy as a result of taking measures and reducing activities are not considered. Neither are future developments that might be expected involved in the approach. These are not taken into consideration, firstly because the exercise is aimed at a correction of the figure of national income and not at the development of a vision for the future, and secondly because, in the model to be used, a large number of assumptions would have to be incorporated. The following may be regarded as an exception to this.

Reduction of Y by double counting, by the costs of the measures needed to attain a sustainable society and by the added value of the activities which have to be reduced in volume, provides a first approach to Y'. The activities burdening the environment which are to be discontinued will, in most cases, be replaced by environmentally acceptable alternatives. The problem of the environment is, in fact, a problem of allocation. It is a question of shifting the patterns of activities in an ecologically sound direction. This shift will be brought about both by increases in the prices of products resulting from measures taken and by a direct reduction in activities placing a heavy burden on the environment.

The first estimate of Y' must therefore be raised by the added value of activities that will come into being after reduction of the harmful activities and through the disappearance of the compensation measures. An iterative calculation becomes here apparent, as there are very few activities that do not adversely affect the environment at all. The replacement activities may lead to the standards being exceeded and thus to the need for further re-allocation. My proposition is to postpone this more dynamic approach until the second phase of the research and to limit the first phase to an initial estimate of Y'.

The familiar objection to entering restoration measures as final delivery instead of as an intermediate (costs) does not apply to Y'. The objection is to the fact that the environment remains outside the System of National Accounts when environmental losses occur (loss is not written off), but is included in the SNA, albeit partially, when the loss is restored (restoration is written up). This means in fact that a comparison cannot be made between various years. Hence the continual pressure for correction of double counting which has been going on for decades now. Since environmental loss at Y' is written off, it is only logical that restoration should be written up. Naturally, an increase in Y' will also occur as clean technology and flow energy become cheaper, as then the deduction becomes less.

Standards and the measures based on them may relate to the occupation of space, the use of soil, the availability of stocks of natural resources, the composition of products, the consumption of raw materials and energy, the emission by activities and the concentration of chemical and other agents.

The standards can be related to environmental functions. Thus it is possible to formulate the way in which a forest should be exploited in order to attain a sustainable use of its functions such as 'supplier of wood', 'regulator of the water management', 'object of study for ecological research', 'supplier of natural products for the local population' and 'source of income from tourism'. The estimated expenditure on the measures required to meet these standards then indicate in monetary terms how far a nation has drifted away from its (supposed) end or standard of sustainable use of its forest resources. Likewise it is possible to formulate the way in which surface water and ground water should be exploited in order to arrive at a sustainable use of its functions such as 'waste-dumping site', 'water as raw material for drinking water', 'water for agriculture', 'cooling water', 'water for flushing and transport', 'process water', 'water for recreation', 'water for navigation' and 'water allowing the existence of natural ecosystems'. And the estimated expenditures on the measures required to meet those standards tell us in monetary terms how far a nation has drifted away from a sustainable use of its water resources. The same holds true for the use of air, soil and space.

The measures may range from selective cutting of trees, reforestation, building terraces, draining roads, maintaining buffers in the landscape, selective use of pesticides and fertilizers to building treatment plants, recirculation of materials, introducing flow energy, altering industrial processes, making more use of public transport and bicycles instead of private cars and making use of space that leaves sufficient room for the survival of plant and animal species.

Of course, no measures can be formulated for irreversible losses. If plant and animal species become extinct, no restoration measures are possible. The same probably holds for the total loss of the top-soil of a mountainous area. An arbitrary value then has to be assigned to these losses, of which only one thing can be said for certain: the value is higher than zero.

A more or less similar problem seems to arise in the case of non-renewable resources. When oil has been exploited and exported or used, it is gone for ever. Since oil reserves are finite, this loss constitutes a cost for the country. So if no alternatives are developed, the generation which experiences the depletion (or a sharp rise of the operating costs) of the resource will suffer a severe economic loss. And since the prospect of a safe and prosperous future for one's children and one's children's children is a normal human need, the diminution of the reserves of non-renewable resources such as oil constitutes a cost here and now.

The valuation of the depreciation of non-renewable resources can be done by estimating the costs involved in the development and practical introduction of alternatives like solar energy, substitutes for minerals and recycling methods.

Points of application concerning the concept of sustainability can be found in ecological literature. Thus Odum (1971) stated that through human activities a development is increasingly taking place which results in mature, stable ecosystems being replaced by more recent, less stable stages. This is the opposite of natural development. As fewer stable stages remain, restoration of impaired systems becomes increasingly difficult and of ever-longer duration, and the number of potential and actual possible uses falls steadily. An irreversible situation can come into being when harm is done on a large scale to predators; substantial numbers of species are lost or general biological activity is suppressed. This is a disruption of food chains that may lead *inter alia* to disruption of the life-support functions of the Earth. The process of the decline and disappearance of species can be seen as an indicator of the extent to which we are already on the way to the disruption of the life-support functions. The chance of severe disruption can be minimized if human activities, through the use of recycling processes, (again) become part of the biological cycle, whereby the height of the level of activities is limited by the condition that the degree of stability of this cycle does not decrease. A sustainable activity pattern would amount to recycling of natural resources, changing to non-polluting sources of flow energy and a use of land that leaves sufficient room for natural ecosystems to function.

Sustainability is linked to environmental functions, possible uses of the environment, as described and listed in Hueting (1980). Sustainability means that functions must remain intact so that all present and future uses remain available. As for renewable resources such as forests, water, soil and air, so long as the regenerative capacity remains intact, the functions remain intact, *e.g.* the function 'supplier of wood' of forests, the function 'drinking water' of water, the function 'soil for raising crops' of soil and the function 'air for physiological functioning' of air. In practical terms this means that things like emissions of cumulating matters such as PCB's, heavy metals, nitrates and carbondioxide may not exceed the natural buffering capacity of the environment and that the erosion rate may not exceed the regenerative power of the soil. As for non-renewable resources, like oil and copper, 'regeneration' takes the form of research and bringing into practice flow resources such as energy derived from the sun (wind, tidal, collectors, photo-voltaic cells), the recycling of materials and the development of substitutes for these.

At the request of Professor Emil Salim, Minister of Population and Environment of Indonesia (see above), I elaborated the method for the case of erosion, designing a co-ordinated set of tables in which the information to arrive at the required figures would fit. My reasoning is as follows.

Suppose the standard for erosion, necessary to arrive at a sustainable economic development is equal to the natural rate of increment of the top soil. This means that the erosion rate in all regions of Indonesia has to be measured (quite a bit of measurement has been done already). For places where the erosion rate exceeds the natural rate of increment, measures to bring the erosion back to the natural rate must be formulated. These measures may differ from place to place. But let us suppose that in a certain region the following measures have to be taken to meet the erosion standard and to maintain the standard in the course of time.[14]

1. Reforestation of the mountain above the agricultural zone or, when farm land has expanded too far uphill, above a certain, not too high, contour line.
2. Building terraces.
3. Setting up a drainage and irrigation system to prevent the origination of gullies.
4. Draining roads and, if necessary, rebuilding them as far as possible along the contour lines of the mountain.
5. Giving information on the need for the measures.
6. Installation of officials, chosen from the local population, to check that nobody obstructs the rules necessary to meet the standard.

The expenditure necessary to carry out these measures (and other similar measures) can be estimated.

In the case of erosion, the following steps have to be taken to arrive at the figure with which the national income figures over a certain period have to be confronted. Which period this should be is not discussed here, because it is not essential to get an idea of the method.

1. *Making a review of the erosion rate (for each province)*. This requires the information in Table 1.

14 A result of the measures may be a decrease in the area of arable land and the employment in agriculture. This necessitates, for instance, investments for local industry or rehabilitation of waste land. Furthermore measures such as making tenancies more secure and other land reform may be necessary to maintain a stable situation. This kind of secondary measure is not taken into account because correction of national income allows only for the direct measures that are necessary to meet the standard for a sustainable use of the environmental functions.

Table 1: Erosion rate by region (per slope class) (in year x).

Erosion rate (times the natural rate of increment)	region (in km^2) 1	2	3	..	..	n	Total km^2 in the province with a certain erosion rate
1 time	a km^2	b km^2	c km^2				
2-3 times	*etc.*						
3-5 times							
5-7 times							
etc.							
Total km^2 of the region							

2. *Establishing the causes of the erosion (for each province).* The findings should be collected in Table 2.

Table 2: Causes of erosion by region (in year x).

Main cause	region (in km^2) 1	2	3	..	..	n	Total km^2 per cause in the province
1	a km^2	b km^2	c km^2				
2	*etc.*						
etc.							
Total km^2 per cause in a region							

Examples of the causes of erosion:
1. Agricultural mismanagement, using land not suitable for agriculture, *e.g.* on too steep slopes.
2. Overcutting of wood, *e.g.* for cooking.
3. Concessionaires not cutting according to rules *etc.*
4. Natural disaster.

More than one cause at the same time can lead to erosion in one area. This has not yet been elaborated in Table 2.

3. *Formulation of the necessary measures (for each province) to meet the erosion standard.* These measures might differ by local geographic situation and by cause. The findings should be collected in Table 3.

Table 3: Measures to meet the erosion standard, by region (in year x).

Measure	region (in km^2) 1	2	3	..	..	n	Total km^2 per measure in a province
1	a km^2	b km^2	c km^2				
2	*etc.*						
3							
etc.							
Total km^2 of the region							

Examples of measures are given above.

4. *Estimate of the costs to meet the erosion standard,* including foregoing farm land, where necessary. The results of the estimates should be collected in Table 4.

Table 4: Costs of the measures by province.

Measure	Costs per province 1	2	3	..	..	n	Total costs for Indonesia per measure
1	a Rp	b Rp	c Rp				
2	*etc.*						
3							
etc.							
Total costs to meet the erosion standard							Total costs for Indonesia to meet the erosion standard

The necessary calculations of the costs of the measures to meet the standards for a sustainable use of environmental functions are not new. In the Netherlands, the first publications of the Department for Environmental Statistics of the Central Bureau of Statistics resulted in estimates of the costs incurred by measures for various degrees of restoration of function (the supply curve, see above) (CBS, 1972, 1973, 1975; Hueting, 1980). Later, the CBS undertook such calculations for the Netherlands Scientific Council for Government Policy (1978) and for the scenario studies in the context of Broad Social Discussion on the future energy supply (Hueting, 1987). A number of 'supply curves' are included in the chapter on costs and benefits of environmental measures in a recent report by the National Institute of Public Health and Environmental Hygiene (1988). The institute uses these data for scenario studies. In other countries similar estimates have been carried out, for instance by the Economic Council of Japan (1974). Apart from these and other, more integral, approaches, numerous studies notably on the measures and costs involved in the reduction of emissions of harmful agents have been carried out in quite a number of countries.

The static volume estimates proposed here, based on standards for sustainable use, have the same character. The principal requirement is scientific and technical knowledge.

On the ground of the experiences mentioned above I believe that a correction of national income figures on the basis of standards for a sustainable use of the environment is feasible. The method has certain advantages and disadvantages.

The disadvantages (or imperfections) are as follows.

1. The results of the approach do not represent individual valuations in the true sense, as has been extensively explained above. This is because, among other things, the intensity of the preferences for a sustainable use of the environment cannot be measured. However, this simultaneously implies that the intensity of the preferences for the acceptation of the adverse effects and future risks involved in the present growth pattern of production and consumption, and thus for the growth of GNP, is equally unknown. Both of these aspects should be clearly mentioned in the presentation of the results of the method in the publications of the National Accounts.
2. The approach is strictly static. Only first-order effects are taken into account (see above). In reality, two additional movements take place. The technical measures and the reduction of activities bring about a contraction or an expansion of related industry, depending on the type of industry. Presumably the net effect is an increase in the correction amount.

In the course of time, however, the economy will adapt itself to the new situation. A second movement takes place as a reaction to the reduction of polluting activities: people are seeking environmentally acceptable alternatives. This reduces the correction amount. Both effects could, in principle, be estimated with the aid of a dynamic model. However, the reliability of the results of such a model would be questionable, since changing to sustainable use of the environment means, in actual fact, a break in the trend, the consequences of which exceed the predicting capacity of the current models.

3. The method ignores the loss of welfare suffered by those people who have a strong preference for the survival of plant and animal species apart from their role in the maintenance of the life-support functions of our planet (which is a prerequisite for sustainable development). These preferences could be compared to the preferences for creating and maintaining art or churches, which might not be considered indispensable for sustainable development and yields, but the loss of which would constitute a decrease in welfare for those who need them. A solution would be to class the diversity of species under the function 'gene reserve'. Another conspicuous example of the same kind is noise. Noise does not affect sustainability, but it can be very disturbing. A solution would be to class this under the function 'quiet in the living area'. Standards for noise levels are already operational in many countries. This too should be mentioned in the presentation of the results.
4. The results of the approach do not indicate the state of the environment. If, for instance, a cheaper anti-pollution technology is invented, the distance between national income (Y) and the estimated sustainable activity level (Y') becomes smaller. But if the technology is not or not generally applied, the state of the environment hardly changes at all. Furthermore, a decrease in costs does not necessarily run parallel to changes in physical parameters. Therefore environmental statistics in physical units remain indispensable.
5. No measures can be formulated for irreversible losses. This holds true for any method.
6. The method is laborious.

The advantages are as follows.

1. As far as we can see, the method is the only way to confront the national income figures with the losses of environmental functions in monetary terms.
2. The method compels the definition of an exact content of the term 'sustainable economic development'. Without such a content the term remains vague and not operational in economic policy regarding the environment.
3. The physical data required for comparison with the standards come down to basic environmental statistics which have to be made anyhow if a government is to get a grip on the state of the environment. The formulation of the measures to meet the standards and the estimates of the expenditure involved are indispensable for policy decisions. In other words, the work for supplementing national income figures might be laborious, but it has to be done anyway if one wants to practise a deliberate policy with respect to the environment.

On the strength of the arguments mentioned above, in order to arrive at a figure for national income alongside the current one, I recommend a correction of national income for environmental losses (including resources) on the basis of standards for a sustainable use of environmental functions.

References

Central Bureau of Statistics, *Waterverontreiniging met afbreekbaar organisch en eutrofiërend materiaal* (Water pollution by biodegradable organic and eutrophicating matter). The Hague, 1972.

Central Bureau of Statistics, *Waterverontreiniging ten gevolge van verzilting, 1950-1970* (Water pollution caused by salinization, 1950-1970). The Hague, 1973.

Central Bureau of Statistics, *Luchtverontreiniging door verbranding van fossiele brandstoffen 1960-1972* (Air pollution resulting from the combustion of fossil fuels 1960-1972). The Hague, 1975.

Central Bureau of Statistics, *Functieverliezen in het milieu* (Losses of function in the environment). Statistische en Econometrische Onderzoekingen No. 18, The Hague, 1975.

Economic Council of Japan, *Measuring net national welfare of Japan.* Tokyo, 1974.

Hicks J.R., The valuation of social income, *Economica* Vol. 15 (1948), pp. 163-172.

Hueting R., Moet de natuur worden gekwantificeerd? (Should nature be quantified?). *Economisch-Statistische Berichten*, 21 January 1970.

Hueting R., *New scarcity and economic growth.* Amsterdam, New York, Oxford, 1980 (first edition 1974).

Hueting R., Some comments on the report 'A low energy strategy for the United Kingdom', compiled by Gerald Leach *et al.* for the International Institute for Environment and Development (IIED). Paper prepared for the Working Party on Integral Energy Scenarios, The Hague, 20 May 1981. Also published under the title: De relatie tussen produktiegroei en energieverbruik. Maakt groeifanatisme blind? (The relation between production growth and energy use. Does growth fanaticism blind?). *Economisch-Statistische Berichten*, 24 June 1981, pp. 609-611.

Hueting R., An economic scenario that gives top priority to saving the environment. *Ecological Modelling* Vol. 38, (1987) pp. 123-140.

Hueting R., Correcting national income for environmental losses: towards a practical solution. In: Y. Ahmad, S. El Serafy, E. Lutz (eds), *Environmental accounting for sustainable development*. The World Bank, Washington, D.C., 1989.

Hueting R., The use of the discount rate in a cost-benefit analysis for different uses of a humid tropical forest area. *Ecological Economics* Vol. 3 (1991), pp. 43-57.

Jansen H.M.A. and J.B. Opschoor, De Invloed van Geluidshinder op de Prijzen van Woningen - Verslag van een Enquête onder Makelaars in en rond de Haarlemmermeer (The Influence of Noise-nuisance on the Prices of Houses - Report of a Survey among House-Agents in and around the Haarlemmermeer). Instituut voor Milieuvraagstukken van de Vrije Universiteit. Werknota No. 15. Amsterdam, 1972.

Johansson P., *The economic theory and measurement of environmental benefits*. Cambridge University Press, Cambridge, 1987.

Kapp K.W., Social costs, neo-classical economics, environmental planning: a reply. *Social Science Information* Vol. 11 (1972) Number 1 pp. 17-28.

Kneese A.V., *Measuring the benefits of clean air and water*. Resources for the Future, Inc., Washington D.C., 1984.

Kuznets S., National income and industrial structure. In: The econometric society meeting, September 6-18, 1947, Washington, D.C., *Proceedings of the International Statistical Conferences* Volume V. Calcutta, 1947, p. 205.

Kuznets S., On the valuation of social income. *Economica* Vol. 15 (1948) pp. 1-16 (February), pp. 116-131 (May).

Leipert C., Social costs of the economic process and national accounts: the example of defensive expenditures. *Journal of Interdisciplinary Economics* Vol. 3 Number 1 (1989) pp. 27-46.

National Institute of Public Health and Environmental Hygiene, *Concern for tomorrow*. Alphen aan den Rijn, 1988.

Netherlands Scientific Council for Government Policy, *The next twenty five years*. The Hague, 1978.

Odum E.P., *Fundamentals of ecology*, 3rd edition. Philadelphia, 1971.

Pearce D., A. Markandya and E.B. Barbier, *Blueprint for a green economy*. Earthscan Publications Limited, London, 1989.

Pigou A.C., *Income*. London, 1949.

Praag B.M.S. van and J.S. Spit, *The social filter process and income evaluation - an empirical study in the social reference mechanism*. Report 82.08, Centre for Research in Public Economics, Leyden University, Leiden, 1982.

World Commission on Environment and Development (WCED), *Our common future*. Oxford, New York, 1987.

Chapter 3

THE MIRROR OF CLEANLINESS: on the construction and use of an environmental index

Frank den Butter*

The almost compulsive drive for cleanliness has been noted as one of the mysteries of Dutch temperament. A Dutch housemaid washing the stoop, although to the casual eye there seems precious little dirt to get rid of, symbolizes this lust for cleanliness. The English historian, Simon Schama (1987, p. 375), in his brilliant account of Dutch social and cultural history said that "no visitor to Holland failed to notice the pains that the Dutch take to keep their streets, their houses and themselves - though there is less unanimity about this - brilliantly clean. The spick and span towns shone from hours of tireless sweeping, scrubbing, scraping, burnishing, mopping, rubbing and washing". But that is history.

Today the Netherlands is no clean country at all. Like most countries in the industrialized world, it suffers from a severe pollution of the environment. There are even a number of reasons why the pollution problem is especially serious in the Netherlands. In the first place, the density of population in the Netherlands is the highest in Europe and hence its urbanization and its density of traffic is also. Secondly, the Netherlands lies in the midst of a circle with a radius of only 500 kilometres, which has about 200 million inhabitants. Thirdly, the Netherlands is the end basin of a number of large rivers which flow through industrialized areas and hence become very polluted. A major internal problem is the intensive use of agricultural land: the Netherlands utilizes the highest amount of fertilizer per acre of land of all agricultural countries. Therefore, because of its special topography and characteristics, in addition to the traditional drive for cleanliness, the Netherlands has a strong need for a stringent anti-pollution environmental policy.

---

* F. den Butter is Professor of Economics and head of the Applied Labour Economics Research Team (ALERT), Free University, Amsterdam, the Netherlands. This paper was first presented at the workshop on Environmental Problems and Policies in Small Open Economies, Schiermonnikoog, The Netherlands, 17-20 June 1991. Critical remarks by J.C. van Ours on a previous version and excellent research assistence by H.P. Kramer and A.M. van Veen are gratefully aknowledged.

Anti-pollution policy measures have been announced in the 'national environmental policy plan' (VROM, 1989), which should, 25 years from now, yield a sustainable economic development and a cleaned-up environment. However, there is no fixed general standard for the cleanliness that the plan aims at. With a sense of romanticism, the plan only formulates a large number of specific goals for the next 25 years. It states that the Dutch should be able to swim in all inland lakes and rivers without becoming ill by 2010. Salmon should be able to breed in the upstream waters of the Rhine and the Dutch Waddenzee should again provide a good habitat for the common seals.

Obviously the debate on environmental policy needs a clear measurement of the pollution or 'mirror of cleanliness'. This environmental index, which summarizes all available data on the state of pollution and environmental damage, is to indicate to what extent the country has been polluted (den Butter, 1990). Such an index may be very helpful to the proponents of environmental policy in the economic debate, as it makes the environment a rival of other policy problems, such as unemployment, government deficit, inflation, or disposable income, all of which are summarized in appealing indices.

This chapter discusses the scope for the construction of an appropriate environmental index for the Netherlands and illustrates how it can be used in policy analysis. Section 1 is a survey of some general notions on the concept of the pollution index. Section 2 is on the relation between the environment and welfare economics. Section 3 indicates how the price of the environment can be determined in the context of welfare economics using the concept of the pollution index. Section 4 gives some suggestions of how a pollution index can ideally be constructed if enough expert information and data were to be available. Section 5 illustrates some environmental indicators for which time series already are available but which are far from ideal. Section 6, these environmental indicators for the Netherlands are combined to a prototype of a mirror of cleanliness. However, the main lesson from this combination exercise is that we need much better data and more sophisticated combination techniques in order to arrive at an index of practical relevance. This and some other conclusions are drawn in Section 7.

1. An index for environmental pollution

The need for summarizing the state of the environment in one index, or at least in a small number of appropriate indices, has obtained general acceptance. Opschoor (1987) and the Social Economic Council (Sociaal Economische Raad, 1989) have underlined that such set of operational and quantitative indicators is essential from the standpoint of economic analysis in the Netherlands. However, the experts doubt whether these indicators can be combined into one overall index for the state of the environment. The argument is that it is far more difficult to aggregate the great variety of aspects of pollution such as the extinction of animals and traffic noise than it is to add up apples and pears which consumer theory has taught us to do.

However, the impossibility of designing a perfect environmental index should not prevent us from constructing one which is less than perfect. In fact, the same argument applies to calculating the national income, which has obtained general acceptance as a useful summary statistic for economic analysis. Moreover, a clear analogy exists between the measuring of the state of the environment and that of the trade cycle. The various trades cycle indices which are used in policy analysis combine a great variety of time series on economic phenomena which are seemingly incomparable.

This analogy with the trade cycle can be taken further by labelling the various ways in which the state of the environment can be summarized in one index. The first form is an index just like the cyclical index, which summarizes the extent to which the country has been polluted, or inversely, has remained clean. We can think of an index with value 100 in the base year. However, it seems more appropriate to let the index express the extent to which the country is polluted in a direct way and to use a scale which runs, say, from 0 to 100. This could be interpreted as the 'percentage' of pollution of the environment. An index value of zero would, in that case, indicate the ideal state of Arcadia with no pollution at all, 5% would for instance be the goal to be reached in future, 20% a critical value above which human life becomes unbearable, and 100% as the level of pollution which destroys all life on earth.

The second form of appearance of the environmental index is analogous to the leading indicator in cyclical analysis. This kind of *environmental barometer* would provide a prediction of the future state of the environment. The need for such an index is obvious as it generally takes a long time for a policy measure to have a final effect on the state of the environment (see *e.g.* the long lags between reductions of sulphite emissions and the decrease of acidification of surface water).

As an alternative to the environmental index and barometer, ecologists usually express the need for an index as a kind of Plimsoll line. It is a maximum utilization rate for the various elements of the environment. Above this limit nature loses its self- regenerating character and the environmental situation becomes unstable. Although this Plimsoll line is easy enough to establish for a ship, drawing the line for the environment appears to be very difficult. Whereas the environmental index and barometer have a mere descriptive character, the Plimsoll line is used in a normative sense; pollution is not allowed to surpass its critical value.

The environmental index is crucial for making the concept of sustainable economic growth operational. In this context sustainable economic growth can be defined as equilibrium growth at a constant value of the environmental index. Obviously, no monetization of the environmental capital is needed for this definition of sustainability. Therefore there is no necessity to calculate a green GNP, which is the actual GNP from the National Accounts corrected for the user costs of the environmental capital which that growth involves. As a matter of fact, such correction of the GNP may very well obscure the question of whether the growth has been sustainable or not. A 3 % growth of the green GNP can, for instance, either be the result of a 5% growth of actual GNP and 2% additional pollution or a 1% growth of actual GNP and a reduction of the level of environmental damage with 2 %. Of course, calculation of both the actual GNP and green GNP implicitly defines an environmental index. However, this monetized index will only be equal to the 'true' index where the (implicit or explicit) price determination of the environment is fully correct. In practice, such price formation which fully reflects environmental damage seems impossible. Therefore a non-monetized index has the advantage over a monetized index in that a serious type of pollution which carries a large weight in the overall environmental index, but which has relatively low abatement costs, will be reduced first.

2. Environment and welfare

The relation between pollution and welfare takes a prominent place in the economic debate on the environment (see Opschoor, 1990 and Heertje,

1990). From the viewpoint of social welfare Heertje regarded the environment, or more broadly formulated, nature, as a consumer product since refraining from the destruction of nature (woods, meadows, lakes, seashores, with all their living plants and animals) directly satisfies the needs of human beings at present and in the future. That is why Heertje advocated including the amount of unspoiled nature in the social welfare function. Economic policy should be directed at a welfare growth in which the environment is weighted heavily. Moreover, Opschoor argued for the inclusion of the environment, not only in the welfare function, but also in the production function.

In the 1950's the Social Economic Council formulated five goals for macroeconomic policy in the Netherlands; low unemployment, price stability, steady economic growth, balance of payments equilibrium and a reasonable income distribution (see Schouten, 1985, for a survey). The arguments above imply that the social welfare function defined by these five policy goals has to be extended by a sixth goal: the environment. Obviously the five traditional policy goals can be quantified in simple summary statistics. These numbers are weighted heavily in actual policy. The dramatic increase in unemployment contributed to the consensus on the policy of wage restraint in order to enhance employment. The increase of the government deficit, which is not on the original list of policy goals of the Social Economic Council, obtained large publicity and the attention of policy makers in the 1980's as well. Here there is also one number which directly reflects policy effectiveness.

The environment will only be able to compete with these traditional policy goals if it can be summarized in one number in the same appealing way. This is a major reason why an environmental index is needed. The index may show the success or failure of the proposed measures of environmental policy. Policy goals for the environment can be formalized, just as they can for the budgetary policy and the employment policy in the 'government agreement', when a new government is formed. If, for instance, at the date of the formation of the government, pollution has reached the level of say 15%, the government could aim at a reduction over the next four years to a level of say 10%. Anyhow, the Prime Minister could promise to resign if his government does not succeed in reducing the level of pollution and bringing it under 15%.

It should be noted that the Social Economic Council has not completely disregarded the environment when discussing the economic policy goals. In the 1960's an ambiguous formulation combined environment and economic growth as policy goals. In the Netherlands the publication of the Meadows Report for the Club of Rome Project in 1972 caused, unlike in most other countries, a temporary upgrading of the role of the environment in economic thinking. However, the result was that in the 1970's the environment disappeared as a policy goal and became a (necessary) condition for economic policy. Nowadays, the Social Economic Council argues that the goal of maintaining ecological equilibrium has a higher ranking than the five traditional goals of macroeconomic policy. However, in practice this high rank of the environment is similar to that of the ceremonial head of state; the position is not really powerful. A better position for the environment would be, as already argued, to include it in the welfare function and to let the trade-offs with the other policy goals be determined openly in the policy process.

The inclusion of the environment in the social welfare function still poses a number of intellectual problems. The repair of environmental damage may take a long time, and sometimes the damage cannot be repaired at all. That is why the environment, as a part of social welfare, affects many generations. The present environmental policy is not only directed towards the welfare of our own generation, but also towards the welfare of future generations. However, we do not know what the trade-offs of these future generations will be for environment and other policy goals. A solution to this problem is the identification principle, according to which the present generation identifies the preferences of the future generation to its own. The next question that arises is what discount rate we should use in the resulting optimization problem for the welfare of future generations. The discount rate commonly used in such circumstances reflects the time preference. Environmental problems, however, have such a long horizon, that the market interest rate as discount rate would serve the interests of future generations very poorly. For that reason, some economists prefer a discount rate of zero in this case. This solution invokes another problem since it is inconsistent not to discount the assets, while the liabilities are to be discounted at the normal market rate payable for the environmental investments made for future generations.

3. The price of the environment

A major question in the economic debate of the environment is who determines the price of the environment and who pays for it. This question can be answered in the context of welfare theory. We have seen in the previous section that the environment, or nature, can be considered both as a consumption good and a production factor. In principle price formation of the environment can be treated analogously as the price formation of exhaustible and partly renewable natural resources. If exhaustion increases and the stock of environment becomes scarce, the price of the latter will rise. This makes the use of alternatives more profitable and automatically sets a limit to exhaustion. However, the self-regenerating power of the environment, which disappears when a certain limit has been surpassed, complicates the price formation process.

The vital question is whether we can leave this price determination process to the market, as classical welfare theory would prescribe, or whether the price of the environment should be determined in a more autocratic way. If full information were available on the remaining stock of the environment and on its self-regenerating power, and if the interests of the future generations were to be fully taken into account, not much objection could be made to allowing the price of the environment to be determined by the market. Obviously these conditions do not hold, as our knowledge on the environment and the altruism towards future generations is rather limited. The impression is that, at the moment, the market price of the environment is much too low. A large gap still exists between the actual utilization price of the environment and its social or welfare costs. Therefore, from the welfare point of view, the use of the environment is far from optimal. For that reason it does not seem wise to let the market determine the price of the environment at this moment.

But who else can determine that price? Maybe those who enjoy nature as a consumption good. Such price determination is possible by using questionnaires, which, for instance, ask visitors to a recreation area how much they would be willing to pay for the song of the nightingale, or it can be determined by revealed preferences in this respect (see Folmer, 1990, for a survey on economic valuation methods for the environment). However, this leaves the determination of the price of the environment to the specific preferences of nature lovers; it does not take the interests of future generations into account. Moreover, the nature lovers will tend to overvalue the spectacular but exterior aspects of natural beauty and undervalue those hidden aspects which are vital for ecological equilibrium.

Therefore I see no other way than to allow price of the environment to be determined by experts. This price determination can, as we shall see, proceed along the same lines as the construction of an environmental index which is based on expert opinions. It should be noted that this form of interventionist price formation does not exclude the role of the market when the prices are to be paid. On the contrary, it seems desirable, once the price of the environment has been determined, that the goals of the environmental policy should be reached by the use of market conforming instruments, such as taxes or transferable pollution rights, and not by quota or prohibition orders.

4. The construction of an environmental index

The state of the environment can be characterized by a large number of aspects, which are again quantifiable in many ways. Such quantification is relatively easy for those aspects which play an important part in the discussions on the 'national environmental policy plan', such as the sulphite and nitrogen emissions which cause acidification, the emission of CFK's, and pollution of surface water. However, aspects which are less easily quantifiable such as noise, air pollution, actual pollution of the soil, threat of the greenhouse effect, the extent of disruption of ecosystems, and the extinction of wildlife should also have their place in the overall pollution index.

For the construction of a proper environmental index all available time series information on the various aspects of the environmental problem should first be collected, and if information is not available on important aspects, action should be taken to set up indicators for that aspect. In this respect a lot of work has recently been done in the field of sustainability indicators. However, some of these indicators have a prospective character and, although it would be appropriate to include them in an environmental barometer, it would not be so good to include them in an environmental index which solely describes the present state of the environment.

In spite of this restriction a lot of indicators will, in principle, be adequate for inclusion in the Dutch environmental index. All these measures of various aspects of the environment should be grouped and weighted according to their importance. Here the experts enter the stage. Environmental experts like biologists, ecologists, should determine the trade-offs for these various environmental aspects. Economic valuation methods and consensus techniques may be helpful for the determination of these trade-offs.

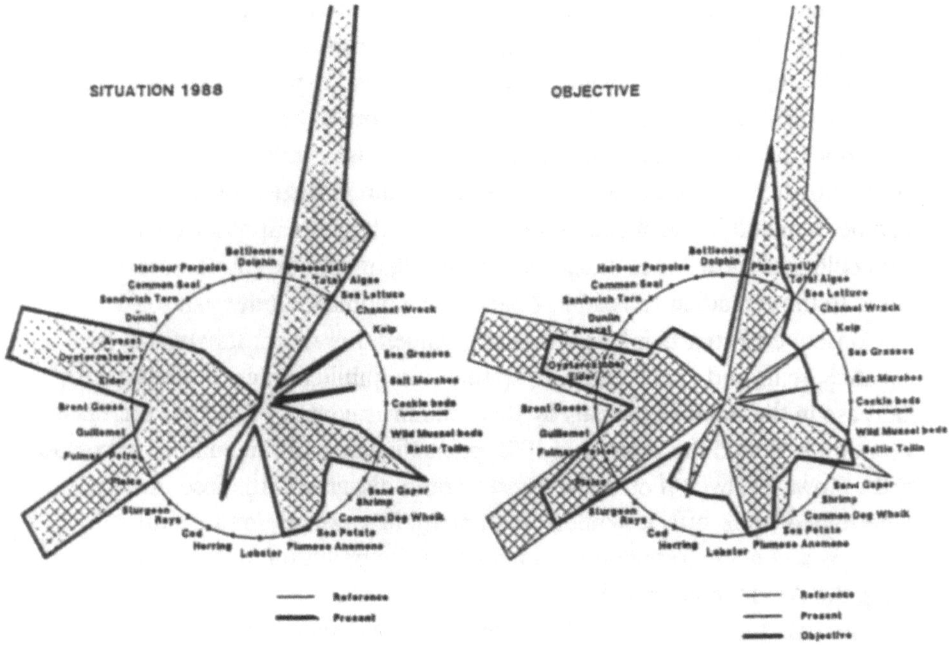

Figure 1: The 'Amoebe approach' for the construction of an ecological Dow Jones index for pollution of the North Sea.
Source: ten Brink (1989).

An interesting example of such a weighting exercise for one aspect of pollution is the 'Amoebe-approach' of ten Brink (1989), Tidal Waters Division of the Dutch institute of 'Rijkswaterstaat'. The Amoebe-approach yields what ten Brink called an ecological Dow Jones index for the ecosystem of the North Sea. This approach is based on an estimation of the numbers of 32 plant and animals species in the Dutch part of the continental shelf. These 32 species were, as far as possible, a cross section of the entire system. As reference, the numbers of these species found in 1930 (a year considered to represent the perfect situation of no pollution) were taken. Numbers for all species were standardised to lie on a unit circle. When the depiction of the actual numbers of these species gives an image of what looks like an amoeba:

some of these species like the common seal, the bottlenose dolphin and the cockle beds, have become much smaller in number than in 1930 while others like total algae and the oystercatcher have become much more numerous compared to 1930 (see Figure 1). For the construction of the index, the percentage change of the actual situation as compared to the reference situation is calculated for each species. The differences of these percentages from 100 are, in absolute values, added up for the 32 species, and this yields the ecological Dow Jones. Hence, when the shape of the amoeba approaches the circle, the ecological Dow Jones index decreases, indicating less pollution of the North Sea. In this way a policy goal for the reduction of pollution can also be depicted in the shape of an amoeba, with a corresponding value for the ecological Dow Jones index, which should, of course, not necessarily be equal to the Arcadian situation of the circle yielding an index value of zero.

Consequently ten Brink has implicitly valued the trade-off between, for instance, seals and cockle beds. In spite of the public interest in seals, an increase in the number of seals by 10%-points as compared to the reference situation is valued the same as a 10%-points increase of the number of cockle beds. However, even if other biologists would disagree with these implicitly determined trade-offs, it would still be possible to weigh up the conflicting opinions and come to one index number for the pollution of the North Sea using the Amoebe-approach.

The next step in the construction of the environmental index is to combine all these ecological Dow Jones indices, which describe just one aspect of pollution, to one index value, again using expert opinions for the determination of weighting. This index number would mirror the general situation of the environment in the Netherlands and would therefore indicate the extent to which the country has been polluted.

As mentioned before, the concept of sustainable economic development can now be made operational by defining it as development under the condition of a constant overall pollution index. However, this definition does not determine the level of pollution at which the sustainable development has to take place. Environmental specialists usually consider a more restricted definition of sustainable development. Their definition often includes explicit norms for a reduction of pollution. For example, one of the norms for ecological sustainability of the North Sea is a reduction of pollution so that the amoeba comes to a shape where the number of each species lies within the 75%- 125% interval around the reference value. For that reason it is essential to dispose of reference values for all component parts of the combined index which describes sustainable development from an ecological or an economic point of view. Moreover, critical load values should be determined for each component part of the index. These may not be surpassed because otherwise nature will completely lose its regenerating power. In this way, elements of the Plimsoll line can be introduced into the index.

After environmental experts have established the various trade-offs between the component parts of the index, politicians should then determine the trade-offs between the pollution of the environment and the other policy goals in the macroeconomic welfare function. Thus politicians are asked to value the environment against things like economic growth, unemployment and inflation. The traditional theory of economic policy assumes that politicians are able to assess, for instance, the trade-off between inflation and unemployment and can quantify how many percentage points of additional inflation they are willing to pay for one percentage point reduction of unemployment. Equally they should be able to make their preference for a clean environment explicit by expressing how much growth they are prepared to forego for a reduction of the environmental index with, say, 10 points. Once these policy choices have been made explicit, economists are able to calculate the shadow price of the environment.

However, such perfect quantification is still a Utopia. At present there is an enormous lack of appropriate time series data on all specific aspects of pollution and there is no consensus amongst experts on the trade-offs between these aspects. Therefore we have to dispense with the idea of constructing an ideal index and concentrate on some scarce time series information on pollution which is readily available.

5. Environmental indicators

Although a lot of environmental data have been collected in the Netherlands, remarkably little time series information is available which can be regarded as overall indicator for the state of the environment. In a survey of measurements of cleanliness, which would appropriately cover most aspects of environmental pollution, the Institute for Environmental Studies of the Free University (IvM) (see Vos *et al.*, 1985, 1986) gave a list of 15 prospective indicators. For the indicators to be included in an overall index, reliable time series should exist on a yearly basis over a period of say 20 years. However, for the majority of the indicators on the IvM list, only data for one specific year are available, or at most for 2 or 3 years. Opschoor (1990, p. 32) presented a qualitative survey of the state of the environment using time series data collected by the CBS for 26 indicators associated with environmental pollution. However, these indicators cover only some aspects of the environment.

Therefore, at present, the construction of an environmental index for the Netherlands, albeit a prototype, is severely hampered by the lack of appropriate data. Nevertheless, in order to show how the various indicators can be combined into one index, we have selected a number of annual time series data from public statistical sources. These data are readily available and contain enough information for time series analysis. The data used in this study are depicted in the appendix to this chapter.

We appreciate that some of these indicators in the appendix represent aspects which can be directly linked to pollution (chloride load of the Rhine, domestic and industrial garbage, common seals in the Waddenzee, acidity of rainfall and vitality of woods), while the other indicators (manure production, use of fertilizer, total mobility, and use of land for industry and buildings) are related to pollution in more indirect ways. Moreover, some of these indicators to a large extent relate to imported pollution (acidity of rainfall, number of seals, vitality of woods, and, in particular, chloride load of the Rhine), whereas the others mainly measure domestic pollution. It should be noted that, with the exception of common seals in the Waddenzee and the vitality of woods, a higher level of the indicator represents a higher level of pollution. In order to standardize the series in this respect, the series of common seals in the Waddenzee has been inverted in the combination exercise in the next section (due to a lack of observations, the series on vitality of woods is not used in this exercise).

The figures in the appendix show that five series (manure production, use of fertilizer, domestic and industrial garbage, total mobility and use of land for industry and buildings) exhibit a clear positive trend over the reference period 1970-1988, which indicates an increase of pollution. On the other hand the emission of mobile sources shows a clear downward trend. Although in selecting these indicators we have tried to represent different aspects of pollution with each indicator, we have included both a series on emission of mobile sources and on total mobility, because the first series only indicates a very specific part of the pollution caused by traffic, whereas total mobility includes all external costs. The data on acidity of rainfall appear to be very erratic and therefore do not provide a reliable indicator. We have left this series out of our analysis. Unfortunately only a few observations are available for the vitality of woods (see Ministerie van Landbouw, Natuurbeheer en Visserij, 1990), which can be regarded as a good example of an indicator to be included in the environmental index. The series for the chloride load of the Rhine and the common seals of the Waddenzee do not exhibit a clear trend over the whole reference period. The low number of common seals in the Waddenzee in 1988 is due to an infection disease which decimated the seals in that year.

In the economic debate on the environment, pollution is often associated with economic growth. In order to illustrate a possible link between growth and pollution, Table 1 gives the correlations of the selected environmental indicators and the volume of national product. Obviously all indicators with an upward trend are positively correlated with national product and, inversely, the indicators with a clear downward trend show a negative correlation.

Table 1: Correlation of environmental indicators and national income.

Indicator	Correlation coefficient
Chloride load of the Rhine	0.41
Manure	0.95
Fertiliser	0.86
Garbage	0.95
Common seals	0.12
Emission of mobile sources	-0.91
Mobility	0.98
Acidity of rainfall	0.72
Vitality of woods	-0.66
Land for industry and buildings	0.94

6. Combining environmental indicators

Using the time series data on the indicators discussed above, this section illustrates some features of the methodology for the construction of an overall environmental index outlined in Section 4 and the problems associated with it. The obvious analogy with the construction of a cyclical indicator which provides a measure for the state of the trade cycle has already been noted. In trade cycle analysis, the technique of principal components is often used as a method for integrating and summarizing information from various data sources. Principal component analysis, which is related to factor analysis, tries to condense the information content of time series into a limited number of components with the minimum loss of information.[1] As well as its use in cyclical analysis, this technique was also used, for instance, by Fase (1973, 1976) for the identification of common patterns in interest rate movements. More specifically, principal component analysis aims at distracting shared but unobserved factors underlying the original data. Whereas the input data may be correlated, the principal components are, by definition, orthogonal. The principal components are arranged in the order of size so that the first principal component explains the highest amount of variance in the original data. In other words, the first principal component can be regarded as an unobserved dependent variable in a regression equation where the indicators act as explanatory variables, and in which the data for this unobserved dependent variable are constructed in such a way that the regression has the highest explanatory power (highest R^2). Technically, the principal components are derived by calculating latent roots of the standardized sample matrix. The first principal component is associated with the highest latent root, the second principal component with the second highest root, *etc*.

In first instance we tried to compute the principal components for all indicators described in the previous section for which data were available over the whole reference period 1970-1988. Hence we excluded the acidity of rainfall and the vitality of woods from our analysis. However, for the interpretation of the principal components it was necessary in the case of a specific interpretation of the underlying indicators - such as in this case where higher values of the indicators were associated with more pollution - that all indicators pointed more or less in the same direction. This was not the case with the emission of mobile sources which showed a downward trend, while the majority of the other series had an upward trend. This resulted in a high negative weighting for the emission of mobile sources in the first principal component, so that this component could no longer be interpreted as an index of pollution since less emission of mobile sources causes a rise of the value of the pollution index.

1 Unlike factor analysis, principal component analysis is a method of descriptive statistics, which is not based on formal statistical theory.

Therefore we have left the emission of mobile sources out of the calculation and computed the principal components for the remaining seven indicators in order to obtain some further information on the relation between these environmental indicators with an upward trend and economic growth. Table 2 shows that the first component explains almost 70% of the total variance of the indicators, whereas the second component yields an additional explanation of about 18%. Hence the first two components adequately summarize the information content of the indicators under review. As shown in Figure 2, the first principal component exhibits a clear upward trend. Therefore it can be associated with economic growth represented by the volume of the national product which is also depicted in the figure.

Table 2: Two largest latent roots and percentages of variation for 7 indicators.

Component	Latent root	% of variance	cumulative %
1	4.89	69.8	69.8
2	1.24	17.6	87.5

However, the interpretation of the second principal component is far less clear. This is illustrated in Table 3, which gives the weightings or factor loadings for the seven indicators in the first and second principal components. The second principal component appears to be highly (but negatively) correlated with the number of common seals in the Waddenzee, which shows no correlation with the first component. It looks like an interesting result as we can identify the second principal component as a (policy induced) deflection of pollution from economic growth. However, the other indicator which is not highly correlated with the first component, the chloride load of the Rhine, obtains an opposite weighting in the second component. That is what makes the interpretation of this component impossible. It also shows that we should be very cautious in using the number of seals as a major indicator of overall pollution in the Netherlands, although at first sight it seems a neat series for this purpose.

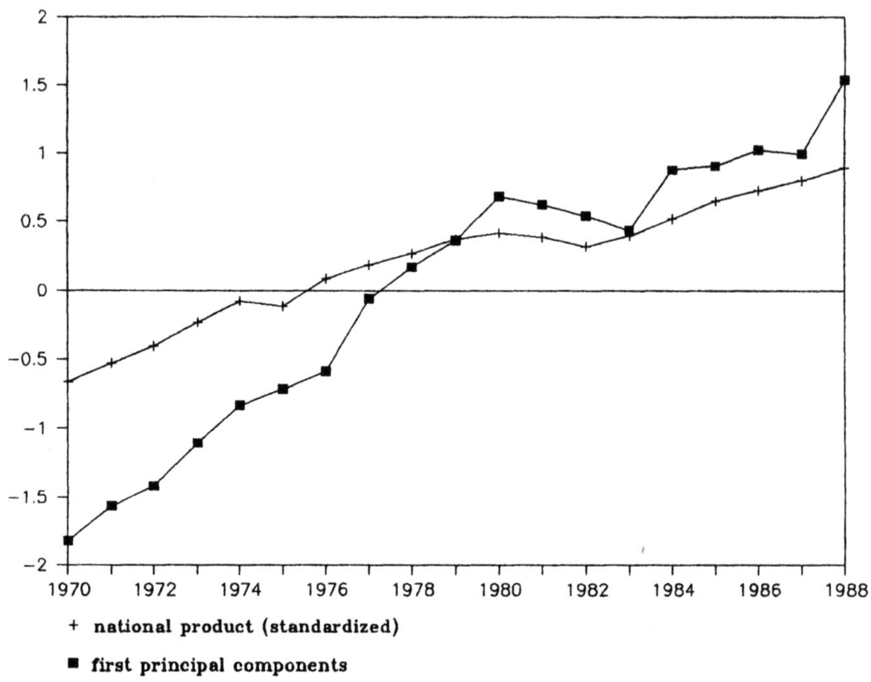

Figure 2: First principal component of 7 indicators, and national product.

Table 3: Factor loadings for 7 indicators (after varimax rotation).

Indicator	Component 1	Component 2
Chloride load of the Rhine	0.50	0.61
Manure	0.96	0.11
Fertiliser	0.87	0.34
Garbage	0.96	-0.07
Common seals	0.13	-0.91
Mobility	0.98	0.01
Land for industry and buildings	0.97	0.09

Hence, principal component analysis did not prove very useful for the construction of an environmental index. An alternative analysis was to combine the indicators by calculating simple index values. For each of the eight series for which data are available over the whole reference period, an index was constructed with 1970 = 1. Figure 3 shows both the arithmetic and the geometric mean index for these eight indicators. It should be noted that in this combined index no weightings have been used and hence that all indicators are valued equally in the index. The figure indicates that the geometric mean index assesses the increase of pollution over the reference period as somewhat larger than the arithmetic mean. However, the combined index appears not to be very sensitive to that specification change.

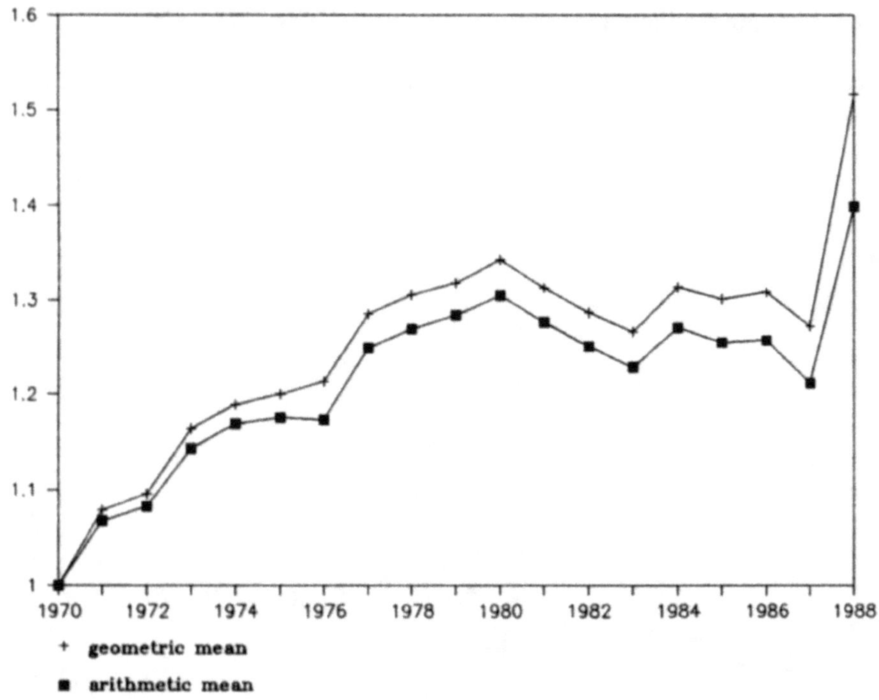

Figure 3: Geometric and arithmetic mean index of 8 indicators.

In addition to these simple indices we considered the following more flexible form for combining the indicators:

$$I_t = (\sum x_{it}^{\rho})^{1/\rho},$$

with I_t the index value in year t, and x_{it} the value of the indicator i in year t, and where the index I_t is normalized in such a way that $I_{1970} = 1$. This specification resembles a CES-function and parameter ρ in the formula indicates the extent of 'substitution' between the indicators. In the case of $\rho = 1$ we have the arithmetic mean, while for large values of ρ the indicator with the highest value obtains the largest weighting. In this way the construction of the index allows for critical load effects where high levels of pollution are associated with large weights (see also Ott, 1978, p. 341, who called it a root-sum-power damage function). Figure 4 depicts three different indices, constructed by means of the CES-function, with values for ρ of 1, 5, and 50. The figure shows that the index with a high value of ρ exhibits relative strong fluctuations.

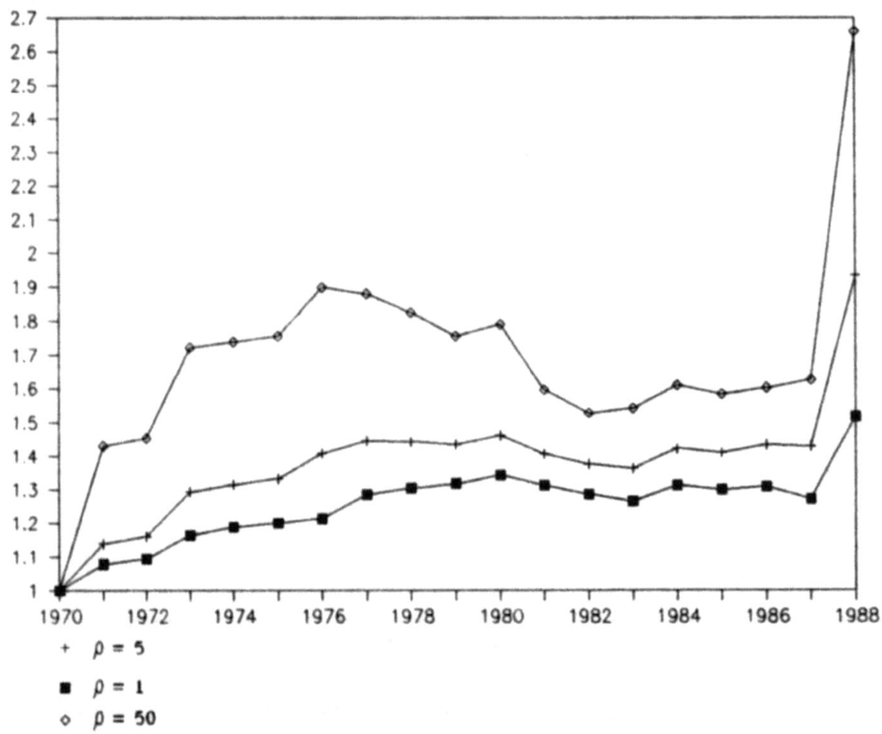

Figure 4: Mean index of 8 indicators, constructed by means of CES-function ($\rho = 1$, $\rho = 5$, $\rho = 50$).

Finally, Table 4 gives the correlation of the combined indices calculated above with economic growth and with the other indicators for environmental pollution. The table shows that the aritmethic mean index (CES with $\rho = 1$) and the geometric mean index are highly correlated with economic growth and hence with the first principal component of the seven indicators. The correlation between the CES index with $\rho = 50$ and economic growth is smaller. There is a rather high correlation with the number of seals. However, to a large extent this is due to the huge decrease in the number of seals in 1988 because of the infection disease. Obviously it does not reflect a sudden increase in actual pollution. This incident exemplifies that in constructing an environmental index it is always necessary to monitor whether the indicators which underlie the combined index are still appropriate for the purpose. A similar incident happened with the construction of the cyclical index after the stock market crash of October 1987 (Black Monday). In that case a cyclical indicator which included the stock exchange index as component, suggested a sudden deterioration of the business cycle. However, no such deterioration took place. Therefore the stock exchange index had to be removed from the cyclical indicator.

Table 4: Correlation of the mean indices of the 8 indicators with other indicators.

Indicator	Arithmetic mean	Geometric mean	CES ($\rho = 1$)	CES ($\rho = 50$)
National product	0.91	0.89	0.91	0.54
Acidity of rainfall	-0.15	-0.33	-0.15	0.06
Vitality of woods	0.14	0.29	0.14	-0.03
Common seals (inv.)	0.50	0.48	0.50	0.86
First principal component of 7 indicators	0.92	0.91	0.92	0.50

7. Conclusions

The environment is still very much understated in the macroeconomic debate. The main reason is the lack of a clear index which mirrors the state of the environment, in terms of which policy goals can be formulated in the same way as goals for reducing unemployment or for reducing the government deficit. This chapter advocates construction of such an index or 'mirror of cleanliness' for use in policy analysis. Moreover, the index can be used for quantification of the environmental policy in macro-economic models (see *e.g.* den Hartog and Maas, 1990; Mulder, 1990).

The construction of an environmental index is by no means an easy task, and many experts will even consider it impossible. This is certainly true for an ideal index on which all agree. Yet, for the construction of a less than ideal index, as outlined in Section 4, much more information is needed: time series on various aspects of pollution and experts' opinions on how to value these aspects in relation to each other. Moreover, the description of how the index should be constructed, abstracts from the different dimensions both in time (long lags between policy measures and final effects on the environment) and space (local, regional, national, worldwide scale of the problem, import and export of pollution to and from abroad). In the case of a small, open economy, the spatial aspect of the environmental index portrays another aspect of its possible use in policy analysis. If similar indices are constructed, for several neighbouring countries, regression and/or causality analysis may reveal how much domestic pollution can be attributed to pollution abroad, and to what extent a reduction of the level of pollution can be induced by domestic environmental policy measures. In this way, the pollution indices and the resulting environmental 'trade balances' may constitute a basis for international negotiations on worldwide policy measures to deflect pollution.

In order to illustrate techniques for the construction of an environmental index, and problems associated with it, this chapter presents calculations for the prototype of such an index, based on the scantly available time series information for the Netherlands. The application of principal components analysis, which is done by analogy of the construction of a trade cycle index, is hampered by the fact that some of the pollution indicators exhibit opposite trends. As an alternative, unweighted indices can be used, but we should be aware that these indices are quite sensitive to the specification of the combination formula. Moreover, the indicators on which information is available by no means cover all aspects of pollution in the Netherlands. Yet we see that the majority of the indices we have constructed still show an apparent correlation with national product. It does not imply that deflecting economic growth is a necessary condition for our environment becoming less polluted, but it does imply that stringent policy measures are needed to stop pollution from running parallel to economic growth (see also Pen, 1990). The main conclusion of this chapter is, however, that much more time series data and experts' opinions on trade-offs are needed for the construction of a mirror of cleanliness, in order to grant it just some practical relevance.

Appendix: Environmental indicators for the Netherlands

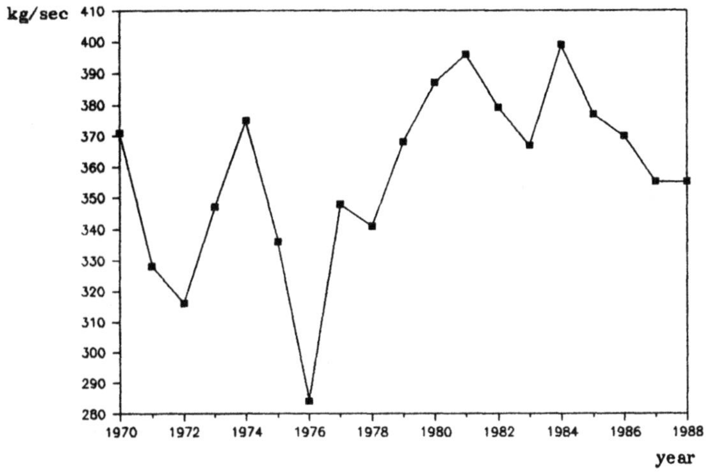

Chloride load of the Rhine.

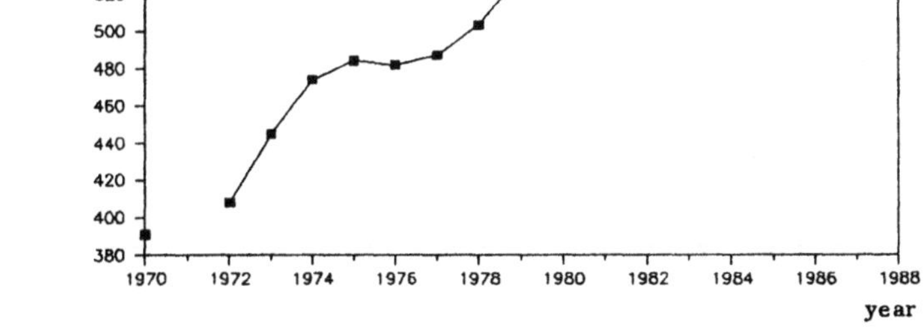

Manure production

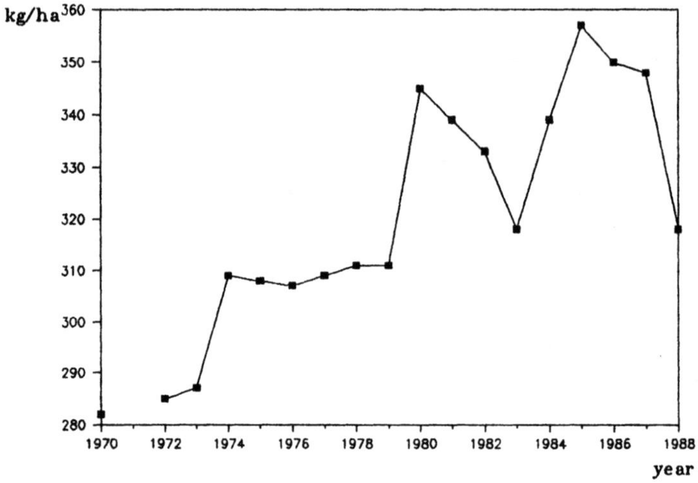

Use of fertiliser.

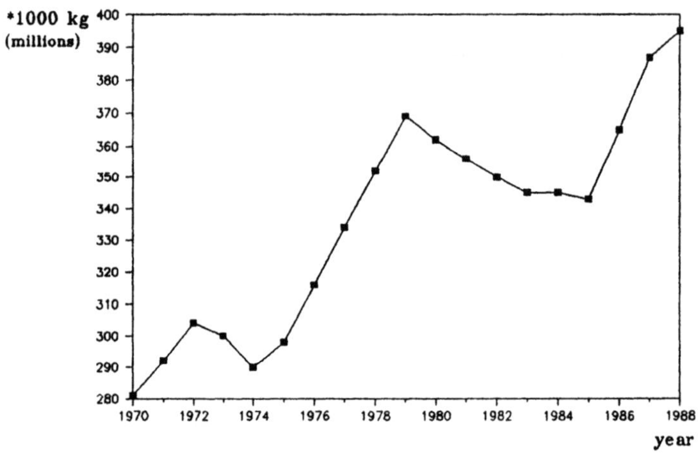

Domestic and industrial garbage.

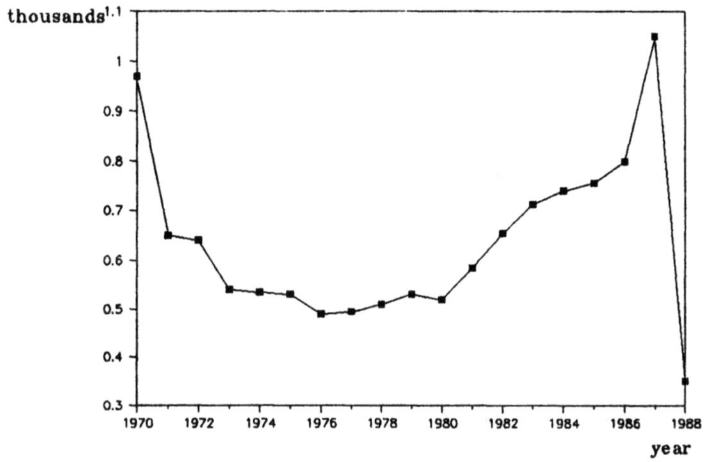

Common seals in de 'Waddenzee'.

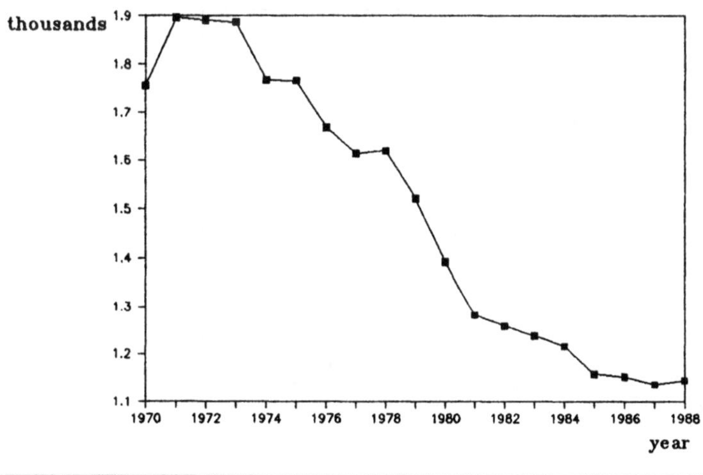

Emissions of mobile sources.

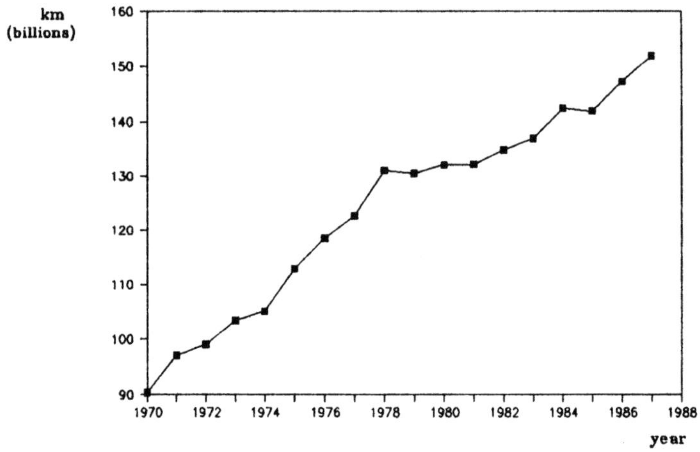

Total mobility.

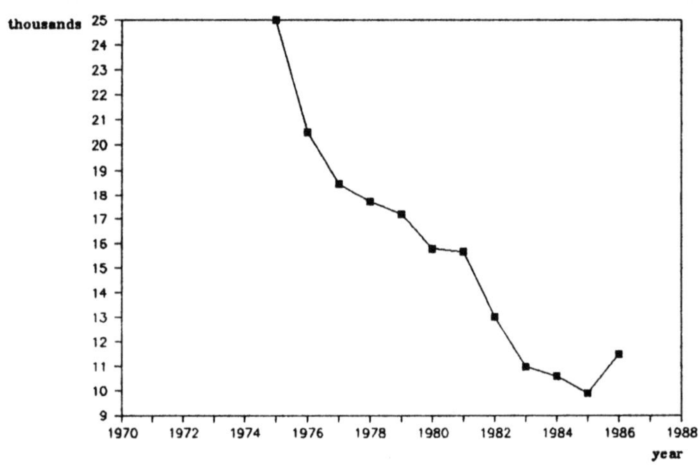

Oxygen drainage of households on surface waters.

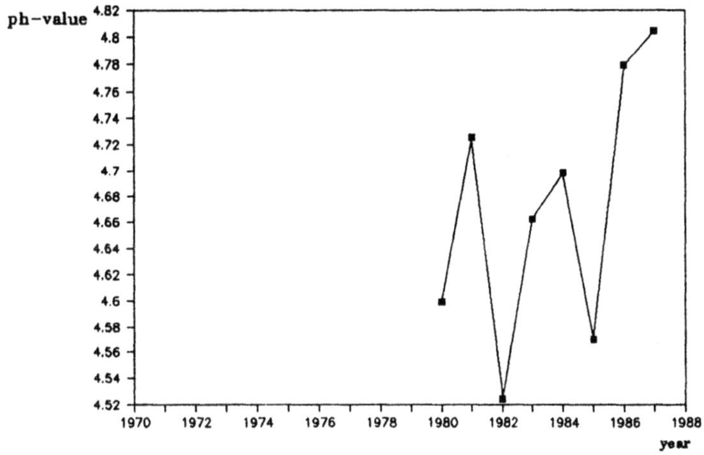

Acidity of rainfall.

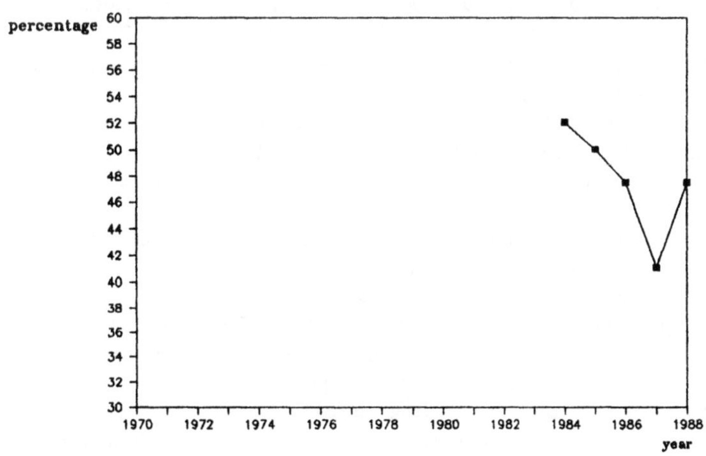

Vitality of woods.

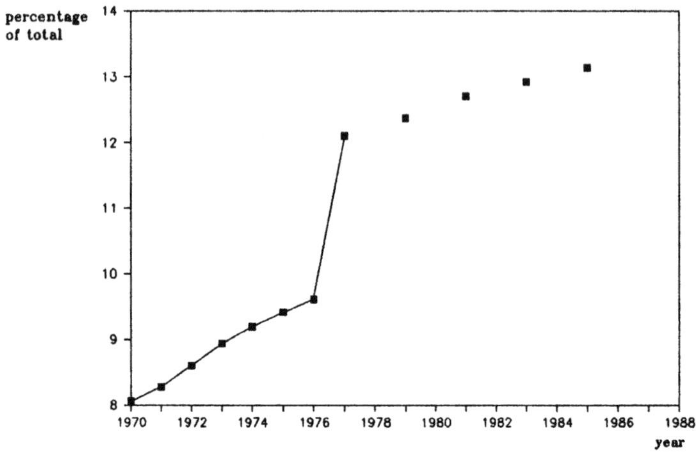

Use of land for industry and buildings.

References

Brink B.J.E. ten, *Amoebe approach; a method for description and assessment of ecosystems*, Summary Poster, 3rd North Sea Seminar 1989. Distress Signals, Rotterdam 1989.

Butter F.A.G. den, Op zoek naar een milieuspiegel: hoe vuil is Nederland? *Economisch Statistische Berichten.* Vol 75 (1990), pp. 196-199.

Fase M.M.G., A principal components analysis of market interest rates in the Netherlands, 1962-1970. *European Economic Review.* Vol 4 (1973), pp. 107-134.

Fase M.M.G., The interdependence of short-term interest rates in the major financial centres of the world. *Kyklos*, Vol 29 (1976), pp. 63-96.

Folmer H., De prijs van het milieu. In: *Geïntegreerd milieuonderzoek* (Koninklijke Nederlandse Academie van Wetenschappen). Amsterdam 1990, pp. 41-55.

Hartog H. den and R.J.M. Maas, Een duurzame economische ontwikkeling: macro-economische aspecten van een prioriteit voor het milieu. In: Nijkamp P. and H. Verbruggen (eds), *Het Nederlands milieu in de Europese ruimte*, Preadviezen van de Koninklijke Vereniging voor de Staathuishoudkunde. Stenfert Kroese, Leiden 1990, pp. 77-126.

Heertje A., Groei en krimp bij duurzame ontwikkeling: welke kennis is nodig? In Nijkamp P. and H. Verbruggen (eds), *Het Nederlands Milieu in de Europese Ruimte*, Preadviezen van de Koninklijke Vereniging voor de Staathuishoudkunde. Stenfert Kroese, Leiden 1990, pp. 43-75.

Ministerie van Landbouw, Natuurbeheer en Visserij, *De vitaliteit van het Nederlandse bos 8, Verslag van de landelijke Vitaliteitsinventarisatie 1990.* Directie Bos- en Landschapsbouw, Rapport 1990-19, The Hague 1990.

Mulder R.J., Milieubeleid en macro-economie. *Maandschrift Economie*, Vol. 54, (1990), pp. 347-363.

Opschoor J.B., Duurzame ontwikkeling: een pleidooi voor herverdeling en herregulering. In: Amstel A. van and H. Jansen (eds), *Environment and development the year 2000 and beyond.* IvM, Amsterdam 1987, pp. 71-81.

Opschoor J.B., Ecologisch duurzame economische ontwikkeling: een theoretisch idee en een weerbarstige praktijk. In: Nijkamp P. and H. Verbruggen (eds), *Het Nederlands milieu in de Europese ruimte*, Preadviezen van de Koninklijke Vereniging voor de Staathuishoudkunde 1990. Stenfert Kroese, Leiden 1990, pp. 7-41.

Ott W.R., *Environmental indices; theory and practice.* Ann Arbor Science, Michigan (1978).

Pen J., Kunnen economen het milieubederf begrijpen? *Hollands Maandblad.* Vol. 31, (1990), Nr. 5-6, pp. 16-20.

Schama S., *The embarrassment of riches; an interpretation of Dutch culture in the Golden Age.* Collins, London 1987.

Schouten D.B.J., De sociaal-economische doelstellingen en hun ontwikkeling. In: Galan C. de *et al.* (eds), *Economische orde en beleid.* Kluwer/ SER, The Hague 1985, pp. 19-33.

Sociaal Economische Raad, *Advies over het rapport Our common future*, Publicatie Nr. 6 - 17. SER, The Hague 1989.

Vos J.B. *et al.*, *Indicators for the state of the environment*, IvM-VU publication R/85/1. IvM-VU, Amsterdam 1985.

Vos J.B. *et al.*, *Vijftien indicatoren voor de toestand van het milieu*, IvM- VU publication R/86/5. IvM-VU, Amsterdam 1986.

VROM, *Nationaal milieubeleidsplan.* SDU, The Hague 1989.

Chapter 4

LAND USE EXTERNALITIES IN NATIONAL ACCOUNTING

Neil Adger and Martin Whitby*

The literature on natural resources reflects a general consensus that the standard identities of national welfare (GNP, NNP) give erroneous measures of economic growth for international and intertemporal comparisons, because they imply that increased welfare requires both increased production and consumption; a goal which may not be compatible with sustainable environmental resource management. In the last decade there has been intense activity to extend the system of national accounts to include those discrepancies long recognised; non-monetized economic activity and the use of natural resources. Although a range of revisions has been suggested (Ahmad *et al.*, 1989), there is little consensus as to correct procedures. The reasons for this stem from the inconsistencies in the underlying economic model of income generated in an economy (Norgaard, 1989) and from suggested revisions requiring large capacities for data collection (Hueting, 1990; Blades, 1989). The alternative rationales of particular solutions for incorporation of environmental data into a physical accounting system, or the value of these into the revision of net product, is to provide an indicator of growth or economic well being, or a tool for development planning.

1. The subject

This study explores the methodology for revising the relative contribution of sectors to economic well being, for policy makers. Stern (1991) asserts that theory and empirical evidence on the determinants of growth are not yet

---

* W.N. Adger and M.C. Whitby are respectively, Research Associate in and Director of the Countryside Change Unit, Department of Agricultural Economics and Food Marketing, University of Newcastle upon Tyne, UK. The Countryside Change Unit is funded by the UK Economic and Social Research Council. Research assistance from Peter van den Berg is gratefully acknowledged. Errors remain the responsibility of the authors.

advanced to the stage where confident assertions on policies for growth can be made. Growth can take different forms, with implications for distribution and for the environment. The incorporation of environmental information into the system of national accounts can better inform policy makers on the effects of policies on the sectors of the economy.

The premise underlying the revision of accounts for environmental quality is that there is a stock of natural capital, the consumption of which is equivalent to the consumption of man-made capital, and which decreases the capacity to generate income (or welfare) in the future. There is consensus on certain revisions that can feasibly be made to the existing accounts. These are to take those parts of the accounts which are already enumerated, but which involve the use of natural capital and revise them to give a measure of 'sustainable income', that level of income which does not jeopardise future income.

The following discussion first reviews current thought on bringing environmental quality into a national accounting framework. Within this debate there are those who advocate the refinement of the accounts from information already held within them. Those who urge a more radical revision favour values being assigned to non-marketed capital at the aggregate level[1]. The framework fits into the latter of the two approaches mentioned above in that non-marketed externalities are valued. Most of the work on evaluating environmental externalities has focused at the micro level, on individual projects. However, the recognition of broader transboundary externalities, such as acid rain, the pollution of the seas and global warming urges a case for evaluation of such effects at the national and international level. This requirement for revision is reflected in the debate on national income accounting arising from the production of the new UN System of National Accounts and experience in developing and developed countries (see Peskin, 1989; Peskin and Lutz, 1990, for example).

Much of the available natural capital is associated with land, so that an accounting system which produces physical and monetary evaluations of land-using sectors will be essential for accurate measurement of environmental quality. The recognition of the characteristics of 'land' as a non-renewable stock resource with renewable service flows (McInerney, 1976) is useful in examining irreversible allocation decisions of the kind

1 In the the UK, for instance, it is intended that environmental externalities be included in policy decision-making under the 1990 Environmental Protection Act for all sectors (see Power, 1990).

involved in land conversion to other uses or development. The identification of these modifications is outlined here for a case study of the UK primary land-using sector. There are clearly problems of delineating boundaries for sectoral analysis in order to assign externalities to particular sectors. Indeed Harrison (1989) advocated aggregate modifications for environmental quality to be made at the national level for this reason. The advantages of the chosen approach are to show the relative importance of sectors across the economy in policy making. The object is to set up a system that is replicable across all sectors.

The framework for the UK primary land using sector highlights the problems of sectoring the economy when externalities have multiple sources. The land use designation process is introduced as the identifier of externalities and a net environmental benefit is calculated for the sector taking the externalities and the costs of defensive expenditure and degradation of natural capital into account. Willingness to pay (WTP) estimates are taken as a measure of utility foregone. The initial partial results for this method show a positive net environmental benefit for the sector, though this in part reflects the incompleteness of the data, especially with respect to negative physical externalities; the comprehensive result may be either positive or negative.

2. Sustainable income and modified welfare

The measure of income which is the object of the modifications recommended by Daly (1989) for example, is that level of consumption which can be consumed without jeopardising future generations of income or welfare. This, according to Daly (1989) is consistent with the original Hicksian definition. Income is not an exact measure of welfare or standard of living (at the national level); various income measures (GNP, GDP) are used as proxies for welfare and income has numerous definitions.[2]

Net product rather than gross product, more closely represents the level of consumption which will not leave the economy worse off in the long run as it incorporates allowance for the run down of the stock of capital. At present, UK national accounts do not recognise the contribution of environmental

---

2 In the UK agricultural sector (a major object of the case study) for instance, net farming income is a residual measure to balance net product with estimated depreciation and factor incomes other than for personal labour.

capital to the production process (absorption of pollution by the environment and the stocks of renewable and non-renewable resources) in allowing income to be generated without damaging sustainability. Part of the proposed adjustments to the national accounting framework address this particular problem.

The non-recognition of the contribution of the stock of natural capital to the generation of sustainable income gives an erroneous measure of welfare due to implicit zero valuation of non-monetized goods. As well as the degradation of the environment through pollution externalities of production and consumption, national accounts also exclude measures of household non-monetized production and the utility of leisure and disutility of labour. All these would have to be accounted for if estimation of welfare is the goal of the national accounting framework.

From the identified requirement to revise the national account to make the income measure 'sustainable' there follow certain adjustments which can feasibly be made. Daly's (1988) adjustments lead to what he describes as 'sustainable social net national product', which is found by subtracting defensive expenditures and depreciation of natural capital from traditional net product measure.

Sustainable Social Net National Product = Net National product
less Defensive Expenditures
less Depreciation of Natural Capital

Hartwick's (1990) 'true' net national product is traditional gross product less a rental for each type of natural capital (marketed and non-marketed). This rent is the price less marginal cost multiplied by the change in stock. Hartwick's analysis, however, does not reduce net product by defensive expenditure, a point agreed by Mäler (1990).[3] The fundamental difficulty with defensive expenditures is that they consist of final and intermediate expenditures, and therefore the identity of factor incomes and expenditures is broken (Bartelmus, 1989). Daly's (1989) 'sustainable social net national product' is then a welfare-based estimation and the proposed set of defensive expenditure adjustments is extensive.

---

3 Mäler (1990) also considers the possibility of taking defensive expenditure as a proxy for the degradation of natural capital, which is a necessary adjustment in his framework, but concludes that this is feasible only when they are perfect substitutes for each other.

Defensive expenditures are those expenditures normally counted in the national accounts which are incurred due to the presence of negative externalities so as to bring the level of welfare back to its original level. Expenditures, which could be regarded as defensive when incurred by firms are counted as increases in costs to that firm and therefore as intermediate expenditures. The same expenditures by households and firms are final expenditures. The proposed adjustment is to treat these as intermediate, which would reduce the level of measured income. This would resolve anomalies such as GNP rising when clean up costs are incurred after an oil spillage for example. Harrison (1989) in her proposed system said that an estimate of these should be taken from Net Product even if the expenditure does not take place to reflect decreased welfare.

The over-riding problem with this modification, as with others is the delineation of the categories of expenditure. In the case of defensive expenditure, it has been suggested that the minimum expenditures which should logically be subtracted from Net Product are the costs of environmental protection and expenditures for damage compensation. Additional categories reported by Daly (1989) reflect concerns in post-industrial societies of decreased quality of mainly urban environments. They include the costs of transport congestion, including health service costs of accidents; increased costs of crime prevention (implicitly regarding high crime levels as a cost of higher levels of economic activity); and increased expenditures incurred due to unhealthy working and living conditions and addictions such as alcohol and tobacco. This is clearly a large agenda of issues to be tackled through social policy and would widen the 'environmental' modifications proposed here. Again the fundamental objective of the measurement of welfare is the guiding rule for determining the revision of the accounts.

The revisions for environmental quality considered in this study are the incurred defensive expenditures by government to maintain the environment (in this case in the primary land using sector). Policies leading to central and local government expenditures are multi-objective, so assumptions of the main purposes of these expenditures must be made to enable identification of the externalities.[4] Although this does not reflect Daly's advocacy of reduction of net product by household defensive expenditure, the measurement of government defensive expenditure moves the estimated sustainable income measure towards an indicator of welfare rather than sustainable income as advocated by Mäler's (1990) framework.

The second major revision of Net Product is based on the premise that natural resources are essential to production and consumption (one of the traditional 'factors of production' being land, or natural resources) for the maintenance of life supporting systems, as well as having intrinsic value in existence for intergenerational and other reasons. This leads to the conclusion that natural capital should be treated in a similar manner to man-made capital in accounting terms, since running down of the stock of capital reduces ability to generate income in the future. If an agreed correct value can be placed on natural capital under an accounting system, the implication is that if stocks of natural capital are depleted to increase stocks of man-made capital, then the ability to recreate income in the future will be maintained. As an example, the study by Repetto *et al.* (1989) of the growth in net product of Indonesia revised the average growth of GDP downwards from 7.1 per cent per annum to 4.0 per cent per annum for the 1971-1984 period, as the observed rapid growth was greatly enhanced by the depletion of primary resources by the logging of natural hardwood forest and extraction of oil.

The case study primary land using sector example does not involve pricing exhaustible resource stocks. The stock of natural capital in UK forestry is taken as semi-natural and broadleaved forest. The stock of commercial softwood forestry is increasing, with the mean annual increment greater than the yield. Modifications are made for the effect of forestry on the stock of soil and biomass organic matter with public good externalities which are incorporated under the next heading; non-marketed natural capital.

Account must be taken of the degradation of the stock of natural capital which is essential to the sustainable level of income, but which is not marketed. This includes elements of the environment such as clean air, the

---

4 Adger and Whitby (1991) show the implications of calculating a Net Environmental Benefit for the land using sector, but the framework of increasing net product by the service of the environment as a sink for pollution and subtracting the cost of providing this service fundamentally depends on counting consumption of natural capital as an increase in Gross Product, and environmental deterioration as a decrease in Net Product. This has been revised in the present chapter to treat defensive expenditures in the same manner as intermediate expenditures by firms.

stock of soil or fisheries, and bio-diversity; some of which are more easily measured than others. Techniques include the cost of replacing the recreatable stock. Part of the role of the environment in determining sustainability is the ability to assimilate pollutants, a role which often has low potential for substitution with man-made capital. The substitutability of man-made and natural capital depends on the irreversibility of depletion decisions; and attitudes to uncertainty in decisions (see Pearce and Turner, 1990, for a discussion of these assumptions). In this study the stock of carbon and changes in it due to continued land use are investigated and costed by the effects on global climatic change. Quantities of agricultural pollutants such as nitrogen and phosphorus are investigated.

3. Modified welfare

The framework envisaged here departs from the debate as to the optimal definition of sustainable income. It shows the relative contribution of non-marketed externalities, and therefore a modified welfare adjustment is included to quantify the aggregate consumer surplus for certain non-use, indirect use and existence values. The total value of a resource can be envisaged as the sum of use, indirect use and existence values (see Johansson, 1990, for example), which can be identified through revealed and expressed preference techniques. Changes in these service flows result in changes in the 'quality of life' or aggregate welfare within an economy. Increases in pollution and negative landscape externalities will reduce the non-marketed benefit from the depleted stock of natural capital. For the primary land using sector these service flows from the non-renewable resource (McInerney, 1976) are mainly associated with the major land users - agriculture and forestry; because of the intimate mixture of these in the landscape it would be difficult to attribute the derived aggregate benefits specifically to one use or the other.

The justification for this addition to sectoral income accounts is to show the relative contribution of various sectors to welfare. This does not relate to sustainable income but shows the implications of policy changes within the sector. Although sectors such as the land using sector appear to make a relatively large contribution to aggregate welfare this reflects the predominance of 'land' (natural resources) associated with this part of the economy.

4. Great Britain case study

The case study of the primary land using sector illustrates a number of important dilemmas in the implementation of environmental accounting as discussed above. The first of these is to delineate the sector in a meaningful way to highlight the environmental externalities. The primary land using sector in Great Britain (GB) is not normally considered as an accounting unit; the study highlights the need for this. The results are critically dependent on the limits set. Modifications for pollution caused by the use of fossil fuels are counted against this sector only when they are directly used, modifications for the depletion of stocks of oil reserves are set against the oil extraction sector. Thus, pollution of water courses by run off and leaching of nitrate fertiliser is a degradation of the stock of natural capital, but the raw materials used in their manufacture accrue against the manufacturing sector.

In Table 1 the sectoral accounts for agriculture and forestry are summarized. These two sectors are not normally reported together in the national context, but this is a necessary step in the recognition of the interdependence of the externalities within primary land using sectors of the economy. The continued expansion of forestry in the post-war period in GB, together with its long production cycle, ensures that its annual net product remains negative. This situation will be reversed as the national forest estate approaches sustained yield. It is an *a priori* expectation that environmental modifications will be relatively large in this sector because of the predominance of natural capital, and because UK agriculture has a Net Product equivalent to 1.4% of GDP in 1988.

The environmental modifications are estimated in the sections below to give a measure of sustainable income for the primary land use sector. The adjustments are separated into defensive expenditures and degradation of natural capital. The use of non-renewable resources was not investigated in this study for the reasons explained above. The modifications for environmental quality are taken from this baseline sectoral account. A modified welfare adjustment is then calculated from expressed and revealed preference studies of GB land use and recreation.

Defensive expenditure adjustments

The modified account for the primary land using sector attempts to estimate government defensive expenditure but ignores household defensive

Table 1: Agricultural and forestry outputs, inputs and net product: Great Britain.[5]

		(£ million current prices) 1988
Final Output		11161
Net Input		5663
Gross Product		5498
less Depreciation		1470
Net Product		4028
of which:	Interest	660
	Rent and Labour	1664
	Farming Income	1816
	Forestry Income	-112

Sources: Ministry of Agriculture, Fisheries and Food (1990); Forestry Commission (1990); Department of Agriculture for Northern Ireland (1990).

expenditure directly associated with the land use sector for reasons explained above. Defensive expenditure allocated specifically designed to maintain the factor 'land' in its present state includes expenditure on national parks, management agreement payments to maintain sites of special scientific interest, and the cost of river clean up after agricultural pollution.

The defensive expenditures required to maintain the landscape and wildlife amenity of rural Britain include payments through management agreements to farmers to avoid depleting the stock of particular habitats as well as expenditure to promote recreation and education. These are the expenditures on the designations aggregated in Table 6, such as Environmentally Sensitive Areas, National Parks, Sites of Special Scientific Interest, as well as policies such as set-aside where a farmer receives payment for returning arable land to semi-natural state for an agreed time-period. Agricultural policies such as those in the Less Favoured Areas (LFA) have not been included here, though it may be argued that such policies have a partial objective of the maintenance of upland farming practices and landscape. Since the conservation objective is only one unknown portion of this policy (which, arguably is present in *most* agricultural public expenditure) and since LFA policies have controversially created negative

5 As well as the problem of setting sectoral limits to the land use sector, a statistical collation problem is experienced in the UK. The Departmental National Income Calculation for agriculture is compiled for the UK. Forestry Commission data on the forestry estate is for Great Britain only. Since many of the environmental externalities studies refer to Great Britain, this was taken as the accounting unit, the equivalent Northern Ireland data being subtracted.

environmental benefit through local over-stocking, this item of defensive expenditure has been ignored. The total of government defensive expenditures identified here specifically targetted at the primary land using sector in 1988 was £43 million.

Defensive expenditure on cleaning up the results of agricultural pollution incidents in UK can be inferred from the prosecutions of farmers. This non-point pollution stems from deliberate and accidental flows of silage effluent into water courses.[6] The National Rivers Authority attempts to recover the full cost of pollution and therefore the average level of fine over the 3.6 per cent of the reported cases prosecuted, has been imputed to all reported incidents. This indicates a total identified agricultural pollution cost of £5.6 million in imputed defensive expenditure.

Other agricultural pollution stems from the use of nitrate fertiliser, resulting in lower drinking water quality. The area most greatly affected in Great Britain by the concentration of the outputs of nitrogen reported in Table 5 is East Anglia. Imputed defensive expenditure in this area by Anglian Water to meet EC standards for drinking water in 1988 had a present value of £9 million, as reported by Hanley (1989).[7] The three indicative figures for government defensive expenditure to redress pollution and conserve the rural environment sum to £58 million, and constitute adjustment (2) in Table 5. Defensive expenditures incurred by households to reverse environmental externalities by the primary land using industries could not be evaluated, but would need to be identified in a full sectoral account. An example is an expansion of the market for water purification equipment and the extra expenditure on bottled water when water quality standards are uncertain.

Adjustments for the degradation of natural capital

The main stock of natural capital associated with the primary land using sector is soil and water; although the limit of the study is such that the water supply industry is outside its scope. The physical pollution by the industries focused on here are nitrogen and phosphate pollution. Additionally, the role of primary land using industries as a sink for carbon emissions from other

6 Other forms of agricultural pollution, such as the nuisance value of straw burning are not considered here, though this is enumerated in the nitrogen satellite account, reported in Table 3.

7 The subsequent privatisation of the water industry in the UK would mean these expenditures would become an intermediate expenditure by the private sector and would be deducted at source. This highlights the anomaly of the treatment of defensive expenditures across sectors.

sectors is investigated. This debate reflects concern about sustainability of modern farming and forestry practices (stock of carbon), and their impact on the greenhouse effect. Forestry, in particular, has been prominent in debate where the carbon sequestration properties of tropical and temperate forests provide justification for afforestation policies or particular projects (see Kayes *et al.*, 1990; Trexler *et al.*, 1989, for examples).

The carbon sequestration properties of the land uses alternative to forestry, and the effect of different land uses on soil carbon are often underemphasised. To redress this, Adger *et al.* (1991) develop a model of carbon dynamics for the GB land using sector, based on reported land use data obtained by aerial photography over the period 1947 to 1980. This shows that the stock of carbon in present land use is increasing, mainly due to accumulation in the soil under long term uses such as forestry. However most changes in land use, especially in felling broadleaved forestry, draining land for conifer planting, and continuous arable production lead to net emissions of carbon. The policy implications of these findings underline the pressures for conservation and an understanding of carbon dynamics in relation to changing land use patterns. Table 2 shows a carbon balance for GB land use for 1988. The retained land use and land use change figures assume trends in land use to have continued after the sample period modelled (1947 to 1980), except where other data, such as forestry harvesting and planting data, were available. Other sources of carbon emissions are the use of lime, the methane emissions from livestock on the land, and the loss of soil carbon from arable cultivation of peatland. The net effects is the difference between emissions and fixations in Table 2, or 4.75 million tonnes of carbon *per annum*.

Table 2: Carbon fixation and emissions by GB land using sector, 1988.

Fixed	'000 tC/pa	Emitted	'000 tC/pa
Crops for consumption	6032	From livestock as methane	2574
As meat	319	Fossil fuel consumed	707
Livestock Products	161	Liming	348
Harvested timber	1049	Peat wastage	500
Retained land use	2224	Land use change	903
Total	9785	Total	5032

Source: Adger *et al.* (1991).

The annual figures for 1988 reflect both changes in land use in GB in the post war period and changes in management practices over the same period. There has been a gradual change in land use practices towards more intensive agricultural systems - for example arable yields have increased steeply over the last century or so. The methods of forest cultivation have also increased in intensity with concentration on clear-felling of single-age stands of trees and re-planting in large blocks. These methods have replaced traditional semi-natural systems where plant nutrients were recycled by adding waste to the soils and where intensive land management techniques such as drainage and liming were not widely used.

The significance of these findings in terms of the stock of carbon, and of the economic implications, if these are to be incorporated into a national accounting framework, are based on their impact on the environment to humans. Two alternative evaluations have been analysed, both based on the premise that global climatic change will have costs to society. These costs may be actual costs of decreased levels of welfare or production, or they may be simply increased uncertainty. The method favoured by Nordhaus (1990) to investigate this is to take the best scientific estimates of the likely effects of climatic change on particular sectors and place a value on these. The optimum policy is then to equate the marginal cost of abatement of emissions with the marginal benefit of avoiding the estimated costs. An alternative (Anderson, 1991) is adapted from optimum pricing of a depletable resource: the cost of each tonne of carbon emitted is the bringing forward of the date when carbon accumulation will have reached an unacceptable limit and non-carbon emitting technologies (or land uses) will have to be substituted. It is assumed that there is some unacceptable level of accumulated atmospheric carbon. When this level is reached, carbon emitting technologies will be forced to be substituted for non-carbon emitting technologies. The damage to society at this level of accumulated carbon cannot be accurately predicted, but costs associated with uncertainty are present, and this level may be decided by international agreement and revised over time with increasing information. The solution of the problem gives the social cost of carbon emissions or the optimal tax on emissions and subsidy on sequestration.

Nordhaus estimated the value of the predicted damage to various sectors of the US economy from global climatic change and sea level rise. The avoidance of this cost is the benefit of sequestrating carbon now. Nordhaus gave a range of damage scenarios and hence projected costs per tonne of carbon emitted, the mean, medium damage scenario being around £7/tC.[8] The use of this estimate for land use in Great Britain would assume the domestic economy to be spatially, climatically and sectorally similar to the economy of the land mass of the US, which is erroneous. The Anderson (1991) estimate, although relying on a total carbon accumulation point thought to be a threshold beyond which it would be undesirable to emit at the global level, has the advantage of including estimates of costs of energy production relating to the UK economy.

Anderson investigated the implications on the forestry industry of the imposition of taxes on emissions (and subsidies on sequestrations) of the calculated social cost (and social benefit) of carbon. Sequestrations through growth and emissions through harvesting occur at different times, and so have been converted to present values in the analysis.[9] The social cost estimate of £30.77/tC in this study is simply applied to the net emissions from agriculture and forestry, given present land use. The results from the carbon balance table are net of changes in soil and biomass carbon, and of the other emissions from agriculture and forestry, so the per tonne of carbon figure can simply be applied to these. The difference between the emissions and fixation of carbon from the carbon balance table is 4.75 million tC which leads to a carbon credit benefit of £146.2 m, given present agricultural and forestry practices and land use.[10]

Similar accounts of the sources of agricultural pollution are presented in Tables 3 and 4. These are nitrogen and phosphorus inputs into agricultural and forestry production. Each has separate environmental consequences, some of which are easy to separate into contributions from the land use sector, while others are additive to emissions from other sectors. The varying importance of the different nitrogen based substances in Table 3 should be recognized. The figures are based on a study of 1978 land use by the Royal

8 This figure is used to calculate carbon credits of afforestation by Pearce (1991).

9 In the growing popularity of market incentives for the tackling of environmental problems, where markets may or may not exist, carbon emission taxes have been offered as one means of achieving the desired environmental policy objective, even within a set of international quota type agreements. If these policies were implemented, and a serious attempt was made to measure carbon emissions from various sectors in the economy, then the equivalent to carbon emission taxes in the fossil fuel using industries would be subsidies and taxes to those parts of the primary land using sector fixing or emitting carbon. The problems of measurement, as found in Adger *et al.* (1991), are major, and subsidies formulated at a multinational level, across a wide range of agroclimatic conditions make the proposal unrealistic.

10 This figure is sensitive, as are all the carbon results, to the delineation of the limits of the study. The fixing of carbon for consumption by the primary land using sector, for instance, would be a net export from households.

Society (1983), but updated in line with 1988 land use data. Nitrate found in drinking water is alleged to have adverse health effects, including methaemoglobinaemia and stomach cancer, and is one aspect of the EC's Directive on drinking water quality (Council of the European Communities, 1980). However, the toxic effects of nitrates are still debated and it is probably the case that health hazards from nitrates are much less than those from NO_x. All of the source substances (7 - 10) listed in Table 3 are judged to be noxious in some sense but they vary in their impact and the way in which they affect the environment.

Table 3: Environmental impact of nitrogen for UK agriculture: 1988.

		kilotonnes
1	Sink for sewage	5
2	Sink for other waste (non-vegetable feed)	40
3	Sink for deposition	372
4	Creating organic-N suitable for human consumption	500
5	Maintaining soil fertility	165
6	Biological N2 fixation (avoiding fertiliser)	196
7	NO_x emissions	26
8	N_2O emissions from denitrification	84
9	NO_3 leaching - water pollution	841
10	NH_3 volatilisation	376

The net nitrogen balance for UK agriculture, shows that, in the period since the Royal Society (1983) study, between 1978 and 1988, use of nitrogen in agriculture grew considerably. Table 3 shows the quantities of nitrogen added to, accumulating in and leaving the agriculture sector in 1988. Only those quantities of environmental significance are included. It should be noted that items 1-3, totalling 417 kt are sinks for pollution, while items 7-10 are immediate sources of pollution and amount to 1327 kt. Item (4) refers to its production of proteins for food and (5) and (6) refer in turn to improvement in soil fertility by handling animal wastes and by the activity of bacteria in fixing nitrogen which is subsequently available as a plant nutrient. These two effects have a more ambiguous benefit in that it could be argued that fixing nitrogen has the same effect as adding fertiliser nitrogen to the soil; namely, it increases the amount of nitrate reaching the water courses. NO_x is now recognized as a serious pollutant, adding substantially to the greenhouse problem, being many times more potent in its impact than CO_2. An unknown part of (8) is also in the form of NO_x.

There has been less specific research on the costs of this pollution, partly because such impacts are disputed (Hanley, 1989). The benefits of pollution control can be shown indirectly through revealed and expressed preference techniques.[11] In the case of nitrate pollution, the minimum estimate of the benefits of the abatement of agricultural nitrate pollution was cleaner drinking water valued at £12.97 per household surveyed in 1988 in the Anglian Water Authority area (the greatest affected area in the UK). This gave an aggregate yearly benefit of £10.8 million (adjustment (1) in Table 5) for the estimated number of consumers affected by excess nitrates in drinking water (Hanley, 1989).

Table 4: Environmental impacts of phosphorus from agriculture: 1988.

		kilotonnes
1	Net sink for sewage	11
2	Addition to soil P-stock (maintaining soil fertility)	134
3	Creation of organic P suitable for human consumption	91
4	Sink for P-deposition	1
5	Soil losses of P to water courses, imposing the risk of eutrophication	40

Table 4 shows that agriculture is a net source of phosphate which reaches the water courses as a result of leaching processes. The quantities are based on a report by the Centre for Agricultural Strategy (1978), but again updated to reflect 1988 land use. The effect of leaching is to promote eutrophication of water courses and to encourage the growth of plants which may seriously reduce water quality. Phosphorus, however, is a non-point pollutant with output from households, and some point sources from industrial outputs. Compared with nitrogen, much smaller quantities of pollutant are involved, and environmental impacts are generally less damaging. In terms of the sink-source balance, agriculture is again a net source with 40 kt entering the wider environment from the sector and only 12 kt from outside pollutant sources being retained.

Although the costs associated with phosphorus use in agricultural production seem to be declining, due to changing management practices, information such as that in Table 4 gives a picture of the physical stocks and

11 Critics of techniques of environmental valuation tend not to be in favour of measures of the costs of pollution. Blades (1989), for instance, concluded that the state of environmental evaluation is such that the benefits of pollution control are best assumed to be equal to the defensive expenditures.

flows involved in the land use sector. No attempt was made to estimate a phosphorus modification, though this could be feasibly carried out through an investigation of the economic costs of algal bloom for the fishing industries; impacts on human health of increased pollution leading to lower labour productivity and increased health expenditures. Some of these would be counted in the defensive expenditure adjustment, some would show as a degradation of the stock of natural capital. Adjustment (1) in Table 5 is then the sum of £10.8 million degradation for decline in water quality and £146.2 million enhancement of the stock of carbon in 1988.

Table 5: Environmental sustainability in agriculture and forestry accounts.

		(£ million current prices) 1988
Net Product		4028
Sustainability modifications:		
(1) degradation of Natural Capital		135
(2) defensive expenditures		-58
Sustainable Net Product		4105
of which:	Interest	660
	Rent and Labour	1664
	Farming Income	1816
	Forestry Income	-112
(1+2) Environmental adjustment		77

The physical accounts and valuation estimates reported above are brought together as a consolidated account in Table 5. The combined effect of the degradation of natural capital and defensive expenditures increases net product by £77 million. As noted previously, this estimate of sustainable income from the land using sector excludes estimates of household defensive expenditure, and full valuation of the costs of agricultural and forestry pollution; and includes an estimate for carbon fixing by the sector as carbon fixed for extended consumption is treated as a net fixation by the land use sector.

Positive externalities

The positive externalities arising from land use are mainly experienced in the form of landscape, wildlife and recreational benefits. Since most of these externalities are associated with public goods of which the more important ones receive some form of official protection, the protection mechanism itself yields indications of their relative size and significance. Thus the defensive expenditures incurred in protecting these features is part of the defensive expenditure adjustment already made. In the UK a very wide ranging and diverse system of designation has been in operation for more than four decades and it has produced a complex overlapping pattern of designation for particular uses.

The critical assumptions for the valuation of the service flows from the land using sector are that the designation process of land for conservation and access purposes is the basis for the valuation of the contribution of the non-marketed stock of natural capital to aggregate welfare in the economy, and that environmental evaluation techniques give an acceptable estimate of the valuation of service flows. On the first of these assumptions, it could be argued that common property resources are valued by means of the political decision-making process. Buchanan (1968) and Steiner (1977) for example, argued that particular public goods are those goods which are provided through collective public action. This inversion of traditional analysis, whereby public goods are defined by the inherent technical characteristics which lead to non-rivalness and non-excludability in consumption, treats the land use designation process as an indicator of value for non-marketed resources in this sector. Public goods are here defined by the political process.

Mäler (1990) argued that, for particular externalities, defensive expenditures are weak indicators of environmental damage. The alternative welfare measures of these externalities, as discussed below, rely on revealed and expressed preferences of consumers of these public goods and the defensive expenditures incurred in maintaining the landscape or abating pollution. Environmental evaluation has progressed in the last two decades (Smith, 1990), but the estimates remain critically affected by the set of inherent property rights of the public goods involved, as well as the acceptability to consumers of a hypothetical market for the good or service (Cummings *et al.*, 1986)[12]. There are also large differences between estimates of willingness to pay (WTP) and willingness to accept (WTA) compensation for the same externality. The usefulness of all essentially micro, site-specific studies in national accounting depends critically on the extent of aggregation biases. These biases specifically depend on the substitutability and

12 These studies are becoming more consistent over time, but their results remain sensitive to choice of technique for measuring demand, and functional form, among other assumptions (see Smith and Kaoru, 1990, and Walsh *et al.*, 1989, for instance).

complementarity within and between land use designations, as discussed with reference to the value of wildlife conservation below. These factors will be critical if WTP estimates are to be of use for aggregation to national income accounting.

Table 6: Areas of land designated for different uses in Great Britain.

Designated Use	Total Area (000 hectares)
Recreation Designations	5250.7
Green Belts	1962.5
Conservation Designations	2242.8
Environmentally Sensitive Areas	785.6

Sources: Department of Environment (1984, 1990), Ministry of Agriculture, Fisheries and Food (1990), Countryside Commission (1990) and Countryside Commission for Scotland (1990).

Note: Several of these designations are not mutually exclusive, so that a total would include some areas more than once.

There is much overlap in the designations between the groups in Table 6. There may also be some overlap between the categories within groups, especially that relating to conservation. It is assumed here that, for example, if a 'site of special scientific interest' (SSSI) is designated in a National Park, then the benefits arising from the two designations will be additive even where they relate to the same area of land. Similarly, if a site is protected by two different forms of conservation designation, then it is reasonable to assume that the benefits from each will be additive for such a particularly valuable area. The list also treats separately the most recent environmental designation, namely Environmentally Sensitive Areas, which was first applied in 1987. The list excludes the major network of footpaths and bridleways for which a specific willingness to pay could be elicited.

The environmental benefits of the land use designations in Table 6, shown in adjustment (3) of the account in Table 7, are derived from WTP estimates of the annual amenity value of particular designations, using revealed and expressed preference techniques. The estimate of the amenity value of Green Belt land is based on a contingent valuation survey of willingness to pay for Green Belt to be retained as a proportion of existing local taxes, for a particular Green Belt (Willis and Whitby, 1985). This estimate of £327 per ha (1988 prices) was aggregated across the present Green Belt area in the UK to give £642 million.

The major designation objectives of National Parks are the promotion of access and conservation, a multi-objective set, as indicated by the different types of defensive expenditure within national parks. They will here be assumed to have a mixture of non-use, indirect use and option values. Estimates from a contingent valuation survey in the Yorkshire Dales National Park (Garrod and Willis, 1991) indicate a mean bid price of £24.56 per visitor (based on 296 observations) to maintain the present landscape in perpetuity. Estimates of householders' willingness to pay for those residents of the national park area were remarkably similar. Latest visitor numbers to all national parks of England and Wales are estimated at 103 million visitors, though no information is available on repeat visits (Countryside Commission, 1991). These figures give a total hypothetical trust fund to ensure these demands are met, of nearly £2.6 billion. If a 6 per cent discount rate is assumed (in line with current UK public sector appraisal of non-marketed public sector operations) this gives an annual value of £152 million.

Visitors form part of the landscape they experience, and as numbers increase the disutility from the lessening of opportunities for unique wilderness experience decreases as use of the goods reach congestible levels (Randall, 1987). Due to this, and because of the substitutability of one designated area for another, the aggregation may be an overestimate for 1988.

Information on the existence value of areas of the UK designated to conserve species and habitats is scarce (see Willis, 1989). A proxy for the environmental benefits of these sites was their use value as revealed through visits specifically to view wildlife rather than general recreation. A study of three 'sites of special scientific interest' (Willis and Benson, 1988) provided an average consumer surplus of £41.97 per hectare, which when aggregated over the existing designations gave an environmental benefit of £94.12 million. The figure presented does not measure the existence value, which has not been estimated but would be additional to the use value calculated. Some of the designations overlap, so that a SSSI may also be designated under the EC's Bird Directive. Whilst it could be argued that aggregation across sites overestimates existence value, equally double-designation is defensible where it signifies international as well as national importance of the existence of some sites.

Extension of site-specific estimates of locally determined value may not be simply raised to the national level without consideration of the problems of aggregation, due to the related problems of substitution and complementarity. If a particular site were to disappear, part of the value attributed to it would simply be transferred to some other site, a bias evident from recreation demand studies of the use value of sites. For National Parks and other recreation sites, the availability of substitutes giving similar levels of utility will lead to overestimates of willingness to pay for the recreation experience. However, for those environmental goods which are complementary, to include only the irreducible, non-substitutable value of the site would under-estimate the appropriate value. The underestimate would be to the extent that sites may be complementary to other designated sites in another locality in the provision of particular ecosystems or corridors for wildlife. This would lead to an underestimate of the willingness to pay for those designations with low use values but large existence values.

Table 7: Modified agriculture and forestry accounts.

		(£ million current prices) 1988
Net Product		4028
Sustainability modifications		
(1) degradation of Natural Capital		135
(2) defensive expenditures		-58
(3) Non-marketed Service flows		888
Modified Net Product		4993
of which:	Interest	660
	Rent and Labour	1664
	Farming Income	1816
	Forestry Income	-112
(1+2) Sustainability adjustment		77
(3) Service flows		888

The adjustment for positive service flows leads to the account shown in Table 7 above, with a positive service flow of £888 million from the land use sector, associated with the maintenance of bio-diversity, landscape and recreation. Large gaps in the estimated benefits and costs of pollution and landscape remain, such as the defensive expenditures on Green Belts, the recreation and existence value of Environmentally Sensitive Areas, and the incurred costs of nitrate pollution latent in the ground from accumulated agricultural use. The modifications to the account are therefore incomplete, omitting many of the adjustments required to give a full indication of the role of the land-using industries in the national economy.

Similar figures for other sectors would be expected *a priori* to be negative. The water supply sector, the externalities of which are closely related to those of the land use sector, would have similar positive flows from aspects of biological conservation. The service flow adjustment is dependent on the nature of the natural resource: 'land' being defined as a non-renewable resource with renewable service flows (McInerney, 1976) or a mixture of fund, flow and biological resources (Randall, 1987), for example.

5. Conclusions

The chapter has reviewed available methodology for modifying National Income Accounts and applied it to the case of the main land using industries, agriculture and forestry, in the UK. The need for sustainability modifications in national accounting systems has been recognized as an important contribution to resource management as well as to the recognition that economic growth as measured by growth in economic indicators will not necessarily reduce poverty or protect the environment. If the modified accounts are ignored, then the collection of sectoral physical data, especially in a developing country context, will, in any case be, beneficial (Repetto *et al.*, 1989, p. 53).

The results of the case study above point to large data requirements and analytical problems if sustainability modifications are to be implemented in a revised System of National Accounts. The aggregate estimates for defensive expenditure in the case of the land using sector are likely to be underestimated, since they have ignored household defensive expenditure. Many economic activities have some aspect within them that could be regarded as not enhancing welfare, but necessary defensive expenditure. This extends to many aspects of government expenditure. There is also the paradox that the greater the government efforts in conserving the environment, the lower the modified net product. A government wishing to see economic growth, as indicated by modified net product, will either have the incentive not to undertake such expenditure or to have it redefined as other than defensive expenditure.

Adjustments to depletion of marketed and non-marketed natural capital for sustainability will necessarily initiate 'satellite accounts' for physical flows of natural resources. The valuation of marketed reserves of extractable resources may be in terms of present value, given present technology, or of projected future prices and reserves. These issues are not addressed in the study of the land using sector, where land has been treated as a sink for pollution and as a store of organic matter in the soil and biomass. The importance of negative externalities in terms of degradation of natural capital is fully covered in the carbon balance estimates, but provides no value for the degradation attributable to phosphate and completely ignores other means of degradation such as accumulated pesticide residues and other effluents and pollutants. The environmental concentration of many substances associated with land using industries are unrecognised as pollutants till they have an impact on society. The physical information required, along with land use modelling, may be useful for showing the effects of agricultural and environmental policies on physical indicators. An example here is the carbon emission estimates, which are a prerequisite for an analysis of the effectiveness of carbon emission taxes and subsidies on total greenhouse gas emissions.

The adjustment to sustainable net product for the service flows again shows the large data requirements for completion of the modified account. The usefulness of the adjustment depends on the acceptance of the assumptions involved. Aggregation problems and the use of the designation process may deter the acceptance of this adjustment. The use of the designation process could focus attention on conservation issues but would lead to the designation of one site exactly comparable in monetary terms to another site in the same designation. The replication of service flows from the land use and other sectors would depend on annual data being available to show changes in these from year to year.

Since the sector dealt with here has been defined to include activities taking place on land, the resulting accounts will not reflect the fact that, for example, expenditure on fertiliser by these industries promotes consumption of non-renewable resources upstream, whilst sales of biological products to users who quickly reconvert them to wastes adds further to global pollution loads. This deficiency in these accounts can be rectified either by providing supplementary detail of upstream and downstream activities for the sector or by the production of a full set of satellite accounts for all sectors. The latter is a matter for public policy and will require several years for completion. If policy makers were to be provided with information enabling them to be sensitive to the impact of their decisions on the global commons, then the sectoral accounts offered here would necessarily be augmented with further data on the transactions between this sector and others regarding the ultimate origin of its inputs and the final fate of its outputs.

References

Adger W.N., K. Brown, R. Shiel, and M.C. Whitby, *Dynamics of land use change and the carbon balance.* ESRC Countryside Change Initiative. Working Paper 15, University of Newcastle upon Tyne 1991.

Adger W. N. and M.C. Whitby, Accounting for the impact of agriculture and forestry on environmental quality. *European Economic Review* Vol. 35 (1991).

Ahmad Y. J., S. El Serafy, and E. Lutz (eds), *Environmental accounting for sustainable development.* World Bank, Washington DC 1989.

Anderson D., *The forestry industry and the greenhouse effect.* Forestry Commission and the Scottish Forestry Trust, Edinburgh 1991.

Bartelmus P., Environmental accounting and the system of national accounts. In: Ahmad, Y. J., S. El Serafy, and E. Lutz (eds), *Environmental accounting for sustainable development.* World Bank, Washington DC 1989.

Blades D. W., Measuring pollution within the framework of the national accounts. In: Ahmad, Y. J., S. El Serafy, and E. Lutz (eds), *Environmental accounting for sustainable development.* World Bank, Washington DC 1989.

Buchanan J. M. *The demand and supply of public goods.* Rand McNally and Co., Chicago 1968.

Centre for Agricultural Strategy, *Phosphorus: a resource for UK agriculture.* Centre for Agricultural Strategy, Reading 1978.

Council of the European Communities (1980) Council Directive of 15 July 1980 relating to the quality of water intended for human consumption, *Official Journal of the European Communities* Vol. L229, (1980) pp. 11-29.

Countryside Commission, *Country Parks.* Countryside Commission, Cheltenham 1990.

Countryside Commission, *Fit for the future: report of the National Parks Review Panel.* Countryside Commission, Cheltenham 1991.

Countryside Commission for Scotland, Personal Communication.

Cummings R., D. Brookshire, and W. Schulze, *Valuing environmental goods: an assessment of the contingent valuation method.* Rowman and Allenheld, Totowa NJ 1986.

Daly H. E., Toward a measure of sustainable social net national product. In: Ahmad, Y. J., S. El Serafy, and E. Lutz (eds), *Environmental accounting for sustainable development.* World Bank, Washington DC 1989.

Department of Agriculture for Northern Ireland, *Statistical Review of Northern Ireland Agriculture 1989.* HMSO, London 1990.

Department of Environment, *Evidence to the House of Commons Select Committee on the Environment.* HMSO, London 1984.

Department of Environment, *The nitrate issue.* HMSO, London 1988.

Department of the Environment, *Digest of environmental protection and water statistics.* Government Statistical Service. HMSO, London 1990

Forestry Commission, Personal Communication 1990.

Garrod G. D. and K. G. Willis, Estimating the willingness to pay for landscape in the Yorkshire Dales. ESRC Countryside Change Initiative Working Paper, University of Newcastle upon Tyne (forthcoming).

Hanley N., Problems in valuing environmental improvements resulting from agricultural policy changes: the case of nitrate pollution. In: Dubgaard, A. and A. Nielsen (eds), *Economic aspects of environmental regulations in agriculture.* Wissenschaftsverlag Vauk, Kiel 1989.

Harrison A., Introducing natural capital into the SNA. In: Ahmad Y.J., A. El Serafy, and E. Lutz (eds), *Environmental accounting for sustainable development.* World Bank, Washington DC 1989.

Hartwick J. M., Natural resources, national accounting and economic depreciation. *Journal of Public Economics* Vol. 43, (1990) pp. 291-304.

Hueting R., The Brundtland Report: a matter of conflicting goals. *Ecological Economics,* Vol. 2, (1990) pp. 109-117.

Johansson P.-O., Valuing environmental damage. *Oxford Review of Economic Policy,* Vol. 6, (1990) pp. 34-50.

Kayes R. J., C. Carden, and P. J. Taylor, *An assessment of the feasibility of large scale afforestation in Britain to offset carbon dioxide emissions.* Political Ecology Research Group for the National Power Division of the Central Electricity Generating Board 1990.

Mäler K.-G., National accounts and environmental resources. European Association of Environmental and Resource Economists Conference, Venice 1990.

McInerney J., The simple analytics of natural resource economics. *Journal of Agricultural Economics,* Vol. 27, (1976) pp. 31-52.

Ministry of Agriculture Fisheries and Food. *Agriculture in the United Kingdom.* HMSO, London 1990.

Nordhaus W., To slow or not to slow: the economics of the greenhouse effect. Yale University mimeo 1990.

Norgaard R., Three dilemmas of environmental accounting. *Ecological Economics.* Vol. 1, (1989) pp. 303-314.

Pearce D. W. and R. K. Turner, *Economics of natural resources and the environment.* Harvester Wheatsheaf, London 1990.

Pearce D., *Assessing the returns to the economy and society from investment in forestry.* Forestry Commission, Edinburgh 1991.

Peskin H. M., *Accounting for natural resource depletion and degradation in developing countries.* Environment Department Working Paper 13, World Bank, Washington DC 1989.

Peskin H. M. and E. Lutz, *A survey of resource and environmental accounting in industrialised countries.* Environment Department Working Paper 37, World Bank, Washington DC 1990.

Power A., The role of externalities in the determination of policy for agriculture. In: Centre for Agricultural Strategy (ed.), *The role of externalities in the determination of policy for agriculture.* Centre for Agricultural Strategy, Reading 1990.

Randall A., *Resource economics: an economic approach to natural resource and environmental policy.* Wiley, London 1987.

Repetto R., W. Magrath, M. Wells, C. Beer, and F. Rossini, *Wasting assets: natural resources in the national income accounts.* World Resources Institute, Washington 1989.

Royal Society, *The nitrogen cycle of the UK.* Royal Society, London 1983.

Smith V. K., Can we measure the economic value of environmental amenities? *Southern Economic Journal,* Vol. 57, (1990) pp. 865-878.

Smith V. K. and Y. Kaoru, Signals or noise? Explaining the variation in recreation benefit estimates. *American Journal of Agricultural Economics*, Vol. 72 (1990) pp. 419-433.
Steiner P. O., The public sector and the public interest. In: Haveman, R. H. and J. Margolis (eds), *Public expenditure and policy analysis*, 2nd edition, Rand McNally, Chicago 1977.
Stern N., The determinants of growth. *Economic Journal*, Vol. 101, (1991) pp. 122-133.
Trexler M. A., P. E. Faeth, and J. M. Kramer, *Forestry as a response to global warming: an analysis of the Guatemala agroforestry and carbon sequestration project.* World Resources Institute, Washington DC 1989.
Walsh R. G., D. M. Johnson, and J. R. McKean, Issues in nonmarket valuation and policy application: a retrospective glance. *Western Journal of Agricultural Economics*, Vol. 14, (19989) pp. 178-188.
Willis K. G. and M. C. Whitby, The value of Green Belt land. *Journal of Rural Studies*, Vol. 1, (1985) pp. 147-162.
Willis K. G. and J. F. Benson, A comparison of user benefits and costs of nature conservation at three reserves. *Regional Studies*, Vol. 22, (1988) pp. 417-428.
Willis K. G., Option Value and Non-User Benefits of Wildlife Conservation. *Journal of Rural Studies*, Vol. 5, (1989) pp. 245-256.

Chapter 5

TAXES *VERSUS* REGULATION IN THE DUTCH INTENSIVE LIVESTOCK SECTOR

Geert Thijssen and Anna Laan*

The environmental effects of agriculture have long been neglected; food security and the farmers' income were the first priorities of agricultural policy. However, the scaling-up and intensification of land use have had adverse side-effects on the environment. Although the use of DDT and PCBs was forbidden in the Netherlands in 1962, it was only in the eighties that consensus grew about the problems caused by agriculture (de Wit, 1988).

Problems caused by intensive livestock farming include the emission of ammonia into the atmosphere. This emission, which contributes significantly to acidification, is caused by the production and spreading of manure. Deposition rates of ammonia in the Netherlands mainly originate from internal sources (75%). Also, over 90% of this internal ammonia emission is caused by the agricultural sector. Therefore national policy which aims at reducing of ammonia caused by agriculture has a considerable impact on the decrease of acidification in the Netherlands itself. In 1989 the Dutch government formulated a plan to allow environment to recover. One of the goals of this National Environmental Policy Plan (NMP) is to reduce total ammonia emissions by 70% of the 1980 level by the year 2000 (VROM, 1989).

The Dutch government is using regulations to reach this goal. Examples are injecting manure, storing manure in covered sheds and the installation of the biofilters in livestock sheds. Farmers are confronted with measures that directly influence behaviour. Another instrument which can be used to reach environmental goals is taxation. Taxes are an incentive to economize on the amount of pollution. For example, prices of inputs used by the farmers can be changed by the government, thus indirectly influencing farmers' behaviour.

* G. Thijssen is Lecturer in the Department of Agricultural Economics and Policy; A. Laan is Ph.D student in the Department of General Economics, Wageningen Agricultural University.
The authors would like to thank H. Folmer, A. Oskam and H. Stolwijk for helpful comments on an earlier draft.

In this study we first examine the advantages and disadvantages of regulations and taxation on a theoretical basis. Taxes seem to be the least-cost method of achieving a given environmental goal. However, other issues are also important in the evaluation of instruments, for example, distributional aspects. The second part of this study evaluates two scenarios for reaching the NMP's goal for reducing ammonia in the Dutch intensive livestock sector by the year 2000. We have done this on the basis of two econometric models, one of the average large Dutch intensive livestock farm and one of the average small Dutch intensive livestock farm. The first scenario contains reduction of the number of animals by 20% of the 1988 level, the second contains taxes on the feed price, and income subsidies. An important aspect in the evaluation is the proposition that in both scenarios the ammonia reduction is 20%. We have assumed that the additional reduction of ammonia is reached by abatement measures. This means that the total reduction will be 75% by the year 2000, which conforms to the government's plan. The model clarifies the effects of the instruments of the two scenarios on farm income, the number of animals, production level and the demand for feed.

The remainder of this chapter is organized as follows. In Section 1 a theoretical evaluation is given of regulation and emission taxes. The model is presented in Section 2. Estimated parameters and elasticities are presented in Section 3, the evaluation of the two scenarios is presented in Section 4, while Section 5 contains some concluding remarks.

1. Instruments of environmental policy

The livestock in the Netherlands has increased considerably since 1950, while the amount of cultivated land and grassland has decreased. The increase is mainly concentrated in the central, eastern and southern sandy areas of the country. Since most of the livestock farms do not have enough land to spread the manure produced, there is a manure surplus. The so-called 'intensive' livestock farms (pig and poultry farms) are particularly land independent and therefore responsible for a large portion of the total manure surplus. The overfertilization of the land where the surpluses are deposited causes several environmental problems, like ammonia emission.

In other words, the agricultural sector uses the environment, particularly the land, not only as a production factor but also as a cheap dump for pollutants. The environment is regarded as a common-property resource, and thus the natural resources are considered to be free goods and no price or too low a price is attached to them. The consequence of this is that there is a discrepancy between private and social costs, and the environment and the production factors are suboptimally allocated. The prices of goods do not always include all social costs that come about during production. This means that the prices of goods the production of which results in severe pollution, like pork, do not reflect the adverse environmental effects of the manure surplus.

The failure to take environmental cost into account results in too high a demand for and production of pollution-intensive goods. So there are two different allocation effects. First, using the environment at a low price leads to the over-production of such things as pork and eggs. Second, the common-property resource soil is overused because no price is charged for it. The consequence is environmental degradation (Siebert, 1987).

The environmental policy proposed by Pigou is to levy a tax equal to the difference between marginal social costs and marginal private costs. The tax would induce the firm to produce the correct socially efficient output, where the output price equals marginal social cost. The firm would bear the external costs in the form of a tax which it will obviously treat as a private cost. The external cost is internalized. A main drawback to the Pigouvian tax solution is that the external cost (damage) function has to be estimated, as otherwise the tax cannot be computed. As this damage function is hard to estimate in practice, only some (inadequate) indications are possible.

Environmental goals (*e.g.* for emission levels) set by the government can be used to overcome this lack of information while implementing control policies. Standards are most likely to be set with reference to some health-related criteria, such as a level of nitrate in the soil that must not be exceeded if that ground water is to be safe for using as drinking water. In the case of ammonia pollution, the government aims at 2400 acid equivalents per hectare per year in 2000[1]. This means that the ammonia emission has to be reduced by 75% of the 1986 level by the year 2000. Politicians and bureaucrats charged with addressing environmental problems can choose

1 The concept of acid equivalent makes it possible to lump all acid and acidifying substances together.

between different instruments, like regulations and taxes, to induce farms to meet this environmental objective. According to many economists, the choice of policy instruments must be based on a criterion like the lowest cost of achieving environmental goals. An instrument like taxes shares this desirable feature; it has the potential to promote economic efficiency. However, theory often diverges from practice. In practice, most environmental policy is implemented via regulations. The Dutch manure policy is also mainly based on regulatory instruments. One of the reasons for this is that economists play a minor role in the administrative groundwork of environmental policy. Administrators with no background in economics tend to overlook economic aspects. Another reason is that the imposition of regulations will, in general, have a more certain effect on environmental quality than taxes on emission, providing the government is capable of controlling the regulation. The government is uncertain of how the firms (*i.e.* farms) will react to a tax. A third reason is the existence of an environmental bureaucracy. The system of environmental regulations fits into an established tradition of regulation with which the bureaucrats are familiar (Bohm and Russell, 1985; Nentjes, 1988).

We need to know whether a tax or regulation is the best means of securing a given uniform standard. First, taxes are the least-cost method of achieving a given standard, and this argument clearly favours the use of taxes. Figure 1 illustrates the general argument. Suppose there are two firms, A and B, with marginal pollution control costs curves dC_A/dR_A and dC_B/dR_B. The origin of farm A is O_A and the origin of farm B is O_B. Starting from O_A the emission reduction R_A is pictured on the right. Starting from O_B the emission reduction R_B increases towards the left. Suppose that an environmental quality standard involving an emission reduction is set. In this there is a 20% reduction in the number of animals. If the standard is enforced, each firm will be required to secure the same pollution reduction, for example, O_AT for firm A which equals O_BT for firm B. The total costs of achieving this uniform standard will be equal to the area under dC_A/dR_A between O_A and T plus the area under dC_B/dR_B between O_B and T; that is the area A + B + C + D. But it is possible to achieve the same emission reduction by imposing a tax of OP_T. The effect is to make firm A secure more pollution reduction than the standard, but to make firm B secure less. The rationale, of course, is that firm B faces the highest marginal costs of pollution reduction so that it should not have to aim at the standard O_BT. After a tax of OP_T, the emission reduction of firm A will be O_AT + TS and the emission reduction of firm B will be O_BT-TS. The total control costs are A + B + C. The tax solution is in fact cheaper overall in terms of resource costs (Wiersma, 1989). Two things must be kept in mind. Whether, for any given pollutant, the costs saved by imposing an uniform tax, rather than enforcing a regulation, will be high depends on the degree of difference between the two cost curves. Secondly, if the total abatement costs for the two farms are low compared with other production costs, then the relative advantage of a tax is going to be small as well (Burrows, 1979).

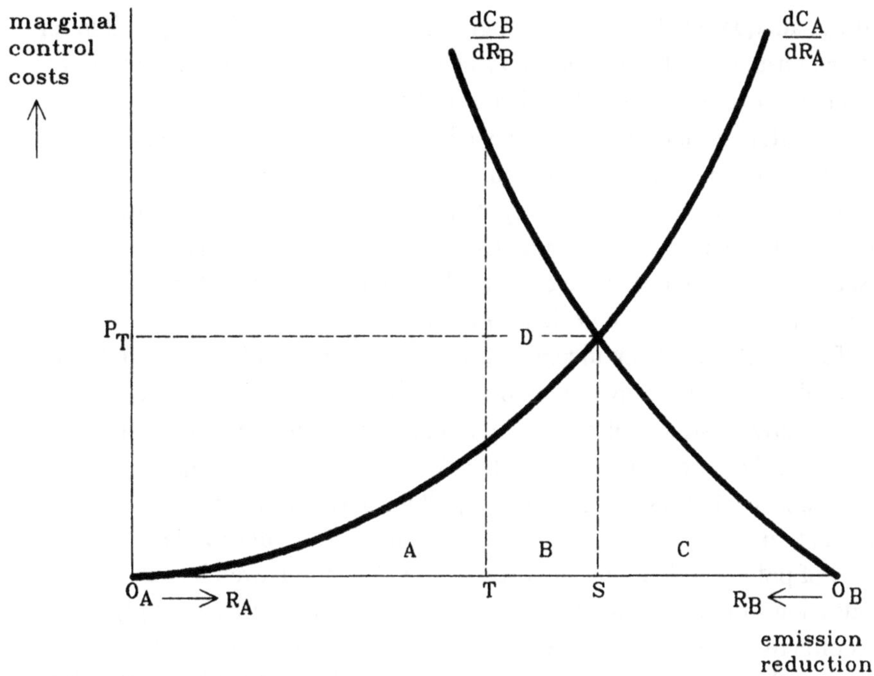

Figure 1: A comparison between taxes and regulation.

Although taxes are the least-cost method of achieving a given standard, instruments can also be evaluated on a variety of other dimensions (Bohm and Russell, 1985, Pearce and Turner, 1990, Siebert, 1987). The distributional aspects of taxation and regulation also have to be accounted for. It is sometimes argued that pollution taxes merely serve to shift the burden of the tax to the consumers. For criteria of economic efficiency, however, such a shift does not matter since the tax reflects the external cost embodied in the product in question, and product prices should change so as to reflect the different external costs embodied in different products. But the government may hesitate to accept these distribution effects. This is true when low-income groups are in a position where reductions in real income are judged to be unacceptable and where a charge system would hit the consumption of this group. Regulations can also have distribution effects, although they may be less striking. The time profile of the price effects of taxes may be very different from that of regulations. It is possible that in the short run, prices will be higher with taxes than with regulations, whereas in the long run, the opposite will occur. It then becomes difficult to compare effects adequately. In the case of agricultural products it is not possible for Dutch farmers to shift the burden to consumers. Dutch farmers are price takers in the output market, which is at the EC level.

It is often argued that taxes give a firm the widest possible choice of mechanisms for reducing pollution, ranging from changes in output to the introduction of 'clean' technology. This cannot, however, be an additional benefit when compared with regulated standards, since in the latter case exactly the same choices are open to the polluter. This is not true if the government prescribes a design standard[2].

Taxes will provide an incentive for the polluter to look for less-polluting technologies, which may reduce pollution below the environmental standard. An incentive system that puts a value on the discharge remaining after control will create a greater incentive for change than a regulation specifying that same level of discharge. Once a polluter has adjusted to the new regulation, there is no longer any incentive for him to attempt to reach a lower level of pollution than that imposed by the regulation, even if such a reduction would be valuable to society. The reason for this is simply that the tax effectively prices all environmental inputs, whereas the standard stipulated in the regulation implies a zero price below the chosen standard and an infinite price above it.

Both regulations and taxes bring administrative and enforcement costs with them. Both administer the standard, but a tax may involve additional costs because of the need to transfer funds (firms presumably have to pay tax on an annual basis to a government organization).

2 A design standard is a method imposed by regulation, which requires producers to use a specific production method.

The conclusion is that there can be no unambiguous recommendation for using one instrument rather than another. Regulations and taxation have their own costs and benefits and, without empirical evidence on actual policies, the net benefits of one measure or the other cannot be clearly known. Setting a standard is unavoidable, given the limited knowledge about what data are relevant for implementing full Pigouvian taxes and the doubts expressed about the efficiency of such taxes. However, it may well be that a given standard is best secured by taxes in some cases and by regulations in others. The comparison we make between the use of these two instruments for environmental policy in the Dutch intensive livestock sector concentrates on the least-cost argument.

2. The theoretical model

Econometric models are used to evaluate the two scenarios, which are based on reduction of the number of animals and on taxes, respectively. Neoclassical production theory lies at the basis of these models. This theory is only briefly described here. For an extensive description see Thijssen (forthcoming). Producers have been assumed to operate under profit-maximizing behaviour over an infinite time-horizon with respect to two inputs. The two inputs are a variable input (mainly feed) and a quasi-fixed input (livestock, buildings and equipment). The farm's objective can be viewed as being twofold; the maximization of short-term profits (resulting in a short-term profit function) and then the maximization of the present value of its long-term expected profits. This means that short-term profit, output supply and variable input demand are conditional upon a fixed level of the capital stock. In the intermediate term the level of capital will change when prices change. This results in a change of output and variable input in the intermediate term and long-term.

According to the duality theory, the short-term profit function represents the production technology. In addition to the variable input and the quasi-fixed input we have distinguished labour as a fixed input[3]. It was decided to use a flexible functional form for the profit function, the quadratic form, for empirical analysis. The profit function has been normalized by the output price, to ensure that the profit function is linearly homogenous in

3 For Dutch intensive livestock farms, land was not an important input for the period 1971-1988.

prices. It is also assumed that the profit function is linearly homogeneous in the quasi-fixed input and the fixed input. Therefore the corresponding production function is linearly homogeneous in inputs. This assumption is necessary at the aggregate level, since only constant returns technologies satisfy linear aggregation (Chambers, 1989, p. 188). The normalized profit function at time t, is written as

$$\pi_t = \alpha_0 + \alpha_1 p_t + \alpha_2 k_t + \alpha_3 p_t k_t + \frac{1}{2}\alpha_4 k_t^2 + \alpha_5 p_t T + \alpha_6 k_t T \qquad (1)$$

where π is the profit normalized by the output price and the labour volume; p is the ratio of the price of the variable input to the price of the output, k is the quasi-fixed input divided by the labour volume; and T is technological change.

If the normalized profit function satisfies certain regularity conditions, it is dual to the production function and its parameters contain sufficient information to describe the farm's production technology at profit-maximizing points in the set of production possibilities. Testable conditions of regularity are that the profit function decreases in the price of the variable input and that it increases in the quasi-fixed input and is concave in the quasi-fixed input $(\alpha_4 < 0)$. This is in line with the convex marginal cost function of Figure 1. To simplify the model, we have assumed that the second derivative of the profit function with respect to the price equals zero. This assumption does not contradict with neoclassical theory, because the profit function should be quasi-convex in the price. A consequence of this assumption is that the short-term price elasticities of the demand for the variable input and the supply of the output are equal to zero. This is a reasonable assumption for the Dutch intensive livestock sector (see Laan and Thijssen, 1990).

According to Hotelling's Lemma, if we differentiate the profit function with respect to the relative price, we obtain the demand function for the variable input

$$v_t = -\alpha_1 - \alpha_3 k_t - \alpha_5 T \qquad (2)$$

where v is the variable input per labour unit. Using the definition of the normalized profit $(\pi_t = q_t - p_t v_t)$, the optimal output for a normalized profit function is

$$q_t = \pi_t - p_t \frac{\partial \pi_t}{\partial p_t} \tag{3}$$

where q is the output per labour unit. The output supply function, therefore, is

$$q_t = \alpha_0 + \alpha_2 k_t + \frac{1}{2}\alpha_4 k_t^2 + \alpha_6 k_t T \tag{4}$$

We have assumed that the demand for the variable input and the supply of the output do not depend on prices in the short term.

The quasi-fixed input (k) is fixed for the period of one year. After one year the quasi-fixed input adjusts according to the partial adjustment theory developed by Lucas (1967). Assumptions made in this theory are that the farm family maximizes the present value of income over an infinite time-horizon with respect to capital facing adjustment costs if it alters its stock of the quasi-fixed input. Changes in this capital stock imply increasing costs associated with integrating new capital into a going concern; reorganizing the way of production, learning process of the farm family members, *etc*. Applications of this theory were made by Denny, Fuss and Wavermann (1981) to manufacturing industries, by Lopez (1985) to the Canadian food processing industry, and by Kuiper and Thijssen (1991) to the Dutch agricultural sector.

Assuming external quadratic adjustment costs, the resulting demand function for capital at the end of the period is a function of the optimal capital stock and the capital stock at the start of the period.

$$k_{t+1} = m k_t^* + (1 - m) k_t \tag{5}$$

where k_t^* is the optimal capital stock and m is the adjustment parameter, which should be larger than zero and smaller than one. The optimal capital stock can be calculated using the well-known static condition that the marginal return to capital should be equal to the user cost of capital

$$\frac{\partial \pi_t}{\partial k_t} = \alpha_2 + \alpha_3 p_t + \alpha_4 k_t + \alpha_6 T = p_{kt} \tag{6}$$

where p_k is the ratio of the cost of the quasi-fixed input to the price of the output. Combining equations (5) and (6), we obtain the demand function for capital

$$k_{t+1} = \frac{m(p_{kt} - \alpha_2 - \alpha_3 p_t - \alpha_6 T)}{\alpha_4} + (1-m)k_t \qquad (7)$$

The net income of the farmer is defined as the difference between the value of output and the value of variable input. Net income is, therefore, equal to the profit multiplied by the amount of labour on the farm.

$$y = (p_q q - p_v v)a \qquad (8)$$

where p_q is the price of the output, p_v is the price of the variable input and a is the labour volume on the farm.

The environmental part of the model consists of a net emission function

$$d_t = \zeta_1 po_t + \zeta_2 bp_t + \zeta_3 pl_t \qquad (9)$$

where d is the net emission of ammonia, po the number of porkers, bp the number of breeding pigs and pl the number of poultry. To simplify the model, abatement measures have been ignored.

The number of pigs and poultry are assumed to be linearly related to the amount of capital. Therefore there are no substitution possibilities between livestock, buildings and machinery.

3. Empirical results

Two econometric models were estimated using the theoretical model derived in Section 2; one model for the average large intensive livestock farm and one model for the average small intensive livestock farm. Data for the period 1971 - 1988 were used to estimate the models. The data set consisted of two parts. The prices of the data on the intensive livestock sector were mainly derived from 'LEI/CBS Landbouwcijfers' (Statistics on Agriculture). The data on the output, the variable input and livestock of the two distinguished farms were taken from 'Bedrijfsuitkomsten in de landbouw', a publication of the Agricultural Economic Institute (LEI)[4]. These statistics are based on a sample of Dutch farms, where accounts of farming activities were kept for the period 1971-1988. Table 1 gives an overview of the data.

Table 1: Data on the average small farm and the average large intensive livestock farm.

	1971	1988	annual change (in %)
small farm			
output[a]	103691	315336	6.3
feed[a]	79455	263780	6.9
capital[a]	50703	120013	4.9
net income	30955	47117	2.3
pigs[b]	74.6	185.1	5.2
poultry	1082	2823	5.5
ammonia emission (kg)	883	2347	5.6
large farm			
output[a]	175078	746285	8.4
feed[a]	146088	611074	8.3
capital[a]	86739	308473	7.3
net income	44020	113739	5.4
pigs[b]	102.9	450.4	8.5
poultry	1754	5715	6.8
ammonia emission (kg)	1429	5446	7.7

a in guilders of 1980.

b total number of porkers and breeding-pigs.

As can be seen from Table 1, the annual changes of output, input *etc.* of the average large farm is higher than the annual changes of the average small farm. The annual change of the net income of the large farm is even more than twice as much as the annual change of the small farm.

Because of the cross-equations symmetry restriction and the possibility that the error terms of equations (2), (4) and (7) may be correlated, these equations were estimated by Zellner SUR (Judge *et al.*, 1988: p. 450)[5].

4 Assuming complementarity, the number of buildings and amount of equipment are linearly related to the amount of livestock. Therefore, it is possible to measure capital solely by the amount of livestock. This assumption is reasonable for the Dutch intensive livestock sector, and is necessary since no data on buildings are available.

5 For computational reasons the output and the variable input have been divided by 10000 and the amount of capital by the average amount of capital.

Equation (9) is a technical equation, the parameters having been obtained from Oudendag and Wijnands (1989). The values for the parameters are 13.75 for ζ_1, 6.5 for ζ_2 and 0.3 for ζ_3.

The estimation results of the model are presented in Table 2. The equations are presented with the *t*-value between brackets. The parameters are all significant at the 10% level and the explained variance is high. The differences between the two models are significant. To get a better insight into these differences elasticities should be calculated. Before calculating these elasticities it is important to test assumptions underlying the methodology of this study.

Table 2: The estimated results of the two models (*t*-values between brackets).

small farm

$$q_t = \underset{(0.92)}{0.14} + \underset{(5.47)}{1.15}\,k_t + 0.5\cdot\underset{(2.46)}{(-0.79)}k_t^2 + \underset{(4.32)}{0.06}\,k\cdot T \qquad R^2 = 0.93$$

$$v_t = -\underset{(0.75)}{0.09} + \underset{(4.42)}{0.94}\,k_t + \underset{(3.01)}{0.04}\,T \qquad R^2 = 0.91$$

$$k_{(t+1)} = \frac{\underset{(2.35)}{0.50}\left(p_{kt} - \underset{(5.47)}{1.15} + \underset{(4.42)}{0.94}\,p_t - \underset{(4.32)}{0.06}\,T\right)}{\underset{(2.46)}{-0.79}} + \underset{(2.35)}{0.50}\,k_t \qquad R^2 = 0.82$$

large farm

$$q_t = -\underset{(1.38)}{0.45} + \underset{(5.73)}{3.39}\,k_t + 0.5\cdot\underset{(4.42)}{(-2.71)}k_t^2 + \underset{(4.17)}{0.09}\,k\cdot T \qquad R^2 = 0.98$$

$$v_t = \underset{(3.27)}{0.44} + \underset{(1.89)}{0.57}\,k_t + \underset{(5.58)}{0.11}\,T \qquad R^2 = 0.98$$

$$k_{t+1} = \frac{\underset{(1.81)}{0.14}\left(p_{kt} - \underset{(5.73)}{3.39} + \underset{(1.89)}{0.57}\,p_t - \underset{(4.17)}{0.09}\,T\right)}{\underset{(4.42)}{-2.71}} + \underset{(1.81)}{0.86}\,k_t \qquad R^2 = 0.88$$

As can be concluded from Table 2, both profit functions are concave in the capital stock, because α_4 equals -0.79 for the small farm and α_4 equals -2.71 for the large farm. The profit functions also decrease in the relative price and increase in the capital stock (see Table 3). The parameter of the lagged capital volume in the demand functions for capital is greater than zero and less than one; therefore both models are stable. The relation between the demand for capital and the prices of capital are negative, as could be expected. Therefore the assumptions underlying the model developed have not been disproved by the data for both farms. Of course, some doubts could be raised about the appropriateness of the data set which has been used. Future research is needed to obtain more reliable results, using the original sample of Dutch farms, where accounts of their farming activities were kept for the period 1971-1988.

Table 3: Elasticities of the two models, at the level of 1988.

	price input	capital (*t*-1)	techn. change	price capital
small farm				
output	0.00[a]	0.50	0.038	
input	0.00[a]	0.72	0.017	
capital	-0.32	0.50	0.021	-0.32
profit	-6.05	3.52	0.181	
large farm				
output	0.00[a]	0.18	0.037	
input	0.00[a]	0.28	0.032	
capital	-0.02	0.86	0.003	-0.03
profit	-5.37	1.15	0.067	

a by assumption

The estimated parameters were used to calculate elasticities (see Table 3). For example, an increase in the capital stock in period *t*-1 by 1%, results in an increase of the output by 0.50 for the small farm. As could be expected, the elasticity of capital is high in the output supply function and the demand function for the variable input, except for the input demand function for the large farm. This unlikely result is compensated by a large constant term (see Table 2) and a high level of technical change, 3.2% per year. Technical change is an important factor in all output supply and variable input demand equations. Remarkable is the difference between the elasticities of the demand function for capital between the small and large farm. The small farm is very sensitive to price changes, while the amount of livestock of the large farm is almost fixed in time (elasticity with respect to the amount of livestock of the previous period is 0.86). The large farm is, therefore, represented by B in Figure 1.

Estimated simulations are carried out with the two models, using the levels of the variables of 1988 (see Table 1). To get an insight into these simulations short-term (one-year), intermediate-term (five years) and long-term (ten years) elasticities with respect to the variable input price are calculated (see Table 4).

As already pointed out, there are remarkable differences between the small farm and the large farm. The large farm is characterized by large fixed inputs (building and equipment) and price change does not have very much influence on the level of the capital stock, output supply and variable input demand, even in the long term. The small farm is more flexible and in the intermediate term a price increase of the variable input by one percent results in a decline of the livestock capital of 0.64%.

Table 4: Short-term, intermediate-term and long-term price elasticities of the two models, at the level of 1988.

	short-term	intermediate-term	long-term
small farm			
output	-0.09	-0.17	-0.18
input	-0.24	-0.47	-0.48
capital	-0.33	-0.64	-0.66
large farm			
output	-0.00	-0.01	-0.01
input	-0.01	-0.02	-0.04
capital	-0.02	-0.07	-0.14

4. Two scenarios evaluated: regulations and taxes

An important goal in the national environmental policy plan, and therefore a basic assumption in both scenarios, is a 70% reduction of the 1980 ammonia emission of the intensive livestock sector by the year 2000 (Stolwijk, 1989). This reduction can be achieved by reducing the number of animals and by abatement measures, such as:

- injecting the manure in grassland;
- ploughing in the manure immediately after it has been sprayed on arable land;
- rapidly introducing more 'ecologically' livestock sheds;

- converting manure into fertilizer;
- storing a quarter of the total manure in covered sheds;
- reducing the nitrogen content in fodder;
- requiring that biofilters be installed in livestock sheds in the immediate vicinity of dwellings.

It is assumed that the reduction of ammonia can be achieved by a 20% reduction of the number of animals of the 1988 level, and that the additional reduction should be achieved by abatement measures.[6]. In this study we examined two scenarios for reducing the number of animals; regulations and taxes. The two models developed in Sections 2 and 3 were used to calculate the effects of the two scenarios on agricultural income, ammonia emission, production and livestock volume. The consequences were compared with the base run. For this base run, calculated using both models, it was assumed that the price of the variable input, output price, price of capital and the number of animals would remain stable between 1988 and 2000.

Table 5 gives the results of the base run. Output of the small farm rises by 3% per year and of the large farm by 3.3% because of technical change. The variable input of the small farm rises by 1.6% per year and the variable input of the large farm by 3.4% per year. This is caused by a higher level of technical change. Net income of the small farm rises by 7.3% per year and of the large farm by 2.6% in the base run. These results are comparable with Table 3. Differences are found only for income, caused by the assumption of constancy of the prices in the simulation period.

The first scenario is that of an animal reduction by 2% per year (see Table 6). In the second, an *ad valorem* abatement tax on the price of the variable input (mainly feed) is introduced.

6 To gain a correct insight into the effect of a reduction of the number of animals on income, *etc.* the assumed abatement measures should also be taken into account. However, the costs of abatement measures and the way farmers react to these measures are not known. Therefore, to compare the two scenarios, we have assumed that abatement measures have no effect on the production and capital level of the two farms.

Table 5: Results of the base run.

Variable	Year 1991	1995	2000
small farm			
production[a]	387271	439945	505787
variable input[a]	306192	326856	352686
capital[a]	120013	120013	120013
net income[a]	70539	98387	133197
ammonia emission[b]	2347	2347	2347
large farm			
production[a]	729156	854606	980058
variable input[a]	455251	525788	613958
capital[a]	308473	308473	308473
net income[a]	253638	286073	318507
ammonia emission[b]	5446	5446	5446

a in guilders of 1980
b in kg

Table 6: Two scenarios: regulations and taxes.

Variable	Year 1991	1995	2000
regulation:			
total animal reduction	2%	10%	20%
taxes:	67%	67%	67%

Table 7 gives the results of the regulation scenario. Output of both farms declines by more than 10% in 2000. The input of the large farm declines less than that of the small farm because of the lower elasticity of capital for the variable input (see Table 3). Therefore, the net income of the large farm declines more than the net income of the small farm. The decrease in the amount of capital and ammonia agrees with the assumptions.

The introduction in the second scenario of an *ad valorem* abatement tax on the input price gives a new equation of the input price:

Table 7: Effects of the regulation scenario, in percentages of the base run.

Variable	Year 1991	1995	2000
small farm			
output	-1.1	-6.3	-14.3
input	-1.4	-6.4	-11.9
capital	-2.0	-10.0	-20.0
net income	-0.1	-6.1	-19.7
ammonia emission	-2.0	-10.0	-20.0
large farm			
output	-0.6	-4.2	-11.2
input	-0.7	-2.9	-5.1
capital	-1.0	-10.0	-20.0
net income	-0.4	-6.2	-21.5
ammonia emission	-2.0	-10.0	-20.0

$$p_{vn} = (1 + s) p_v \tag{10}$$

where p_{vn} is the new input price and *s* is the tax rate. The tax has been chosen at such a level that by 2000 the ammonia pollution reduction will also be 20%. Tax policy will be budgeted neutrally; the revenues of the abatement tax are used to support the farmers' income. In this scenario the numbers of animals are a function of capital:

$$po_t = \delta_1 k_t \tag{11}$$

$$bp_t = \delta_2 k_t \tag{12}$$

$$pl_t = \delta_3 k_t \tag{13}$$

The estimation results of these equations are presented in Table 8.

We begin the tax in 1989 to ensure that the abatement of ammonia begins in 1990. Also, in the tax scenario, the capital function is changed. In the new capital function the value of *T* is fixed at the 1988 level, since it is unlikely that there will be a technical change resulting in an increase of the number of animals after the introduction of environmental policy instruments.

Table 8: The estimated results of the animal equations.

	δ_1	δ_2	δ_3
small farm			
	91.2	23.5	1463.1
t-values	18.7	21.2	8.82
R^2	0.75	0.75	0.32
large farm			
	195.2	64.5	3469.95
t-values	28.6	36.6	23.82
R^2	0.87	0.92	0.81

The ammonia emission has to be reduced by 20% of the 1988 level by the year 2000. The long term price elasticity of the demand function of capital is -0.66 for the small farm and -0.14 for the large farm. The small farm's share of total capital is 0.3 and the large farm's share is 0.7. To be sure that the ammonia reduces by 20% the tax must be:
$0.20/\{(-0.66 \cdot 0.3)+(-0.14 \cdot 0.7)\}$, which equals a tax rate of 0.67.

Table 9: Effects of the tax scenario, in percentages of the base run.

Variable	Year 1991	1995	2000
small farm			
output	-16.2	-35.0	-37.7
input	-17.1	-29.4	-28.0
capital	-25.1	-45.9	-47.2
net income	-12.5	-51.3	-59.9
ammonia emission	-25.1	-45.9	-47.2
large farm			
output	-0.6	-1.1	-4.5
input	-0.8	-2.9	-2.3
capital	-2.3	-6.5	-9.1
net income	-0.5	-3.6	-8.2
ammonia emission	-2.3	-6.5	-9.1

The small farm is much more sensitive to the tax rate than the large farm (see Table 4). Net income of the small farm declines more than 50% despite the income transfer. This is as expected since the absolute values of the input price elasticities of the small farm are much higher than the input price elasticities of the large farm (see Table 4). The tax rate has already had a considerable effect in the intermediate run for the small farm, which is also in accordance with the elasticities of Table 4. The total aggregrated reduction of ammonia is 20%, namely:
$(0.427 \cdot 2347 + 0.091 \cdot 5446)/(2347 + 5446) = 0.20$, where 2347 and 5446 are the ammonia emissions of the small and large farm in 1988, respectively.

Doubts can be raised as to the usefulness of the model when such a price shock is introduced. Coefficients will probably change; for example, the influence of technical change on the demand for capital will decline. However, it is clear that the tax rate should be very high to reduce the amount of capital and therefore the ammonia emission by the year 2000.

If we compare both scenarios we see that taxes have a large effect on small farms and a small effect on large farms. The net income of the small farm declines more in the tax scenario; the large farm's net income declines more in the regulation scenario. However, the differences in the total net income loss of both farms between the tax scenario and the regulation scenario is negligible.

In Section 1 some aspects of the advantages and disadvantages of the two instruments were mentioned. An important argument favouring taxes is that they are the least-cost method of achieving a given standard. This is based on the argument that each firm will respond to its own marginal pollution control cost curve. If we consider the loss of net income as an approximation of the ammonia emission reduction costs then there are no differences in the efficiency of the two scenarios. Another aspect mentioned was the distribution effect of an environmental policy. In the tax scenario, the small farm gives up more net income than the large farm. In fact, there is an income distribution from the small farm to the large farm. In the regulation scenario, the net income loss is more or less the same for both farms.

Another argument in favour of taxation is that taxes leave a farm with a wide choice of ammonia-reducing technology, and provide an incentive for the polluter to seek less polluting technologies which may reduce pollution below the environmental standard. We have assumed the same emission reduction in both the regulation scenario and the tax scenario, and therefore, this possible advantage of a tax has not been examined in the scenarios. Another aspect we did not look at is the administrative and enforcement costs, so a complete comparison cannot be made.

5. Conclusions

We evaluated two scenarios based on taxes and on imposing regulations, respectively, on the basis of the theory and using two models, one of the average small intensive livestock sector farm and one of large average intensive livestock farm in the Netherlands. Our main conclusions are

a. Taxes are theoretically least-cost solutions for securing a given environmental standard. The problem is, however, that the right level of the tax is usually unknown. In this study this problem was solved by using models of an average small and an average large Dutch intensive livestock farm.
b. The models postulated seem to appropriately describe the input decisions of intensive livestock farms in the Netherlands, since the assumptions underlying them are not rejected by the data and the elasticity estimates are reasonable. However, there are considerable differences in the elasticities with respect to the variable input price at the short, intermediate and long term between the average large and the average small farm. The small farm is much more sensitive to changes in the input price than the large farm. Further research using panel data is needed to examine the reliability of these results.
c. The 70% reduction in the ammonia emission by the year 2000 can be achieved by abatement measures and by reducing the numbers of pigs and of poultry. It is assumed that 50% of ammonia reduction is reached by abatement measures. The additional 20% will be reached by either regulations concerning the number of animals or by taxes. A tax of 67% on the variable input price has the same effect on ammonia emission and the number of animals as the use of regulations has.
d. The effect of the regulation scenario on the net income of both size of farms, as a percentage change of net income in the base run, is almost the same for both farms. The effect of the tax scenario on net income of the small farm is more severe than the effect on the large farm's net income.
e. The differences in the efficiency of the regulation scenario and the tax scenario are negligible. In contrast to the regulation scenario there is a large income transfer from the small to the large farm in the tax scenario.

References

Bohm P., C.S. Russell, Comparative analysis of alternative policy instruments. In: Kneese, A.V., J.L. Sweeney, *Handbook of natural resource and energy economics* Vol.1. Elsevier Science Publishers B.V., New York 1985.

Burrows P., *The economic theory of pollution control.* Martin Robertson, Oxford 1979.

Chambers R., *Applied production analysis.* Cambridge University Press, Cambridge 1989.

Denny M., M. Fuss and L. Waverman, Substitution possibilities for energy: evidence from U.S. and Canadian manufacturing industries. In: E. Berndt and B. Field (eds), *Modelling and measuring natural resource substitution.* MIT Press, Cambridge Mass. 1981.

Judge G., R. Hill, W. Griffiths, H. Lütkepohl, T. Lee, *Introduction to the theory and practice of econometrics.* Second edition. John Wiley, New York 1988.

Kuiper W. and G. Thijssen, *Supply response and input demand of the agricultural sector in the Netherlands.* Tinbergen Institute Research Bulletin, Vol. 3 (1991), pp. 149-159.

Laan A. and G. Thijssen, *Towards environmentally accountable agriculture: direct or indirect regulation in the Dutch intensive livestock sector?* Proceedings of the VIth EAAE Congress, The Hague, 1990.

Lopez R., Supply response and investment in the Canadian food processing industry. *American Journal of Agricultural Economics* Vol. 67 (1985), pp. 40-48.

Lucas R., Optimal investment policy and the flexible accelerator. *International Economic Review* Vol. 8 (1976), pp.78-85.

Nentjes A., Martkconform milieubeleid. *Economisch Statistische Berichten* (1988) pp. 401-405.

Oudendag D.A. and J.H.M. Wijnands, *Beperking van de ammoniakemissie uit dierlijke mest,* Onderzoeksverslag 56, Landbouw Economisch Instituut, Den Haag 1989.

Pearce D.W., *Environmental economics.* Longman, London 1976.

Pearce D.W. and R.K. Turner, *Economics of natural resources and the environment.* Harvester Wheatsheaf, New York 1990.

Siebert H., *Economics of the environment.* Springer, Berlin 1987.

Stolwijk H.J.J., *Economische gevolgen voor de veehouderij van een drietal milieuscenario's.* Onderzoeksmemorandum no. 57. Centraal Planbureau, 's-Gravenhage 1989.

Thijssen G., *Microeconomic models of Dutch dairy farms.* Ph.D thesis, Wageningen (forthcoming).

VROM, *Nationaal Milieu Beleidsplan, kiezen of verliezen.* Staatsuitgeverij, 's-Gravenhage 1989.

Wiersma D., *De efficiëntie van een marktconform milieu-beleid.* Groningen 1989.

Wit C.T. de, Environmental impact of the CAP. *European Review of Agricultural Economics* Vol 15 (1988) pp. 283-296.

Chapter 6

EFFICIENCY IN TRANSBOUNDARY POLLUTION ABATEMENT: a scheme for sharing the costs of reducing sulphur emissions in Europe

Lars Bergman, Herman Cesar and Ger Klaassen*

It is becoming common knowledge that a cooperative European programme to reduce sulphur emissions might lead to considerable cost advantages over isolated, national strategies. Shaw (1989) for example showed that the funds required for a 50 percent uniform reduction in emissions could be applied in a more efficient way to reduce sulphur deposition to 3-4 g/m^2 instead of 5-8 g/m^2. Such a cost-effective, targeted abatement strategy, however, implies an uneven distribution of pollution control efforts and associated costs, since the most cost-effective measures will be concentrated in a limited number of countries. Consequently, countries which have to carry the cost burden are likely to oppose to the abatement strategy. To implement cost-effective strategies, inter-country transfers of funds within Europe are therefore probably indispensable. A scheme for these transfers has to be designed such that it is beneficial for all countries to participate.

Countries such as Sweden and the Netherlands are presently discussing the possibilities of paying countries to reduce their emissions instead of taking more stringent, and hence more expensive, abatement measures domestically. The electricity producers in the Netherlands, in their annual report (SEP, 1989), suggested making investments in abatement measures in other countries, especially in Poland. Comparable proposals were discussed in the Swedish Parliament. Several principles can be applied for the sharing

* L. Bergman is Professor of Economics, Stockholm School of Economics, H. Cesar is Ph.D Student, European University Institute, Florence, and G. Klaassen is Research Scholar, International Institute for Applied Systems Analysis, Laxenburg, Austria. The authors wish to thank Markus Amann and Rod Shaw of the Transboundary Air Pollution Project at IIASA, Netherlands for providing valuable advice and comments. The financial support from the Foundation IIASA as well as the University Simulating Fund (USF) and the Institute for Environmental Studies of Free University, Amsterdam, are gratefully acknowledged.

of the costs of reducing sulphur emissions in Europe (Klaassen and Jansen, 1989). It is difficult, however, to find a scheme that provides sufficient incentives for each country to participate (Mäler, 1989).

This paper focuses on a particular scheme for sharing the costs of reducing sulphur emissions in Europe, which is beneficial for all countries. In addition, the incentives for countries to be deceptive, as well as the possibilities for counteracting deception are examined.

Section 1 introduces the scheme. Section 2 gives an overview of the model used to calculate the minimum costs to reach deposition targets. Illustrative results of the cost-sharing scheme are included in Section 3. Section 4 examines ways in which countries can practise deception when cooperating, and the possibility of a fund to counterbalance this. Conclusions are the subject of Section 5.

1. The scheme

Mode of operation

The following scheme for international cost-sharing aims at establishing a mode of operation of a supranational institution, a 'European Environmental Protection Fund', and at exchanging information between individual countries and the 'Fund'. The purpose of the scheme is to give each individual country in Europe the incentives to support a joint programme for sulphur emission reduction and to ensure that the joint programme is designed to attain cost-efficiency. Cost-efficiency implies that target deposition levels are attained at minimum costs with respect for the allocation of abatement measures across countries.

It is assumed that each country has already adopted a plan for emission control, and that these plans are common knowledge for all relevant countries. Thus, unless additional commitments are made, each country expects the emission vector (for list of symbols, see Appendix).

$$\bar{E} = (\bar{E}_1, \bar{E}_2, \ldots \bar{E}_n) \tag{1}$$

for the n countries in the relevant group of countries. However, it is also assumed that the deposition levels resulting from $\bar{E}$ are regarded as unacceptable or at least not low enough by all n countries. Thus there is a serious interest in additional emission control. With this background the scheme can be described in a series of steps:

1. Each country estimates a cost function

$$C_i = C_i(E_i); \quad dC_i/dE_i < 0 \tag{2}$$

for emission reduction in the home country. C_i is the total cost and E_i is the total emission in country i. There are no particular quality requirements for the estimated cost functions, but once the country has submitted itself to the Fund, it has to accept the policy recommendations that the Fund might make on the basis of, among other things, the submitted cost function.

2. On the basis of the submitted cost functions and committed emissions reductions for all countries, the Fund calculates deposition control functions

$$\hat{C}_i = \hat{C}_i(Q_i, \bar{E}, \pi, b) \quad with \quad \frac{d\hat{C}_i}{d\hat{Q}_i} < 0 \tag{3}$$

for each country. Q is the deposition in country i, b is a vector of cost functions parameters while π is the vector of parameters of the atmospheric transportation matrix, for instance, the so-called European Monitoring and Evaluation Programme (EMEP) matrix. In principle, $\hat{C}_i$ is finite for $Q_i = 0$, but low Q_i values are likely to imply emission reductions implemented outside country i but paid by country i. It should be emphasized that $\hat{C}_i$ includes the cost of control measures in other countries, paid by country i, in order to reduce depositions in country i. The cost function $\hat{C}_i$ is interesting as it indicates the cost for country i in attaining additional deposition reductions by independent action.

3. The Fund reports the cost function (3) to country i. On the basis of that function, and its willingness to pay for deposition reduction, country i determines a target deposition level Q_i^*. That level may or may not be equal to the estimated 'critical load' for country i and it may or may not

be the result of an analysis of marginal damage costs and the marginal costs of deposition reduction implied by (3). The cost to country i for the target deposition reduction is

$$\overline{C}_i = \hat{C}_i(Q_i^*; \overline{E}, \pi, b)$$

4. On the basis of this information the Fund identifies a vector $e = (e_1, e_2, \ldots e_n)$ of cost-efficient, additional emission reductions by solving the problem

$$C^* = \min_{e_i} \sum_i \{C_i(\overline{E}_i - e_i) - C_i(\overline{E}_i)\} \tag{4}$$

subject to

$$\sum_j \pi_{ij}(\overline{E}_i - e_i) = Q_i^*; \text{ for every } i$$

where π_{ij} are the coefficients of the EMEP matrix and the summation over i includes all countries willing to collaborate in a joint emission control effort. The equality constraint reflects the necessity of avoiding free riding.

5. The Fund requires all countries in the group of collaborating countries to reduce (or perhaps increase) their emissions by e_i^*. Moreover, in order to finance this additional emission control, the Fund reimburses country i by

$$C_i(\overline{E}_i - e_i^*) - C_i(\overline{E}_i)$$

That is, for the extra cost estimated on the basis of the cost function submitted by country i itself.

6. Finally, each country contributes to the Fund by paying $\alpha \cdot \overline{C}_i$ where

$$\alpha = \frac{C^*}{\sum_i \overline{C}_i} \quad \text{with } \alpha \leq 1 \tag{5}$$

Clearly $\sum_i \alpha \overline{C}_i = C^*$, as the Fund is breaking even and $\alpha \overline{C}_i \leq \overline{C}$ for all i.

That is, each country benefits from the scheme. Thus, given that country i is actually willing to pay $\overline{C}_i$ in order to attain its deposition target, the benefit of being a member of the Fund is equal to $(1-\alpha)\overline{C}_i$. Estimates of 'benefits' defined in this way are presented in Section 3. It should be added that, in the light of the reduced costs of attaining the initially stated deposition target, country i may want to revise its deposition target. In that case the procedure is repeated.

Some observations

A few observations can immediately be made. First, membership of the Fund is implicitly assumed to be voluntary; any country that wishes to become a member is accepted. In practice, the gain to the individual country depends on which countries participate. Thus, from the point of view of the individual country, there is an 'optimal' group of members of the Fund. We have not analyzed this issue in depth, but a few illustrative, numerical results are included in Section 4.

Secondly, in practice, the equality constraints in Equation (4) may be impossible to satisfy. The reason is that there is only one control variable, the emission level, for each country but several receptor points. Thus $(\overline{E} - e)$ is an n-dimensional vector while Q is an m-dimensional vector with $m > n$. In other words there are more goals than means, and (4) has to be rewritten

$$C^* = \min_{e_i} \sum_i \{C_i(\overline{E}_i - e_i) - C_i(\overline{E}_i)\} \tag{4'}$$

subject to:

$$\sum_j \pi_{ij}(\overline{E}_j - e_j) \leq Q_i^*; \ \forall \ i$$

In addition, there should perhaps be a non-negativity constraint on e_i; countries may feel that, in order to reduce depositions, cooperation should not lead to increased emissions in any one of the cooperating countries.

With these modifications of the scheme, however, there is a possibility of free riding. By stating a higher target deposition level than it desires and is willing to pay for, a country can attain the desired deposition level at a lower cost. The numerical results will illustrate this possibility for a few cases (Section 4).

Thirdly, countries may have incentives not to report the true cost functions. To see this, consider the following benefit function for country i

$$B_i = (\bar{C}_i - \alpha K_i \bar{C}_i) + (K_i C_i^* - C_i^*); \ \forall \ i \qquad (6)$$

where B_i are the benefits in country i and C_i^* the cost of additional emission reduction in country i in the coordinated cost minimizing plan over and above the initial emission reduction plans. The parameter K_i is controlled by country i and has the following role. When country i reports its cost function to the Fund it reports the true cost function times K_i, *e.c.* $K_i C_i$. Truthful revelation of the cost function thus implies $K_i = 1$.

With the inclusion of K_i the contribution to the Fund is $\alpha K_i \bar{C}_i$, while the reimbursement from the Fund is $K_i C_i^*$. As the true cost function in the optimum programme is C_i^*, country i can gain from excessive reimbursement by cheating about its cost function. On the other hand $K_i > 1$ means that the contribution to the Fund will be higher than it would be otherwise. In other words, the benefits, B_i, can be seen as a function of K_i. A necessary condition for maximization of B_i with respect to K_i is, after some manipulation and under the simplifying assumption that both C_i and α are independent of K_i,

$$\frac{dB_i}{dK_i} = C_i^* - \alpha \bar{C}_i \left(1 + \frac{\partial \alpha}{\partial K_i} \cdot \frac{k_i}{\alpha} \right) + (K_i - 1) \frac{\partial C_i^*}{\partial K_i} = 0 \qquad (7)$$

with $\partial C_i^* / \partial K_i \leq 0$.

It is obvious that truthful revelation of the cost function, *e.c.* $K_1 = 1$, is only a special case. However, it is also clear that the degree of cheating depends on how sensitive the optimum plan is for the cost level in country i. If country i should carry out more or less the same measures at any cost level, then $\partial C_i^* / \partial K_i$ is small in absolute value, and the optimum K_i deviates significantly from unity. If, on the other hand, a small cost increase in country i could shift a significant share of abatement measures from country i to some other country, there is not much room for cheating with the cost function.

Finally, even if there is no possibility for countries to cheat with the cost functions alone, there can be situations in which a combination of untrue revelation of both the cost function and deposition goals may be beneficial to these countries. The reason is that a country that is the main polluter of some neighbouring countries will be paid by 'the Fund' to abate its pollution, especially when the costs are low. This holds, even when the revealed target deposition in this country is very low. By announcing too low abatement costs and too high deposition goals, it can avoid payments to the Fund. By contrast, the country will be paid by the Fund to reduce emissions. Its only costs are then the true costs of abatement minus the announced costs of abatement. This amount may be much smaller than the costs this country would have had to contribute to the fund had it rightly announced its target deposition and cost function.

2. The model used - RAINS

RAINS (Regional Acidification INformation and Simulation) is an integrated model of acidification in Europe. It describes the set of relations that links the generation of pollutants through deposition with their adverse impacts on natural resources such as forests, ground water and lakes. The emphasis is on the transboundary aspects of air pollution (Alcamo *et al.*, 1987). The model has been developed by the International Institute of Applied Systems Analysis (IIASA) as a tool for evaluating control strategies. Currently the model is mainly sulphur-based, but nitrogen is being incorporated and ammonia emissions are to be included in the near future.

The model consists of a number of submodules (Figure 1): energy pathways, SO_2 control strategies, cost, SO_2 emissions, SO_2 transport, lake acidity, forest soil acidity and direct forest impacts. In this paper the first five submodules were used.

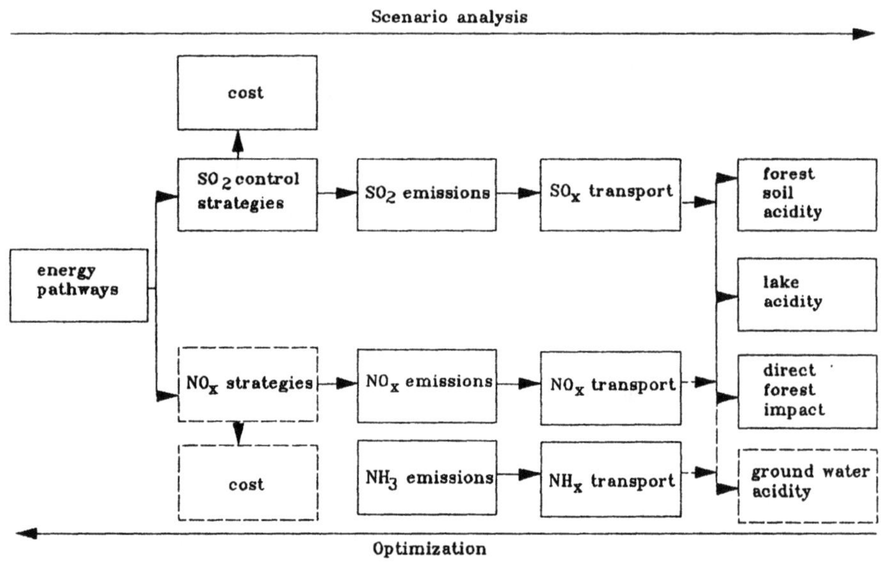

Figure 1: Schematic flowchart for the RAINS model.

In the Energy Pathway and SO_2 emissions submodels, different energy projections can be implemented. The submodel accounts for five emission-producing sectors: conversion (*e.g.*, refineries), power plants, domestic, industry and transportation. Eight fuel types are distinguished: brown coal, hard coal, derived coal (*e.g.*, coke, browncoal briquettes), light oil (*e.g.*, gasoline), medium distillate (gasoil), heavy oil, gas and other fuels. The last two are assumed to produce no sulphur emissions. Moreover, process emissions are taken into account when calculating the total emissions.

In the Pollution Control and Cost submodels, four types of emission reduction are considered: energy conservation, fuel substitution, use of low sulphur fuels and desulphurization. For the last type the following technologies are considered: combustion modification, flue gas desulphurization and regenerative processes. For the option 'energy conservation', no costs are assessed. For the remaining options, costs are based on country and technology-specific parameters (Amann and Kornai, 1987). The resulting national abatement cost functions incorporate the most important cost influencing factors of the European countries in an internationally comparable way. The cost functions are piecewise linear, reflecting that, in order to increase emissions further, a different technique with higher marginal abatement costs has to be applied.

The transport submodel predicts concentration and sulphur deposition for 150 × 150 km grids over Europe from the emission patterns of SO_2. In doing so, it uses source-receptor linkages generated by the long-range atmospheric transport model developed by the Norwegian Meteorological Institute under the European Monitoring and Evaluation Programme (EMEP) of the ECE Convention on Transboundary Air Pollution. Each country has at least several grids so that regional differentiation of deposition loads within a country is possible. As shown in Figure 1, the model can be operated in two ways:

- The *Scenario Analysis mode.* Given a specified pattern of energy use and control strategies, the environmental consequences are assessed.
- The *Optimization mode.* Given environmental targets, specified in terms of sulphur deposition or desired emissions, the optimum (*i.e.*, cost efficient) geographical distribution of sulphur emission reduction is calculated.

In the Scenario Analysis mode, the submodels described above are used to calculate emission and deposition. Furthermore, the optimization mode is used to estimate potential cost savings of more cost-effective policy measures.

3. The cost sharing scheme - an example

In this section, using a specific set of cost functions and target deposition levels, the proposed scheme is illustrated. The contributions of the countries to the Fund as well as reimbursements of the Fund to the countries are calculated for this set.

The cost functions used are the standard, piecewise linear functions given in the RAINS model for the official energy pathway in the year 2000.[1] It is assumed that the initial emissions are those following from current reduction plans as incorporated in RAINS. This means that the costs calculated for the scheme are the extra costs to attain target deposition levels over and above the costs of the current reduction plans. The optimization mode of the RAINS model is used for all minimum cost calculations. Target deposition

1 The fuel burnt in new and existing plants was however based on more detailed information (Cesar and Klaassen, 1990).

levels are quite arbitrarily chosen and summarized in Table 1. Note that these are peak grid levels, the average national sulphur deposition might be much lower.

Table 1: Peak grid target depositions in European countries.[2]

Denmark, Finland, Norway, Sweden	1 g S/m^2
EEC-countries, Austria, Switzerland	2 g S/m^2
Centrally planned economies, Albania, Turkey, Yugoslavia	4 g S/m^2

In order to calculate the payment scheme for this specific example, four calculations have to be carried out. First, the costs to country i $(\overline{C}_i)$ for unilaterally attaining its target deposition levels (Q_i^*) have to be computed. These are the minimum costs of abating air pollution necessary for reaching the deposition targets for this country. This means that abatement measures can be taken both in the country itself and elsewhere, depending on the costs. The results are summarized in Table 2. Note that for some countries, such as Ireland and Bulgaria, deposition goals are met by the current reduction plans without any further costs.

Secondly, the minimum costs (C^*) of jointly attaining target deposition levels (Q^*) in all countries contributing to the Fund have to be calculated. For each country these are the costs of the abatement techniques that it should install to reach the overall deposition goals. In the scheme, these costs would be reimbursed to the countries by the Fund (Table 2). Note that these costs are much lower than the sum of the costs of unilaterally attained reductions $(\overline{C}_i)$, illustrating the gains from cooperation.

Thirdly, the contribution of each country to the Fund is calculated. In order for the Fund to break even, countries only need to pay a fraction α of the cost $\overline{C}_i$ to it. The sum of $\overline{C}_i$ equals the quotient of the sum of C^* and α, with α being about 0.36. Hence, the contribution of country i is $\alpha\overline{C}_i$ and the benefits of each individual country from the scheme is $(1-\alpha)\overline{C}_i$ (Table 2).

Finally, the net payments to the Fund are calculated as the difference between the contribution to the Fund and the reimbursement by the Fund to each country (Table 2). Note that the sum of the net payments is zero which indicates that the Fund is breaking even.

2 A specific grid in Denmark was put to 2 g S/m^2, and one grid in Poland was excluded to find a feasible solution.

Table 2: Calculation of the cost sharing scheme (in mio DM).[3]

Country	Min. costs to unilaterally attain Q^* $(\bar{C}_i)$	Min. costs for jointly attaining Q^* (C_i^*)	Contribution of country *i* to the Fund $(\alpha\bar{C}_i)$	'Benefits' from scheme to country *i* $[(1-\alpha)\bar{C}_i]$	Net payments of country *i* to the Fund $(\alpha\bar{C}_i - C_i^*)$
ALB	0	0	0	0	0
AUS	3,849	0	1,370	2,479	1,370
BEL	5,421	1,245	1,929	3,492	684
BUL	0	0	0	0	0
CSSR	5,121	1,506	1,822	3,299	316
DEN	2,933	32	1,044	1,889	1,012
FIN	4,707	0	1,675	3,032	1,675
FRA	1,359	269	484	875	215
FRG	7,099	1,103	2,526	4,573	1,423
GDR	3,872	1,695	1,378	2,494	-317
GRE	558	532	199	359	-333
HUN	1,450	0	516	934	516
IRE	0	0	0	0	0
ITA	5,164	2,399	1,838	3,326	-561
LUX	883	0	314	569	314
NET	5,420	300	1,929	3,491	1,629
NOR	1,074	0	382	692	382
POL	4,463	885	1,588	2,875	703
POR	22	1	8	14	7
ROM	284	0	101	183	101
SPA	3,700	3,360	1,317	2,383	-2,043
SWE	2,933	0	1,044	1,889	1,044
SWI	2,946	0	1,048	1,898	1,048
TUR	0	0	0	0	0
UK	2,793	2,678	994	1,799	-1,684
USSR	9,589	9,273	3,412	6,177	-5,861
YUG	1,450	2,153	516	934	-1,637
SUM	77,090	27,431	27,431	49,659	0

Once this calculation has been carried out by the Fund, a country might want to revise its deposition target. To balance costs and benefits of such a revision, a country needs to know the marginal costs of changes in its deposition target. For Austria, this is shown in Table 3. A change in deposition goals from 2.0 g S/m^2 to 1.5 g S/m^2 increases annual costs with

3 $\alpha = \frac{27,431}{77,090} = 0.356$

2008 million DM to 3378 million DM. Similarly, loosening of deposition targets to 2.5 g S/m^2 decreases costs with 563 million DM to 807 million DM. Other countries might also want to revise the deposition targets. In that case the process can be repeated until no country wants to make any further changes.

Table 3: Comparison of costs and deposition levels for Austria at different deposition levels (in mio DM).

Target deposition (g S/m^2)	Resulting deposition (g S/m^2)	Min. costs to unilaterally attain Q^* $(\bar{C}_i)$	Min. costs for jointly attaining Q^* (C_i^*)	Contribution of country *i* to the Fund $(\alpha\bar{C}_i)$	Net payments of country *i* to the Fund $(\alpha C_i - C_i^*)$
1.50	1.50	9,801	63	3,378	3,315
2.00	2.00	3,849	0	1,370	1,370
2.50	2.50	2,266	0	807	807

This example shows that, given the deposition targets and cost functions, the cost sharing scheme can be calculated quite easily. However, the problem is to what extent countries will truly reveal their cost functions and deposition goals.

4. Incentive compatibility

Deposition levels

The first possibility for deception originates from the cost effective way of jointly attaining the target deposition levels. This means that some countries might reach low peak depositions because of measures taken to decrease deposition in neighbouring countries. This might even be true if their own deposition goals are high.

This creates the opening for these countries to behave as free riders since denying to the Fund their desire to decrease current deposition levels will lower their costs, while their lower deposition levels will be attained anyhow because of the measures taken for other countries. In our specific example (described in the previous section), ten countries were able to gain by not truly revealing their deposition targets: the Scandinavian countries (Finland, Norway, Sweden), some Western European countries (France, Luxembourg, the Netherlands and Switzerland) as well as Hungary, Rumania and

Yugoslavia. Though this may be different for any other example, it seems that the chance on changes in the composition of the group as well as the number of its participants is quite low. An elevation of the deposition goals for Czechoslovakia, the GDR and Poland to 6 g/m^2, for example, leaving other things unchanged will only lead to the exclusion of Sweden from the group of possible 'cheaters'.

Table 4: Comparison of costs and deposition levels for Sweden and the Netherlands at different deposition levels (in mio DM).

Target deposition (g S/m^2)	Resulting deposition (g S/m^2)	Min. costs to unilaterally attain Q^* ($\bar{C}_i$)	Min. costs for jointly attaining Q^* (C_i^*)	Contribution of country i to the Fund ($\alpha\bar{C}_i$)	Net payments of country i to the Fund ($\alpha C_i - C_i^*$)
Sweden					
1.00	0.95	2,933	0	1,044	1,044
1.25	0.95	778	0	285	285
1.50	0.95	0	0	0	0
Netherlands					
2.00	2.00	5,420	300	1,929	1,629
2.50	2.00	2,473	300	914	614
3.00	2.00	1,212	300	455	155
3.50	2.00	362	300	137	-163
4.00	2.00	0	300	0	-300

The gains from understating the desired deposition level differ per country and per situation. Table 4 summarizes these gains for Sweden and for the Netherlands in our specific case. In Sweden, the peak grid deposition always drops to 0.95 g S/m^2 for every target deposition in Sweden above this number. This means that Sweden's contribution to the Fund (1044 million DM) can drop to zero if their announced target depositions are high enough. A similar situation occurs for the Netherlands, which is able to annually gain as much as DM 1929 million.

Cost functions

As was mentioned in the previous section, countries may also be able to be deceptive with their cost functions. This possibility was also simulated with the RAINS model. Given the target deposition levels and the cost functions, it was assumed that the USSR would overestimate its costs. The USSR was chosen because its dC^*/dk is zero for reasonable values of k, and its $\overline{C}_i$ is close to C_i^*.

In the extreme case with $\overline{C}_i$ and C_i^*. being equal, an overestimation of the true costs with $100 \cdot (k-1)$ percent leads to net payments from the Fund being k times as large (assuming α to remain constant). This was checked in our example with $k = 1.1$ for the USSR. The results are presented in Table 5. The numbers show that, even though the contribution of the USSR to the Fund increases, the additional reimbursement implies an overall gain of about ten percent. It should be noted that the results for the USSR are rather specific due to the fact that, given the selected deposition targets, the USSR always has to take a specific number of domestic abatement measures to meet its own domestic targets. This explains the small difference between the costs of unilateral and cooperative action.

Table 5: Comparison of costs with ten percent overestimation of costs for the USSR.

Country	Min. costs to unilaterally attain Q^* $(\overline{C}_i)$	Min. costs for jointly attaining Q^* C_i^*	Contribution of country i to the Fund $(\alpha\overline{C}_i)$	'Benefits' from scheme to country i $[(1-\alpha)\overline{C}_i]$	Net payments of country i to the Fund $(\alpha\overline{C}_i - C_i^*)$
k=1	9,589	9,273	3,412	6,177	-5,861
k=1.1	10,578	10,292	3,833	6,745	-6,469

More generally, the scope for deception can be analyzed as follows. Recall that the net payment to the Fund is $(\alpha\overline{C}_i - C_i^*)$. As a result of deception $(k_i \neq 1)$ all three factors α, $\overline{C}_i$, and C_i^* change. First of all, unilateral costs $(\overline{C}_i)$ change with $y(k_i - 1)\overline{C}_i$. y is smaller than or equal to one because optimization implies that an increase in costs in country i with $(k_i - 1)$ generally implies that it is cheaper to pay other countries. Hence $\overline{C}_i$ is likely to rise with less than $(k_i - 1)C_i^*$. Secondly, optimal costs of cooperation $(\overline{C}_i^*)$ change as well with $z(k_i - 1)\overline{C}_i^*$. z is smaller than or equal to one. Since cooperation allows for more cost-effective solutions than unilateral action, z is likely to be smaller than y. Thirdly, α (the ratio of optimal cost for country i and the sum of the costs of unilateral action) will change. α is defined as $C_i^*/\sum\overline{C}_i$. Since cooperation generally offers more scope for cost-effective solutions, the change in C_i^*, resulting from a change in country i's reported cost function, is likely to be smaller than the change in $\sum C_i^*$. Consequently the change in α $(\delta\alpha)$ will be smaller than 1. This leads to the following conclusion. Deception with the cost function is beneficial if it reduces net payments of country i to the Fund. That is $\delta(\alpha\bar{C}_i - C_i^*) < 0$. This can be rewritten as: $\delta\alpha y(k-1)\bar{C}_i - z(k-1)C_i^* < 0$. Or , alternatively, as $\delta\alpha y/z < C_i^*/C_i^*/\bar{C}_i$. Recall that, generally, $\delta\alpha < 1$, $y/z > 1$ and $C_i^*/\bar{C}_i < 1$. Thus, deception is beneficial only if the change in α is sufficiently large. The greater the difference between C_i^* and $\bar{C}_i$, the higher $C_i^*/\bar{C}_i$, the smaller is the chance that the $\delta\alpha$, determining the contribution to the Fund, is sufficiently large to reduce net payments. In other words, if C_i^* is close to $\bar{C}_i$, that is for countries such as USSR, Spain, Greece and the United Kingdom (Table 2), deception is more likely to be beneficial.

Optimum group size

The problem of finding the optimal group size has already been mentioned in Section 1. Some numerical results of leaving one specific country out of the Fund are presented here. A Fund excluding Spain would not change peak deposition levels in the countries of the Fund. However, α would decrease with some 7 percent (Table 6). This means that the contribution of the remaining countries is 7 percent lower while deposition levels remain unchanged. Obviously, these countries are interested in leaving Spain out of the Fund.

Table 6: Calculation of the advantages of leaving Spain out of the Fund.

Country	Min. costs to unilaterally attain Q^* $(\bar{C}_i)$	Min. costs for jointly attaining Q^* (C_i^*)	Contribution of country *i* to the Fund $(\alpha\bar{C}_i)$	'Benefits' from scheme to country *i* $[(1-\alpha)\bar{C}_i]$	Net payments of country *i* to the Fund $(\alpha\bar{C}_i - C_i^*)$
Spain in					
Spain	3,700	3,360	1,317	2,383	-2,043
Rest	73,390	24,071	26,114	47,276	2,043
Sum	77,090	27,431	27,431	49,659	0
Spain out					
Spain	0	0	0	0	0
Rest	73,390	24,289	24,289	49,101	0
Sum	73,390	24,289	24,289	49,101	0

The same is true to some extent if the USSR or the UK are left out of the Fund, in which case α decreases by some 5 percent and 1 percent respectively. However, peak deposition in other countries will change in these cases. For instance, leaving USSR out will harm Finland to quite an extent.

Circumventing deception
Whether the possibilities for deception will be a serious threat, in practice, to the establishment and operation of the Fund is difficult to assess but a number of considerations can be mentioned. Firstly, even if some countries overreach, it might still be beneficial for other countries to participate since the costs of attaining target levels unilaterally might be higher. Moreover, attainment of desired deposition levels might not be feasible at all without cooperation. In that case the desire to reach the target deposition levels is to be balanced with the risk of deception.

Secondly, possible attempts by countries to use deception with their deposition targets can be checked in several ways. Submitted deposition targets can be compared to official policy documents in order to reveal discrepancies. Furthermore, deposition targets can be compared to deposition levels resulting from present policies. Clearly, the desired targets should not be higher than the ones achieved with present policies.

Thirdly, cost functions can be checked as well. Groups of experts can check whether the submitted cost-functions seem reasonable in view of available technical studies and empirical data. In addition, the cost function can be compared to the real costs for a number of relevant cases such as the application of flue-gas desulphurization in power plants. This, for example, can be done by a team of independent accountants. The accounting reports can be used to correct cost functions and to adjust countries initial payments and receipts from the Fund.

5. Conclusions

As pointed out there are some fundamental problems in connection with the coordination of abatement strategies in different countries. Deception possibilities in 'our' scheme only reflect this general problem. In spite of the weaknesses, our scheme demonstrates a mode of operation for a 'Fund'. In addition, it is shown that a simple cost-sharing scheme can significantly reduce the *ex-ante* costs of additional emission control for an individual country and can assist in speeding up the process of emission reduction.

Appendix: List of symbols

α	ratio of the optimized costs of co-operation and the costs of unilateral action
b	vector of cost functions
β_i	benefits of co-operating compared to unilateral action
C_i	cost function of country i
$\hat{C}_i$	cost of deposition control function in country i
C_i^*	optimal costs of cooperation
$\overline{C}_i$	costs for unilaterally attaining target deposition levels
E_i	total emission of country i
$\overline{E}$	vector of planned emission reduction
e	vector of cost efficient (additional) emission reductions
k_i	coefficient indicating deviation of revealed from true abatement costs in country i
π	coefficient of the transportation model
Q_i	deposition in country i
Q_1^*	target deposition level of country i
y	coefficient of change in unilateral costs
z	coefficient of change in costs of cooperation

References

Alcamo J., M. Amann, J.-P. Hettelingh, M. Holmberg, L. Hordijk, J. Kämäri, L. Kauppi, P. Kauppi, G. Kornai, and A. Mäkelä, Acidification in Europe: a simulation model for evaluating control strategies. *Ambio* Vol. 16 (5), (1987) pp. 232-245.

Amann M. and G. Kornai, Cost functions for controlling SO_2 emissions in Europe. IIASA Working Paper WP-87-65, IIASA, Laxenburg, 1987.

Cesar H. and G. Klaassen, Costs, sulfur emissions and deposition of the EC directive on large combustion plants. Working paper WP-90-006. IIASA, Laxenburg, 1990.

Klaassen G. and H.M.A. Jansen, Economic principles for allocating the costs of reducing sulfur emissions in Europe. Institute for Environmental Studies, Free University, Amsterdam, 1989.

Mäler K.G., The acid rain game. Paper prepared for ESF Workshop Economic Analysis for Environmental Toxicology, Amsterdam, May 1989.

SEP, Verslag over het jaar 1988, N.V. Samenwerkende Electriciteits-produktiebedrijven, Arnhem, 1989.

Shaw R.W., Using an integrated assessment model for decision-making in transboundary air pollution in Europe. In L.J. Brasser and W.C. Mulder (eds), *Man and his ecosystem, proceedings of the 8th world clean air congress*, The Hague, 11-15 September 1989, Elseviers Science Publishers, Amsterdam, 1989.

Part Two

GROWTH AND STEADY STATE

Chapter 7

ON ECONOMIC GROWTH, TECHNOLOGY AND THE ENVIRONMENT

Andries Nentjes and Doede Wiersma*

Over the last two hundred years the world economy has shown a process of economic growth with only a few interruptions. This development began in the eighteenth century in Great Britain, with the invention of how to organize mass production and how to use technology for that purpose. In the course of time this industrial revolution spread to other countries and technological progress has been incorporated into the system of industrial production. As a result, production has increased substantially, world population has expanded and average world GDP *per capita* has increased from $200 U.S. in 1775 to $1800 in 1975 (Krelle, ed., 1989).

However, besides increasing welfare in large parts of the world, the process of economic growth has had important negative consequences. Because of the unequal spread of industrial development over the world, the differences in *per capita* income between nations have widened enormously. Moreover, the impact of world economic growth on the natural environment has been increasingly becoming a serious problem since the mid fifties of this century. Depletion rates of energy and other non-renewable resources are now faster than ever experienced before in history, and increased environmental pollution has led to a growing awareness of the possible environmental constraints on future economic growth. In this contribution our main objective is to analyse the relation between economic growth and the environment, emphasizing the role of production technology. Economic growth exercises its negative consequences in two ways. Firstly, there is the depletion of energy and other natural resources caused by industrial production and consumption processes. The present depletion rates could result in shortages of supply of these resources which could lead to lower economic growth. Secondly, economic activity generates waste as a

* A. Nentjes is Professor of Economics and D. Wiersma is Senior Lecturer in the Department of Economics, University of Groningen, the Netherlands.

by-product of production and consumption. If the amount of waste that is thrown back into the environment exceeds the absorptive capacity of the environment, the pollution of air, water and soil impairs ecological functions, with negative consequences for human welfare. Both aspects are analysed in Section 1 where a survey is given of the economic growth debate, which began in the seventies. From the survey it will appear that the depletion of resources (*i.e.* energy) will not be man's most serious concern in the next century. Environmental pollution seems to become a more acute problem in the medium term. Because of this we concentrate on environmental pollution in the following sections. Section 2 discusses the relation between economic growth and environmental pollution in a macroeconomic framework. The analysis shows that economic growth is compatible with non-deteriorating environmental quality only if the efficiency of pollution abatement can be raised by way of technological progress. Since technological progress does not fall from heaven like manna but is the result of research and development efforts, environmental policy should contain strong incentives for the stimulation of this sort of technological progress on the level of microeconomic decisions. For this reason incentives for the innovation in pollution control are analysed in (a micro-economic framework) in Section 3. Section 4 gives a summary and some policy recommendations.

1. Economic growth and its limits (a survey)

The discussion in economic literature about the negative effects of economic growth began at the end of the sixties. Contributions to the debate can be divided in two classes. One group is concerned with qualitative analysis and theoretical arguments pro and contra economic growth. The other consists of quantitative methods (global models) for making prospects of the possible limits to growth in the foreseeable future. Both types of studies are briefly reviewed. Our main aim was to find out in which way technological progress is evaluated as a solution for overcoming some of the limits to growth.

Qualitative analyses

Two questions dominate in the qualitative studies of the pros and cons of economic growth.

1. In what way economic growth can contribute to a further increase of social welfare in societies, where the basic needs of life already have been fulfilled.
2. Whether further economic growth in the future will be limited by a shortage of natural resources and/or by environmental pollution. Some researchers included both questions in their analysis (Mishan, Daly, Beckerman). Others only focused on the possible limits to growth caused by a finite natural environment (Boulding, Georgescu-Roegen).

Mishan (1967) analysed in a polemic essay the issue of whether further economic growth could contribute to human welfare. He found that economic growth provides more and better goods, more travel, income equality, more education and more scientific progress and innovation. Against these benefits, continued growth produces negative aspects, such as congestion of traffic, violence, environmental degradation and increased pollution. Mishan argued that, in economies fully supplied with consumer goods, a continued economic growth will lead to satiation. Evaluation of these aspects of economic growth led him to the conclusion that the net effect of future economic growth on human health and happiness could be adverse and possibly disastrous.

In a second book Mishan (1977) worked out his satiation thesis. He formulated constituents of a good life such as food, clothing, housing, education, which can be assumed to be the minimum requirements for life in any society. In most western economies these basic needs are more or less fulfilled. Further economic growth would only lead to cosmetic improvements of these goods, which would not result in a further substantial increase of welfare. Technological progress has been developed in a direction where it produces adverse spillovers with respect to human welfare. Some innovations (nuclear power) generate dangerous pollutants, others (in the information industry) give users a direct power over individuals. To avoid these negative impacts, government control has to be reinforced and individual freedom consequently reduced. Here the key arguments for leaving the present growth path are the satiation of human needs and the socially negative aspects of economic growth. The environmental constraints to growth are an additional argument. Even if environmental spillovers could be completely corrected, which in Mishan's view leads to an increase in welfare, then economic growth is not desirable because of the social aspects. Mishan did not include the possible use of technological progress for pollution abatement in the analysis, nor did he formulate policy proposals for stopping economic growth.

Daly's (1977) plea for a stop to economic growth is based on more or less the same arguments as those of Mishan. Firstly, there is an absolute scarcity of natural resources. When there were low levels of population and low *per capita* consumption there was little need to worry about this type of scarcity. But this situation has changed. Growth of population and of *per capita* consumption push us ever closer to the carrying capacity of the biosphere. Further economic growth will deplete natural resources and environmental pollution will degrade the environment. Secondly, a distinction can be made between absolute wants which are the essential needs of human beings and relative and trivial wants, which satisfy the desire for superiority. Daly argued that in affluent societies the absolute wants are globally fulfilled. Further economic growth for satisfaction of the relative wants is undesirable. This same idea of social limits to growth was also elaborated by Hirsch (1977) and Scitovsky (1976). In contrast to Mishan, Daly formulated an alternative to economic growth. He advocated the concept of a steady state economy, with constant stocks of people and physical capital, maintained at levels that ensure low rates of depletion of non-renewable resources and energy.

To bring about such a society, three institutions have to be created, based on the price system and the system of private property. To impose control on the rate of resource depletion, the government would have to auction a limited quantity of transferable quota rights to buyers. Since depletion of natural resources (including fossil energy) is restricted by this institution, pollution is also restricted. Higher prices for depletion quotas include incentives for recycling and energy-saving technology. Transferable birth licences could be issued to every person to help ensure population control. To limit the degree of inequality in the distribution of income and wealth, an institution has to be established which imposes constraints. In this blueprint of a steady state economy the institutions are directed to impose quantity restrictions for solving the problem of absolute scarcity. The reason for this is that, in Daly's view, the price system deals only with relative scarcity. Correction of environmental pollution alone is insufficient in that it acts only on relative prices. This correction does not stop the increase of absolute scarcity resulting from continuing population growth and *per capita* consumption. Within the quantity constraints set by the institutions higher prices for depletion quota's provide incentives for technological progress in energy saving and pollution abatement activities.

Against the pleas for a stationary state, Beckerman (1974) took an opposite stance in his polemic defence of economic growth. Further economic growth is judged to be needed for abolishing poverty in developing countries and in some parts of western societies. Beckerman expected no shortage of non-renewable resources in the foreseeable future. From historical evidence about the supply of resources, he came to the conclusion that, in the past, supply has always adjusted to demand. Therefore, data on the present supply (stock) of non-renewable resources is not suitable for making predictions about future shortages. Pollution is expected to be a manageable problem if governments apply market instruments in their environmental policy, which also gives incentives for technological progress in pollution abatement equipment.

In contrast to these normative evaluations of both social and environmental pros and cons of economic growth is Boulding's (1966) positive analysis of the relation between economic development and the natural environment. Boulding applied the systems approach to economic development. Systems can be defined as being open or closed for inputs and outputs. In an open system, inputs enter the system from outside and outputs go to the outside. In a closed system, the outputs of all parts of the system are linked to the inputs of other parts. There are no inputs from outside and no outputs to the outside. Boulding distinguished three classes of inputs and outputs for economic development: matter, energy and information. In the traditional view of the economist, the present world economy is an open system for these classes of inputs. Material is used for consumption and production processes and leaves the economic system when its economic value has become zero. In order to create this material throughput, energy has to be used in the system. A problem is that in the past the energy input has shifted from solar and hydro energy sources to the increasing use of fossil energy. There has also been an accumulation of human knowledge, which is, according to Boulding, the most essential factor for economic development. Because of the finite resources of material and fossil energy and the limited storage capacity for waste from production and consumption processes, the economic system has to be viewed as a closed system. In such a closed system, 'the spaceship Earth', growth of production and consumption are not a plausible measure of the success of the system. In a spaceship economy it is the conservation of the total capital stock, material, energy and knowledge that matters. Stock maintenance and technological change which result in the maintenance of the stock by less production and consumption is a gain.

Increased searching and improvement of exploitation techniques can result in a substantial increase of the present supply. Boulding believed that the transformation of the economy to a more closed system is a long-term problem. In his view, many of the immediate problems of pollution and of environmental degradation could be solved by corrective taxation. The impact of technological progress in pollution abatement is not included in this analysis.

A fundamental analysis of the relation between the physical environment and the economic process can be found in Georgescu-Roegen (1971, 1975). Economic activities are governed by the physical laws of thermo-dynamics. According to the first law of thermo-dynamics material resources and energy, which are used for consumption and production, are not lost but only transformed. The second law of thermo-dynamics, the entropy law, states that material and energy degrade by use from order (low entropy) to disorder (high entropy). Energy is transformed into heat by use and heat becomes so dissipated that it cannot be used again. Material resources are transformed by production into valuable economic goods which are consumed. After consumption, the economic value of these goods becomes zero and they are disposed of in the environment as waste. In this way, natural resources, too, are subject to dissipation. The economic process produces an immaterial flow of utilities through depletion of energy and natural resources and through a flow of waste to the environment. Because of the finite stocks of energy and of natural resources and the limits of the storage capacity for waste of the environment, this development cannot go on forever. Georgescu-Roegen (1971) showed that the finite stock of fossil energy is the main hindrance to long-term economic development. Possible future shortages of natural resources could be minimized by more intensive exploitation techniques and by recycling waste, but more energy is usually needed for this. Environmental pollution can be decreased by abatement methods, but for this again additional energy is required. A steady-state economy in itself gives no ultimate solution either, because the use of fossil energy will continue. In order to avoid a shortage of fossil energy and natural resources for future generations, a conversion to a maximal use of solar energy and minimization of the rate of depletion of natural resources is essential. Georgescu-Roegen (1975) made the following specific recommendations. Firstly, goods should be manufactured in such a way that durability increases. Secondly, the research and use of solar energy should be stimulated more. Until the direct use of solar energy becomes convenient, energy waste should be avoided and, if necessary, strictly regulated. Technological innovation can play a role in this.

To sum up, these qualitative contributions to the economic growth debate in the seventies can be divided into in two classes. The first consists of normative evaluations about the social desirability of economic growth. The main issue in these analyses is the judgement about the satiation of human needs. Mishan and Daly believed that most human needs are already globally fulfilled. Beckerman stated that further economic growth is needed to abolish poverty in affluent societies and in developing countries. Environmental constraints to economic growth play a secondary role in this discussion. For Daly and Mishan these constraints were an additional argument to plead for a stationary economy. No (Mishan) or little (Daly) attention was given to possible technological progress in methods for environmental protection. In contrast to this, Beckerman was very optimistic about the role of technology in solving environmental problems, but he did not develop the idea further.

The second part of the growth discussions consists of positive analyses. In these studies, the central subject is the environmental limits to economic growth. Analyses by Boulding and by Georgescu-Roegen are both concerned with the very long term, during which shortages of natural resources and fossil energy may occur. Environmental pollution is a problem for the more immediate future which could be managed by corrective taxes. The role of technological progress in pollution abatement is not denied in these analyses but it receives little attention. All these analyses appeared in the seventies, when environmental pollution was not yet a serious problem on a continental or a global scale. This perhaps explains why environmental pollution and the role of technological progress in abatement methods received relatively little attention in these analyses.

Quantitative analyses

Quantitative prospects and projections about world economic growth and its limits started in 1972 with the publication of *The limits to growth* (Meadows, *et al.*, 1972). Since then other global models and prospective views have been developed. In this section a brief survey is given of those projections in which environmental developments have been included in the analysis.

In 'The limits to growth' world development is approached by means of a number of aggregative variables such as world population, industrial production, agricultural production, natural resources and environmental pollution. These variables are connected by means of feedback loops. For instance, an increase of industrial production widens the possibilities for population growth, but it also increases the rate of depletion of natural resources and of environmental pollution. This in turn can result in a slowdown of production. On the basis of historical data about the development of the main variables from 1900 to 1970, it is assumed that in the future these variables will show a continuous constant exponential rate of growth. Simulation of this unchanged growth pattern by the model showed that world economic development will stagnate, to be followed by a fall in output and income in the next century because of a shortage of non-renewable natural resources (especially zinc, lead, tin, copper, mercury). One result of relaxing this limit in the simulations, by assuming that the stock of natural resources could be doubled through intensive exploration of minerals, increased efficiency in resource use, and by worldwide recycling is that industrial production could be boosted to a higher level. However, the faster rate of growth of environmental pollution (heavy metals, pesticides, coal dioxide, *etc.*) will increase the death rates of population and decrease food production. Additional simulations of the exponential growth model showed that the relaxation of one of the limits always caused the economic system to run into another limit. For instance, by assuming no shortage of natural resources and avoiding pollution by increased abatement, the world population may increase further up to the limit posed by disposable soil for agriculture. Technological progress is only included in this model by relaxing some of the limits, but it has no impact on the assumed exponential growth patterns, nor do changes in human behaviour and government policies.

An alternative approach was worked out by Mesarovic and Pestel (1974). They analysed the world economic system by means of a world model with ten regions connected in a trade network. For each region, a submodel is formulated in which different hierarchical levels of human behaviour and of policymaking are distinguished. At the top of the hierarchy is the individual level, below it the group, demographic-economic, technological and environmental levels. In this way changes in policy decisions and in human behaviour which influence economic growth can be analysed in the model. Prospective calculations with this model to the year 2025 show that, with unchanged economic growth, emergency situations can occur in parts of the world (for instance a food crisis in South-Asia), which may have consequences for development in other regions. A collapse of the world system seems unlikely. In order to avoid such crises Mesarovic and Pestel recommended the directing of human behaviour and government policies in the future towards more cooperation. By this means the undifferentiated exponential growth in parts of the world should be changed in an organic growth path of the world system, which is more sustainable. Organic growth means that fast growth in early stages of development is followed by a slowdown. On environmental problems, Mesarovic and Pestel's analysis mainly focuses on the energy problem. To avoid future shortage of supply a strategy has been developed. In the short term (30 years), energy demands can be provided by oil and natural gas. In the medium term a switch to coal will be necessary and in the very long term (more than 200 years) the use of solar energy is desirable. The effects of environmental pollution are not included in this analysis, nor are the possibilities of technological progress in methods for reducing pollution.

A third global model in which the relation between world economic development and the environment has been analysed was developed by Leontief *et al.* (1977). This model was built specifically to provide a tool for analysing the impact of prospective economic issues and policies within the International Development Strategy of the United Nations. It contains the economies of fifteen world regions, linked by flows of imports and exports, as well as capital flows. Forty-five sectors are distinguished for each region. Their relations are represented by an input-output model. The demand for natural resources and environmental pollution are included in the input-output structure. Using this model, simulations of world economic development until 2000 have been made. For the adequacy of natural and mineral resources, two scenarios have been analysed. In the first scenario the estimates of regional and world resource endowments are based on present data of existing reserves. The second scenario incorporates more optimistic estimates of the levels of resource endowments, but is still fairly conservative as it does not take account of new major potential sources or new discoveries. A comparison of the growth rates of consumption of minerals like copper, bauxite, nickel, zinc, lead, iron and fossil energy with the supply scenarios shows all these resources, except lead and zinc to be fully adequate in 2000. Environmental pollution has been analysed by taking five pollutants for water pollution, one for air pollution (particulates) and solid waste. A proportion of these pollutants (80 à 99 percent) is assumed to be abated at the level of the U.S. standards for abatement in 1970. Worldwide abatement of these pollutants turns out to be manageable in 2000.

As well as these global models, some prospective projections have been made about the future of the world economy. These projections are mostly based on historical evidence which serves as a support for views and policy recommendations for the future.

An optimistic view of the future is presented by Kahn (1979). Kahn sketched human history in a very long term perspective of more than ten thousand years. He distinguished three stages of development. The first stage, running from about 8000 B.C. to 1800 A.D., is characterized by agricultural and pre-industrial activities. The second stage (from 1800 to 2200) is seen as a transition period in which human society is changing from the pre-industrial stage to a third stage of post-industrial conditions where society will be free from economic scarcity. Kahn argued that we are in the midst of the transition period. He began his analysis from the premise that social, political and cultural forces are likely to slowdown the growth of population and production long before the world encounters unmanageable problems of resource shortages and increasing pollution. Evidence for this assumption is the observed slowdown in the growth of population and industrial production in affluent societies. The same development can be expected in the rest of the world when industrialization spreads. In this view, rapid worldwide economic growth is needed to raise wealth and income in developing countries. Environmental limits may temporarily cause a slow down of economic growth but in the longer term that can be avoided by technological progress. When speaking of the supply of natural resources, Kahn referred to the past: additional supplies of existing resources were discovered, and new kinds of resources were taken into use. On the basis of the historical evidence he expected that this development would continue. Environmental pollution would be effectively abated by government regulation directed to the stimulation of technological progress in this area. In this broad prospective view, the possibilities of technological progress for pollution abatement were not worked out in detail.

A more recent view about the future of the world economy is presented in the United Nation's report: *Our common future* (Brundtland *et al.*, 1987). In this report the development of the world economy over the last hundred years has been evaluated in order to explore the potential for reaching a sustainable development in the future. Sustainability is defined as a development that meets the needs of the present without compromising the ability of future generations to meet their own needs. In evaluating the past the report noticed that since 1900 the world economy has expanded 20 times, industrial production has increased by a factor 50 and world population has multiplied more than three times. Four-fifth of this increase has occurred since 1950. As a result living standards and the quality of life have vastly improved in parts of the world. Many of the products and technologies that have gone into this improvement are raw material- and energy-intensive and entail a substantial amount of pollution. Since 1900 the consumption of fossil fuels has grown by a factor 30. Environmental pollution has become more pronounced since the seventies. In Europe and North America acid rain is killing forests and lakes. The burning of fossil fuels puts carbon dioxide in the atmosphere. Global warming caused by a rising CO_2 level can bring about enormous changes in the global pattern of agricultural production and the rise of the sea level will endanger coastal areas. Other industrial gasses threaten to deplete the ozone shield to such an extent that the number of human and animal cancers will rise sharply. Other forms of environmental degradation, such as the destroying of tropical forests and the increasing desertification, continue on a vast scale. In order to reduce poverty in developing countries, economic growth will have to be increased in the future. To bring developing countries' energy use up to that of industrialized countries by the year 2025 would require increasing global energy use by a factor of five. The supply of energy resources is not the main problem. Forecasts of recoverable reserves indicate that oil production will gradually decrease in the next century, but gas supplies should last over 200 years and coal about 3000 years at present rates of use. It is the global ecosystem which cannot wihtstand a further increase in the burning of fossil fuels. Threats of global warming and acidification of the environment most probably rule out even a doubling of energy use. A further increase of growth must, therefore, be less energy-intensive than growth in the past. In order to reach this goal, a reorientation of technology is required. With that aim in mind the Brundtland report makes two recommendations. Firstly, the capacity for technological innovation in developing countries needs to be greatly intensified. Secondly, technology development in the world must be much more oriented towards environmental factors. The U.N. world commission on environment and development has made a great number of policy suggestions that could help to bring about such a change. They range from the enforcement of environmental policies at the national level to the strenghtening of international cooperation on environmental issues. The common theme of these suggestions is still to stimulate the integration of economic and environmental aspects in policy decision-making. In this way technological progress should change in the direction of increasing energy efficiency and pollution abatement.

To sum up, these quantitative studies give a somewhat heterogeneous picture of future world development and its environmental limits. The most extreme views are given in Kahn's (1979) prospective analysis and the world model of *The limits to growth* (Meadows *et al.*, 1972). Both studies have in common that they are concerned with a relatively by long-term horizon and that expected development has a deterministic characteristic in the sense that changes in human behaviour and of policies cannot alter the assumed development. However, in their prediction of future development the two studies differ completely. In the study by Kahn it is the assumed slowdown of economic growth because of 'natural' social factors, such as satiation of basic needs, that prevents the world system from collapsing because of environmental limits. Technological progress directed towards conservation of the environment on a global scale is not needed. In 'The limits to growth', the exponential growth path collapses because of the environmental and resource barriers to economic expansion. Technological progress in the environmental production sector (resource saving and pollution abatement) can delay the stagnation but it cannot alter the growth path.

In contrast to these extremes, the studies by Mesarovic and Pestel (1974) and by Leontief *et al.* (1977) are much less deterministic. Changes in human behaviour and in government policies are allowed to alter the present growth path to a more sustainable development. In Mesarovic and Pestel's model, world economic development can continue if human behaviour and policies are oriented towards organic growth; that is, to a slowdown of growth trends of population and production. In the model by Leontief *et al.* the impact of a number of policy strategies is calculated by model simulations.

On environmental issues, all these models are outdated as recent developments of environmental pollution are not included. In Mesarovic and Pestel's model the analysis of environmental problems is concentrated mainly on energy problems. Leontief *et al.* have included both the development of natural resources and environmental pollution in the model. The time horizon is too short (up to 2000) to expect shortages of resources.

Environmental pollution is not recognized as an important problem since it was expected that it could easily be reduced by implementing the U.S. pollution control standards of 1970.

In the eighties, however, this picture of environmental issues changed. Environmental pollution, such as acid rain, the greenhouse effect and the depletion of the ozone shield were expected to become global threats long before a shortage of fossil energy and other natural resources occurred. The main policy suggestions concerning the environment in *Our common future* (Brundtland *et al.*, 1987) are more directed towards avoiding pollution than to energy saving as such. The report recommends technological progress in pollution abatement as an important tool for solving the pollution problem.

None of the studies discussed in this section analysed the mechanisms for stimulating this type of technological progress in a comprehensive economic framework. In Sections 2 and 3 an effort is made to fill this gap.

2. Pollution and economic growth: a macroeconomic framework

In this section we concentrate on the consequences of environmental pollution for future economic growth. For many pollutants, such as acid rain, carbon dioxide, *etc.*, today's emissions influence environmental quality in the future in a negative way. If the present flow of emissions exceeds the absorptive capacity of the environment, environmental quality degrades. As a result, the absorptive capacity in the future decreases and the damage of accumulated pollution to human welfare increases. Pollution abatement today can prevent these future welfare losses, but only by using resources which cannot be allocated for present consumption. Technological progress in pollution abatement can be defined as reaching a given pollution reduction with lower resources or reaching a higher pollution reduction with given resources. With this kind of technological progress, the use of resources for pollution abatement will be decreased and/or environmental quality will be improved. The impact of pollution abatement and of technological progress in pollution abatement on future economic growth is analysed in a macro economic framework. Firstly, the future allocation of pollution and economic growth are analysed in a situation of intertemporal welfare maximization. Secondly, the impacts of pollution abatement and of technological progress in pollution abatement on economic growth are included in the analysis.

The pollution limit to growth

Air pollution caused by SO_2 emissions is a clear example of the relations between flows and stocks of pollutants and environmental degradation. A large flow of SO_2 emissions causes health damage in the localities or regions where the flow of pollutants is emitted. Dying forests, however, are the consequence of the stock of SO_2 depositions accumulated over the course of time (together with NO_x, NH_3 and ozones). Even in the face of a sharp reduction of the present flow of SO_2 emissions in the atmosphere, forests will continue to die, since the stock of SO_2 deposited will go on growing and the buffering capacity of the soil has been used up in the past. The error of the optimists (Simon and Kahn, 1984; Singer, 1988) who point out that, since the flows of many pollutants have been reduced, our environment is improving, is that they overlook the fact that in almost all areas, stocks of harmful pollutants are still increasing, and therefore potential and actual damage too. As a rule, solutions to environmental problems caused by stocks of pollutants require very drastic reductions of the flow of pollutants emitted into the environment; up to 70 to 95 percent in most cases (RIVM, 1988). The damage caused by SO_2 deposition in the European Community has been estimated at 2848 ECU per ton of sulphur deposited (Bergmann, 1985). To attain a situation in which, according to present scientific knowledge, no significant damage is inflicted, emissions in Western and Eastern Europe have to be reduced by about 80 percent relative to the 1985 level of emissions.

Many other sink problems, ranging from local to global, can be added to the acid rain example; the degradation of the ozone layer, sea pollution by plastics, accumulation of phosphates in agricultural soils, phosphate eutrophication of lakes, accumulation of nitrates and pesticides in agricultural soils and in subsoil drinking-water supplies, accumulation of radioactive ceasium in the humus of forest soils and, in the Netherlands, the gradual increase of cadmium and copper in the soil (Reijnders, 1989). The CO_2 pollution of the atmosphere is the most well-known global problem caused by a stock of pollutants. According to the most recent expert views, a doubling of the natural concentration of CO_2 in the atmosphere will raise the temperature of the global atmosphere by an average of 4°C; a situation which can be reached between the years 2030 and 2050 if present trends continue. The rise in atmospheric temperature will have a worldwide impact on climate, sea level will rise and coastal areas will be flooded. Climates may become more turbulent, affecting wind flows and rainfall, which in turn may make present agricultural areas unsuitable for cultivation. On the other hand the greenhouse effect can stimulate the growth of plants and in some areas more abundant rainfalls can stimulate agriculture.

The potential economic impact of changes in temperature and climate are enormous. About one-third of the world population lives below the two-metre-above-sea-level mark. In a worst-case scenario, the sea level may have risen that much by the second half of the next century. The costs would be immense; floods, loss of land and huge investments in water defence works. The frequency of hot, dry summers in Europe and North America could increase. The cornbelt in the U.S. Midwest is already endangered by desertification and shifting grain production to (North)Canada has its limits (Reijnders, 1989).

To stabilize the level of CO_2 in the global atmosphere, global emissions of CO_2 and CO_2 equivalent gasses should be reduced by about 50 percent. Because of the time lags involved in the atmospheric warming-up process, the temperature would nevertheless go on to rise by 1°C even if the necessary reduction of emission were effectuated today.

These two examples indicate that the accumulation of pollutants is responsible for considerable and growing social costs. Damage to the productive function of the environment caused by the accumulated stock of pollutants decreases the future level of potential output. Deterioration of environmental quality also diminishes the utility that people directly derive from environmental amenities. A drag of present pollution on future welfare cannot be denied. However, the large margins of uncertainty in the physical and biological data and the difficulties involved in economic evaluation of future impacts of sink pollution mean that we do not have a solid empirical base for assessing the extent to which future economic growth will be slowed down by present environmental degradation and whether present pollution is sustainable or not.

In economic literature the dynamics of flows, stocks and the economy has usually been analysed by means of optimum control theory. A general treatment of this approach can be found in Nijkamp (1980) and Ströbele (1986). In particular, the economics of depletable and renewable resources offer many examples of the application of this theory. More recently, efforts have been made by Siebert (1987), Barbier and Markandya (1989) and Nentjes (1989) to apply it to the problem of environmental pollution. The optimum control problem that has to be solved can be formulated as a problem of choice for the decision maker. There is an opportunity to exploit the environment today as a sink for pollutants and to shift the negative consequences for output and welfare to the future. Sustainable growth takes into account the limits set by environmental constraints. In optimum control models it is assumed that the planner intends to maximize the discounted value of welfare over time, subject to some contraints with respect to aggregate production and environmental pollution. A sustainable development, in the sense that environmental quality is maintained in the long run, is reached if the flow of pollutants in each period equals the absorptive capacity of the environment.

One of the main unsolved questions is exactly what the relation between the stock of pollutants that has been accumulated and the capacity of the environment to absorb the present flow of emissions is.

Siebert included in his analysis a constant absorptive capacity for pollution as a limit to economic growth. In Barbier and Markandya and Nentjes the relation between environmental quality and the absorptive capacity of the environment to assimilate pollutants is assumed to be determined by the stock of accumulated pollutants (Barbier and Markandya also incorporated the use of renewable and depletable resources, but for their results these additions are not essential.) According to Nentjes, the capacity of the environment to absorb and neutralize the flow of pollutants increases when the stock of pollutants increases. Barbier and Markyanda assumed that the capacity to absorb pollution is a strictly concave function of the stock of pollutants. However, these are assumptions based on *a priori* arguments. Empirical research still has a long way to go in this area.

Pollution abatement and technological progress in pollution abatement

The impact of pollution abatement on economic growth was analysed by Krelle (1984), Siebert (1987) and Nentjes (1989). The results of these approaches for economic growth are different. According to Krelle pollution abatement is compatible with economic growth. In contrast, Siebert and Nentjes concluded that pollution abatement cannot prevent economic stagnation. This difference in outcomes can be explained by differences in the assumptions about the cost function of pollution abatement. This can be illustrated by analysing the impact of pollution abatement on economic growth. Pollution can be reduced by abatement activities. Let total abatement costs be K and total output Y. Resources have to be shifted to abatement activity. As a result net income is $(Y - K)$. In this situation intertemporal welfare maximization boils down to maximizing $(Y - K)$ over time. Growth of net aggregate production $(Y - K)$ exists if $d(Y - K)/dt > 0$, or $dY/dt > dK/dt$. Such growth will be sustainable, *i.e.* without deteriorating environmental quality, if the additional pollution caused by economic growth is fully compensated by pollution reduction. If economic growth continues over time, sustainability demands an increase of pollution reduction.

Krelle (1984) assumed constant marginal abatement costs in this analysis, which means that with increasing total output, pollution can be reduced by devoting a constant fraction K of Y to pollution abatement. In this case dK/dt is proportional to dY/dt and consequently $d(Y - K)/dt$ does not decrease. Economic growth is compatible with pollution abatement.

However, Krelle's assumption is patently contrary to the established facts. Marginal pollution abatement costs are increasing. Siebert (1987) and Nentjes (1989) began from this assumption. With increasing marginal abatement costs, dK/dt increases at a faster rate than dY/dt, which implies that $(dY/dt - dK/dt)$ approaches zero over time. In this case pollution abatement activity makes economic growth only temporarily possible, but it cannot prevent stagnation in the long run.

Technological progress in pollution abatement could solve the conflict between pollution and economic growth. In the economic literature this idea has been suggested by Siebert (1987) and has been worked out by Kuipers and Nentjes (1973) and Nentjes (1989). In a neo-classical model of economic growth with pollution, Kuipers and Nentjes concluded that economic growth would be compatible with pollution abatement if the rate of technological progress in pollution abatement were to exceed the rate of labour augmenting technological progress plus the rate of growth of the labour force. Nentjes (1989) concentrated on the impact of technological progress on sustainability, *i.e.* on the capacity to maintain environmental quality. In this approach p is the pollution per unit of output and k the cost of reducing pollution per unit of output. Since k is a fraction of a unit of output, $0 \le k \le 1$. The change in pollution control costs needed to be able to reduce pollution per unit of output can be represented in the formula $\tilde{k} = E\,\tilde{p}$ in which $\tilde{k}$ stands for the rate of change of pollution control costs and $\tilde{p}$ for the rate of change in the pollution coefficient; E is the cost elasticity of the pollution coefficient: $(dk/k)/(dp/p)$. The cost elasticity has a negative value since abatement costs increase if pollution per unit of output is reduced. The formula shows that reduction of p raises marginal abatement cost (with $E\,\tilde{p}$). However, the increase of abatement costs can be mitigated by technological progress in pollution control. As a consequence of technological progress, a reduction of p (the pollution per unit of output) may be feasible without increasing k (the cost of pollution control per unit of output). The relation between the rate of change of pollution control costs, of the pollution coefficient and of the rate of cost saving caused by technological progress in pollution control (γ) can be expressed as:

$$\tilde{k} = E\,\tilde{p} - \gamma \tag{1}$$

A constant environmental quality can only be maintained, if the rate of growth of output $(\tilde{Y})$ is equal to the rate of decline of the pollution coefficient:

$$\tilde{Y} = -\tilde{p} \tag{2}$$

Equation (2) shows that when the flow of pollution is sustainable today, every percentage of growth of output from today on asks for an equal percentage of reduction of pollution per unit of output (*cet. par.*). Only on that condition will the total flow of pollutants entering the environment remain constant and equal to the absorptive capacity of the environment. The growth of net income would be the result of the growth in gross output minus the increasing fraction of output allocated to pollution abatement. However, if k rises, the moment will come when the increase in abatement costs exceeds the increase of gross income. A condition for sustained growth of net income is that:

$$\tilde{Y} \leq -\tilde{p} \quad and \quad \tilde{k} \leq 0 \tag{3}$$

Substitution of (3) in equation (1) gives:

$$\gamma \geq E\,\tilde{Y} \tag{4}$$

Condition (4) shows a sustainable positive rate of growth of net income is feasible only if the rate of technological progress in pollution control exceeds a minimum value determined by the rate of output growth and the elasticity of abatement costs. So technological progress is a crucial factor in maintaining sustainable income growth. Section 3 deals with the type of governmental policies that would stimulate the research and development of new environmental technologies.

3. Technological progress in pollution abatement: a microeconomic framework

We can draw the conclusion from Section 2 that sustainable economic growth is feasible if the increase of pollution caused by further economic growth is compensated by a continuous increase of emission reduction, and if the resulting increase of marginal abatement costs are fully offset by technological progress in pollution abatement. In this section we analyse the incentives for stimulating this kind of technological progress. In a market economy the decision whether or not to invest in research and development of new products or production methods is taken at the level of the individual firm. A profit maximizing firm balances the costs of research and development (the supply side of the market) against the expected benefits of exploitation of a new technology (the demand side). In a market economy of produced goods and services, technological progress depends on demand and supply factors governed by the market.

In contrast to this, the demand for technological progress in pollution abatement originates in the environmental policy of the government. Also, the supply of technological progress in pollution abatement is heterogeneous. Some big polluting firms, for whom research and development are a part of their regular activities, may possess a large capacity for developing abatement technology at relatively low costs. Small polluting firms without research and development capacity have to buy new abatement technology from specialized firms. The interaction between the demand for technological progress in abatement technology by the government and the heterogeneous supply of this technology has been analysed by Nentjes and Wiersma (1988) and by Nentjes (1988). From this analysis it appears that the impact of the environmental policy of the government on technological progress in abatement technology has two aspects;

- the stringency of the environmental policy;
- the kind of instruments of environmental policy which will be used.

For sustainable growth a constant amount of pollution, at most equal to the absorptive capacity of the environment, is required in the course of the time.

In order to prevent emissions from growing, the stringency of environmental policy has to be continuously increased in terms of demanded emission reduction. This increase in stringency may have a positive incentive on technological progress in pollution abatement. Big firms may anticipate this trend by developing more efficient abatement technology. For firms specialized in innovation, increasing strictness of environmental regulations provides an opportunity for opening new markets.

A related question has to do with the kind of instruments the government can use for increasing the stringency of the standards and, at the same time, for stimulating technological progress in an efficient way. For the growth of pollution as a consequence of economic growth, a command and control system and a system of constant charges for each unit of emission have disadvantages compared to a bubble concept with emission permits. With a command and control approach, the allowable emission of each polluter is fixed. With a system of constant charges, every polluter has to pay a charge per unit of emission. A cost minimizing polluter will abate pollution as far as the marginal abatement costs are lower than the charge and will pay the charge over the residual emissions. The application of both instruments cannot prevent an increase of total pollution in a situation of economic growth in which the number of polluters increases (Baumol and Oates, 1988). In order to reach sustainable growth, a continuous adjustment of emission standards of the command and control system and of emission charges would be necessary to prevent pollution from growing. A bubble concept has the advantage that such adjustments can be avoided. With this, total aggregative emission can be fixed at the level needed for sustainable growth. Permits can be issued by the government for the allowed total emission. In the case of increasing pollution caused by economic growth, the price of the permits increases. As a consequence of this, pollution will be more costly and additional abatement results in cost savings for polluters. As a result pollution abatement will increase.

The incentives of different instruments of environmental policy for technological progress in pollution abatement was evaluated by Downing and White (1986). The general conclusion to draw from these studies is that in a situation where total emissions are given and are constant, market instruments (charges and an emission permit system) have more effect on technological progress in pollution abatement than a command and control system. In a situation of sustainable growth, for which both a constant pollution in the course of the time and technological progress in pollution abatement is required, a bubble concept with tradeable emission permits is the most suitable instrument of environmental policy.

When introducing tradeable emission permits, an important issue is how to distribute the emission rights among polluters. The emission trading programme under the U.S. Clean Air Act gives an example of a politically feasible solution. Emission rights have been granted to existing polluters according to the emissions that were allowed under direct regulation. As a consequence, a firm has to buy emission permits (from other firms) only in so far as it wants to emit a larger amount of pollutants than it is entitled by the permits in its possession to do.

Limiting the right to pollute, and making the existing rights exchangeable, creates a scarcity rent. Under the distribution that has been proposed, the rent is appropriated by the existing firms according to the extent to which they pollute. Although from the point of view of fairness this may be difficult to accept, it can ease the political acceptance of tradeable pollution rights. Firms that have to acquire emission permits have to buy them from other firms, often within the same industry. Even though expenditure on emission permits is a real cost for the individual firm, for the group of polluting firms as a whole it is a transfer. Since the net costs for the group are not raised, an important ground for political resistance against the use of the financial instrument is removed.

In the context of this chapter a main issue is the relation between a system of tradeable emission permits and economic growth. A plausible assumption is that the price of an emission permit affects economic growth negatively. One can imagine that, as a special case, when no further improvements in abatement efficiency can be obtained, the emission constraint (set by the total of pollution permits) will set a limit to growth. However, the probability that such a stationary state will be reached in the foreseeable future is very small, since the spectre of technological opportunities to reduce pollution is enormous. For example, it has been calculated that in the Netherlands the amount of waste and emissions can be reduced to 60 or 70 percent of the 1985 level with technologies that have already been developed (VROM, 1989).

A general model would have to take into account all the feedbacks between the price of tradeable pollution permits and economic growth. If improvements in abatement efficiency lag behind output growth, the increasing demand for pollution permits will raise its price, and consequently economic growth will slowdown. However, there is a feedback mechanism. If the price of tradeable emission permits increases (and economic growth slows down), a larger part of savings will be invested in research and development efforts to increase abatement efficiency by reducing the marginal costs of pollution abatement. The improvement in abatement efficiency that is attained in this way will counteract the rise in the price of emission permits and, by doing that, stimulate economic growth.

4. Conclusions

The discussions in Sections 1 to 3 can be summarized in the following propositions.

(1) The contributions to the 'economic growth *versus* the environment' debate in the seventies concentrated on the social limits to growth and the constraints posed by finite stocks of depletable natural resources.
(2) During the eighties environmental pollution (and overexploitation of renewable resources) emerged as the main elements of unsustainable economic development.
(3) In its capacity to absorb pollution, the environment can be viewed as a renewable resource that can be exploited within a given limit.
(4) Continuous growth of labour productivity propels an economy that maximizes intertemporal welfare towards a stationary state of zero growth, since in the progressive state, the rate of growth of pollution abatement costs exceeds the rate of growth of gross output.
(5) The coming of the stationary state is prevented if the rate of technological progress in pollution control exceeds the rate of growth of marginal abatement costs arising from the necessity to reduce pollution per unit of output.
(6) The innovation incentives emanating from present environmental regulation are weak; they may not be enough to bring about the rate of technological progress in pollution control that is needed for a sustainable positive rate of economic growth.
(7) Incentives could be strengthened considerably, and without a radical reform of environmental policy, by the introduction of tradeable pollution permits in the existing system of direct regulation.

References

Barbier E.B. and A. Markandya, *The conditions for achieving environmentally sustainable development.* LEEC-Paper 89-01, 1989.

Baumol W.J. and W.E. Oates, *The theory of environmental policy.* Cambridge University Press, Cambridge 1988.

Beckerman W., *In defense of economic growth.* Cape, London 1974.

Bergmann H., *Tentative estimates of damage caused by SO_2-depositions in the European Community and cost of controlling SO_2-emissions,* 5th CIDIE Meeting. European Investment Bank, Luxembourg 1985.

Boulding K.E., The economics of the coming spaceship Earth (1985). In: H. Jarret (ed.), *Environmental quality in a growing economy.* The Johns Hopkins Press, Baltimore 1966.

Brundtland G.H. *et al., Our common future.* Oxford University Press, Oxford 1987.

Daly H.E., *Steady-state economics.* Freeman and Co, San Francisco 1977.

Downing P.B. and L.J. White, Innovation in pollution control. *Journal of Environmental Economics and Management* Vol. 13 (1986) pp. 18-29.

Georgescu-Roegen N., *The entropy law and the economic process.* Harvard University Press, Cambridge Mass. 1971.

Georgescu-Roegen N., *Energy and economic myths.* Pergamon Press, New York 1975.

Hirsch F., *Social limits to growth.* Routledge and Paul, London 1977.

Kahn H., *World economic development.* Westview Press, Boulder Colorado 1979.

Krelle W., Economic growth with exhaustible resources and environmental protection. *Journal of Institutional and Theoretical Economics* Vol. 140 (1984) No. 3.

Krelle W. (ed.), *The future of the world economy.* Springer Verlag, Berlin 1989.

Kuipers S.K., and A. Nentjes, Pollution in a neo-classical world: the classics rehabilitated? *De Economist* Vol. 121 (1973) No. 1 pp. 52-67.

Leontief W. *et al., The future of the world economy.* Oxford University Press, New York 1977.

Meadows D.L. *et al., The limits to growth.* Universe Books, New York 1972.

Mesarovic M.D. and E. Pestel, *Mankind at the turning point.* Agon Elsevier, New York 1974.

Mishan E.J., *The costs of economic growth.* Staples Press, London 1967.

Mishan E.J., *The economic growth debate.* Allen and Unwin, London 1977.

Nentjes A., An economic model of innovation in pollution control. Paper presented at the Annual Meeting of the Association of Environmental and Resource Economists, New York 1988.

Nentjes A. and D. Wiersma, Innovation and pollution control. *International Journal of Social Economics* Vol. 15 (1988) No. 3/4 pp. 51-70.

Nentjes A., An environmental policy for sustainable growth. Paper IIPFF 45th Congress, Buenos Aires, August 1989.

Nijkamp P., *Environmental policy analysis.* John Wiley and Sons, Chichester 1980.

Reijnders L., *Naar een nieuwe ijzertijd?* Van Gennep, Amsterdam 1989.

RIVM, *Zorgen voor morgen.* Samsom/Tjeenk Willink, Bilthoven 1988.

Scitovsky T., *The joyless economy.* Oxford University Press, New York 1976.

Siebert H., *Economics of the environment,* 2nd ed. Springer Verlag, Berlin 1987.

Simon J.L. and H.H. Kahn, *The resourceful earth: a response to global 2000.* Blackwell, Oxford 1984.

Singer M., *Passage to a human world.* Hudson Institute, Indianapolis 1988.

Ströbele W., *Rohstofföokonomik.* Verlag Vahlen, Munich 1987.

VROM, *Nationaal milieubeleidsplan.* Staatsuitgeverij, The Hague 1989.

Chapter 8

THE STEADY STATE ECONOMY

Willem Heijman*

Over the next 85 years world population is expected to grow from five to at least eight billion people. So a no growth economy is not a realistic assumption for the near future. In the long run, however, a realistic option might be a steady state economy in which both population and the human economy are constant. In this chapter I look at the steady state concept in relation to the expected growth of world population. The chapter is organized as follows. In the first section a moderate scenario for world population to the year 2100 is shown. After that three definitions of a steady state are given of which the first two are dealt with further on in the chapter: Stuart Mill's stationary state and the so-called physical steady state. Tinbergen's model of the depletion of an exhaustible resource can be placed within this tradition. The physical steady state was developed mainly by Georgescu-Roegen, Daly and Ehrlich. A specific model that fits in this tradition has been developed by Zoeteman. It appears that the concept of the physical steady state can be applied to both the sustainable depletion of renewable resources and the sustainable depletion of non-renewable resources. The last sections of this chapter deal with the necessity of technical change in view of the growing world population.

1. World population

Table 1 shows how world population has developed in the past and what the expectations for the future are. In this table the *developed countries* are: USA, Canada, western Europe, USSR, eastern Europe, Japan, Australia and New Zealand. All other countries are considered to be *developing countries.*

* W.J.M. Heijman is Senior Lecturer in the Department of General Economics, Wageningen Agricultural University.

Table 1: World population (millions)

Year	Total	Developed countries	Developing countries	Percentage in developing countries
1850	1171	302	869	74
1875	1390	406	984	71
1900	1608	510	1098	68
1925	2062	631	1431	69
1950	2515	751	1764	70
1975	3936	1092	2844	72
2000	5893	1274	4619	78
2025	7364	1380	5984	81
2050	8197	1415	6782	83
2075	8446	1434	7012	83
2100	8500	1445	7055	83

Source: Clark W. C. and R. E. Munn, 1986, pp. 106-107 (adjusted), *The Economist*, 20-1-1990, pp. 21-26 (adjusted).

A look at the world income situation shows that, on average, it improved in the period 1970-1990. In this period the growth rate of the real gross domestic product of the whole world was about 3.5% per year, while the world population rose by about 1.8% per year in the same period. From this it can be concluded that, during this time, real income *per capita* rose on average by about 1.7% each year (Srinivasan, 1988; World Bank, 1989). Of course, these statistics do not say much about the poverty in the world, since this is also a matter of the distribution of the world income. One of the major difficulties in overcoming world poverty is that poor countries tend to have higher rates of population growth than rich countries (van Marrewijk, 1990).

A study of Table 1 shows clearly that in the next hundred years total population is expected to increase, mainly because the population in developing countries will increase. It should be stressed that only a moderate scenario is presented here (see for instance RIVM, 1988, p. 15). The United Nations even reckons with the possibility that in the year 2100 total population will have increased till 13 billion people, of which about 11 billion will live in developing countries (*The Economist*, 1990, p. 21; see also Arvill, 1983). The data of Table 1 are presented as graphs in Figures 1a and 1b. In Figure 1a both total population and the population living in developing countries are shown.

It is noticeable that the expected development of world population shows a logistic pattern, which here means that it is expected that by the end of the twenty-first century world population will be stabilized. Of course, this type of growth is not at all new. See for example Pearl (1925) and also Verhulst (1838).

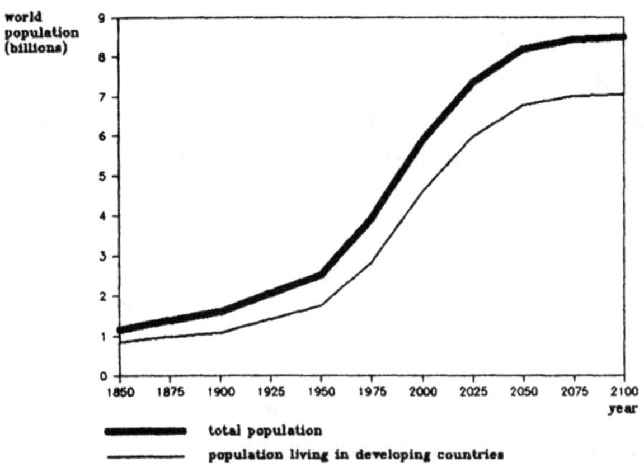

Figure 1a: The world population.

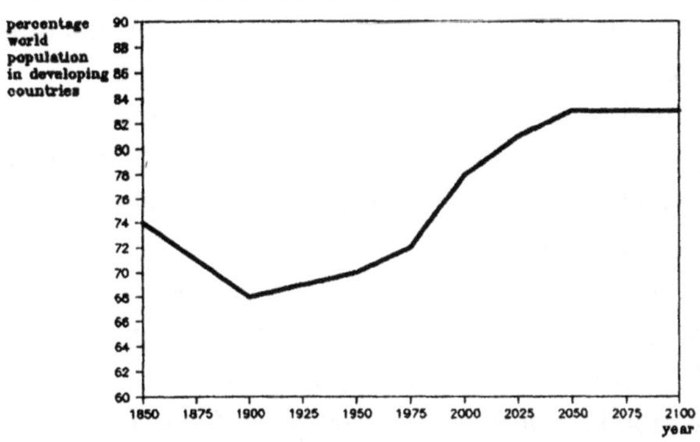

Figure 1b: Percentage population living in developing countries.

In Figure 1b the percentage of the total population living in developing countries is shown. From Table 1 and Figure 1b it is clear that the share of people living in developing countries is increasing. In 1975 it was 72%, and by 2100 it is expected to be 83%.

Taking into account that only a moderate scenario is presented, it has to be concluded that world population in the next 85 years will grow to a relatively high level. This implies that to keep the average income per head at the present level total production must grow. It is clear that the prospected growth of the population can become a danger to the world environment and the stocks of exhaustible and renewable resources (Ehrlich *et al.*, 1968, 1971; Welles, 1971; Heilbroner, 1971). After this coming period of growth, hopefully it will be possible to maintain a stationary situation, which is what John Stuart Mill said would happen. However, what is certain is that the basic assumption made by John Maynard Keynes for the solution of the economic problem 'within a hundred years' (*i.e.* no important increase in population) does not hold (Keynes, 1931).

2. Steady state

There are at least three basic definitions of the steady state:

1. The steady state as a situation in which both production measured through the Gross National Product (GNP) and population are constant. Like Mill (1848), I call this situation the *stationary state*.
2. The steady state defined as a physical concept. In this definition, as far as the renewable resources are concerned, this refers to a situation in which human use of nature expressed in physical terms equals natural production expressed in physical terms. As far as non-renewable resources are concerned it refers to a situation in which the stock-depletion ratio is constant. I use the term *physical steady state* to refer to a situation in which both the stock of renewable resources and the stock-depletion ratio for non-renewable resources are constant.
3. The steady state as a situation in which production, consumption and investment grow with a constant percentage maintaining a constant capital-output ratio. In this definition, which is the one economists are most familiar with, production is measured in terms of the GNP. I refer to this situation as *state of steady growth*.

To define a steady state these three definitions are often combined. For example, the concept *sustainable growth* is a combination of the state of steady growth and the physical steady state (WCED, 1987; VROM, 1989).

This is to illustrate that a physical steady state is not the same as a no growth economy in terms of the GNP. In the next two sections I will deal first with the concept of the stationary state.

3. Stationary state

In his *Principles of political economy* John Stuart Mill wondered:

> Towards what ultimate point is society tending by its industrial progress? When the progress ceases, in what condition are we to expect that it will leave mankind? (Mill, 1848, p. 746).

His answer to this question was *the stationary state,* which he assumed to be ultimately unavoidable. In his time, most economists advocated the so-called *progressive state,* in which the economy of all nations could continue to grow. Mill, Jevons (1866) and also Malthus (1798), who was the first economist to write on the principle of population, were opposed to the assumption:

> that in the natural and normal affairs population must constantly increase, from which it followed that a constant increase of the means of support was essential to the physical comfort of the mass of mankind. (Mill, 1848, p. 747).

Mill considered a conscientious or prudential restraint on population to be indispensable. He saw the progressive state as a necessary condition for reaching the stationary state, which is also a mental and moral state of being:

> The best state for human nature is that in which, while no one is poor, no one desires to be richer, nor has any reason to fear being thrust back by the efforts of others to push themselves forward. (Mill, 1848, pp. 748-749).

He was of the opinion that, because of the accumulation of capital, there is room in the world for a great increase of population, but that there is little reason to desire this. He pointed to the destruction of nature which would be the consequence of this.

> Nor is there much satisfaction in contemplating the world with nothing left to the spontaneous activity of nature; with every rood of land brought into cultivation, which is capable of growing food for human beings; every flowery waste or natural pasture being ploughed up, all quadrupeds or birds which are not domesticated for man's use exterminated as his rivals for food, every hedgerow or superfluous tree rooted out, and scarcely a place left where a wild shrub or flower could grow without being eradicated as a weed in the name of improved agriculture. (Mill, 1848, p. 750).

The stationary state of capital and population does not imply a halt in human improvement. Mill stated that in the stationary state much progress can be made, both morally and socially.

It will be clear that Mill was of the opinion that economic growth should not be continued infinitely. In the end a steady state (or stationary state as he called it) will emerge and this is even a desirable situation, at least socially and morally.

In classical, neoclassical and also Marxist theory[1], in the absence of population growth and technical innovations, the stationary state will generally be reached more or less automatically because of the decreasing marginal productivity of capital (Siebert, 1987; Mandel, 1980). This can be shown as follows. In the described situation total production (y) is a function of the input of capital (k):

$$(1) \qquad y = y(k) \qquad \frac{dy}{dk} > 0, \quad \frac{d^2y}{dk^2} < 0.$$

Savings (s), which equal gross investment, are supposed to be a fixed proportion (σ) of the total product:

$$(2) \qquad s = \sigma \cdot y(k).$$

Depreciation (b) is assumed to be a fixed proportion (π) of capital stock:

$$(3) \qquad b = \pi \cdot k.$$

Net investment (dk/dt), which is the extension of the capital stock, equals gross investment minus depreciation:

$$(4) \qquad \frac{dk}{dt} = \sigma \cdot y_t(k_t) - \pi \cdot k_t.$$

1 In fact the *tendency of the rate of profit to fall* is the Marxist counterpart of the *tendency of the marginal product of capital to decrease* in usual neoclassical theory. One might even consider the latter as the cause of the first.

In Figure 2 the development of an economy without population growth and without technical innovations is shown as a graph.

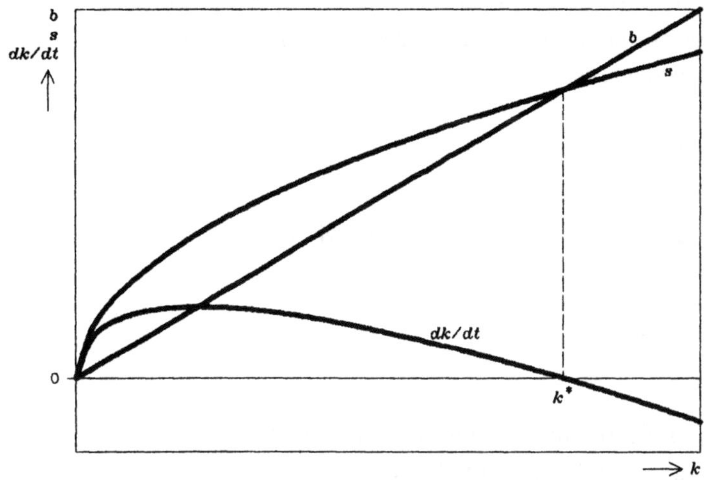

Figure 2: The development of a stationary economy.

To the left of $k*$ in Figure 2 gross investment (s) exceeds depreciation (b). This implies that net investment (dk/dt) exceeds zero and as a consequence the stock of capital will grow. To the right of $k*$ net investment is less than zero implying that capital stock will decrease. This means that $k*$ is a stable equilibrium of the capital stock. In this equilibrium, capital, production, consumption, investment and population will be stationary. Indeed, it has to be admitted here that, since zero population growth and no technical development are both assumed, the above model reflects a rather specific situation. Besides, in the model there is no relation between depletable resources and capital accumulation.

4. Tinbergen's model

A modern contribution to the steady state concept of a stationary state was made by Tinbergen (1987, 1989) for natural resources. For his steady state model, Tinbergen assumed:

- a stable world population,
- a constant consumption for all, present and future, generations,

- that the problem of the unequal world income distribution is solved.

Suppose in year 0 the total stock of a certain natural resource equals H_0, while the use of natural resources in this year equals h_0. The consumption then is c_0, implying a resource productivity of $c_0/h_0 = p_0$. Because of technical innovations, the amount of resource needed to produce c_0 units consumption goods decreases each year by factor f. This gives:

$$(5) \qquad h_t = f \cdot h_{t-1}.$$

Equation (5) implies that all future generations will use:

$$(6) \qquad \sum_{t=0}^{\infty} h_t = \frac{h_0}{(1-f)}.$$

Since the amount indicated in equation (6) must equal H_0, the use of the natural resource in period 0 must equal:

$$(7) \qquad h_0 = (1-f) \cdot H_0.$$

If, for example, factor f equals 0.976, which is the case for the productivity of labour in the past 27 years, then h_0 can be 1/41 part of the total stock (Tinbergen, 1989, p. 677). Though this result is fairly optimistic, it still implies the following *rules of life:*

- Keep population constant,
- Continue technical development at factor f, (see also Baumol, 1985),
- Increase development aid, so that migration will not have to occur for economic reasons,
- Continue the exploration for new natural resources.

Tinbergen's model is based upon the use of exhaustible resources. Also, in his model substitution between the resource (the non-reproductive factor) and capital (the reproductive factor) is not possible. These two circumstances imply that in his model technical renewal is necessary to maintain a constant level of consumption per head for a constant population. Stiglitz (1974) and Solow (1974) showed that, for a production function with a substitution elasticity of one and constant production elasticities, a constant consumption per head can be maintained, even without innovations, if the marginal propensity to save equals the production elasticity of the exhaustible resource (see also Peer, 1990). Proof of this is given in the appendix of this chapter. The economic significance of this is that, in this case, the pessimism of the Club of Rome is not justified (Meadows, 1972; van de Klundert *et al.*, 1983, pp. 98-103). Indeed, the circumstances for which the proof is delivered are rather specific. Another aspect Tinbergen's model does not deal with is the productivity of nature. This aspect is dealt with further on in this chapter.

5. Physical steady state

A definition of a physical steady state was given by Herman E. Daly. According to him

> A steady state is defined by constant stocks of physical wealth (artifacts) and a constant population, each maintained at some chosen, desirable level by a low rate of throughput - *i.e.*, by low birth rates equal to low death rates and by low physical depreciation rates, so that longevity of people and durability of physical stocks are high. (Daly, 1974, p. 15).

Apparently, Daly combined Mill's stationary state with the physical steady state. Three magnitudes are basic to his concept of the steady state: stock, service and throughput. The stock is the total inventory of producer's goods, consumer's goods and human bodies (Daly, 1980(b), p. 325). In fact this stock is equal to the concept of Irving Fisher's *capital goods* (Fisher, 1906, p. 66). The service is the satisfaction experienced by the use of the stock, which is something other than service in the normal acceptation, while the throughput is the entropic physical flow from natural sources through the human economy (see also Boulding, 1966 and Georgescu-Roegen, 1971 and 1980). The relation between these three magnitudes can be specified as follows (Daly, 1980(b), p. 326):

$$(8) \qquad \frac{\text{service}}{\text{throughput}} = \frac{\text{service}}{\text{stock}} \cdot \frac{\text{stock}}{\text{throughput}}$$

A steady state economy exists when: 1. the stock is constant at a sufficient level, 2. service is to be maximized, given the constant stock and 3. throughput is to be minimized, given the constant stock (Daly, 1980(b), p. 327).

In his definition of the steady state Daly deliberately excluded the services, defined as non-material goods. However, economic growth is measured as an increase of the Gross National Product (GNP) *including* the services. According to this definition it still is possible for the GNP to keep on growing on the condition that the physical element in the production remains constant. In fact, Daly was of the opinion that the growth of production must be compensated by a decrease in the resource use per unit product of the same magnitude, which means that his anti-growth argument is not that absolute, though in an earlier article he stated:

> A policy of maximizing GNP is practically equivalent to a policy of maximizing depletion and pollution. (Daly, 1971, p. 83).

This statement is only true, when *'maximizing GNP'* is interpreted as *'maximizing the physical element in the GNP'*.

If it is possible for production to grow, maintaining the physical steady state, it is also possible for population to grow while maintaining this physical steady state and, at the same time, keeping the income per head constant. So it can be concluded that, based upon Daly's own argument, a physical steady state can be maintained while the GNP and the population grow, because his concept of the steady state refers at a physical state of affairs; the GNP is an economic index referring at the economic value of goods and services. Indeed, it should be stressed here that the possibility of a growth of both the GNP and the population are constrained by the physical conditions of the physical steady state. In fact, it might be said that Daly was advocating a state of sustainable growth.

To attack the price mechanism, Daly distinguished between relative and absolute scarcity. According to him, price mechanism can only cope with relative scarcity, inducing substitution as the main solution to the scarcity of resources. Absolute scarcity can only be dealt with by the introduction of the steady state economy with direct regulations (Daly, 1974, p. 18). It is clear enough that absolute scarcity is something that cannot be handled by the price mechanism. However, it is not clear which resources are absolute scarce and which are not. The part that is absolute scarce may be smaller than Daly thought, because the substitution possibilities between exhaustible resources are numerous (Nordhaus *et al.*, 1977).

For institutions, Daly favoured the introduction of the following: 1. an institution for stabilizing population, 2. an institution for stabilizing physical wealth and keeping throughput below ecological limits, and, 3. an institution limiting the degree of inequality in the distribution of the constant stocks among the constant population (Daly, 1974, p. 20). Almost no scientist would disagree about the necessity of these three institutions. However, the question is how far a government can go in enforcing all kind of measures for birth control, income distribution and production limitations. It is possible that in most developed countries these institutions more or less exist, while in the developing countries social structure will have to change radically if such measures are to be succesfully implemented.

Paul Ehrlich's ideas are more or less compatible with Daly's and Georgescu Roegen's. He defined a steady state economy (SSE) as follows.

> An SSE is one in which material throughput is minimized by limiting resource depletion (an thus automatically limiting pollution), the quality of capital stocks is maximized, and the distribution of wealth is made relatively equitable. It is not necessarily a static economy - progress in efficiency and trade-offs among competing firms and activities can go within the constraint of minimal throughput. (Ehrlich *et al.*, 1980b, p. 40).

Ehrlich called a society based on an SSE a *sustainable society*. In such a society economic growth is limited by the constraints of the physical steady state. The most important constraint is the entropy law which says that

> All physical processes proceed in such a way that the entropy of the universe increases. (Ehrlich *et al.*, 1980a, p. 47).

But under the assumption of reaching the sustainable society even this law does not absolutely forbid the growth of the GNP and the population.

6. Zoeteman's model

An interesting contribution to the thinking in terms of physical steady state was made by Zoeteman (1989). His model does not deal directly with the use of natural resources, but with the abatement of environmental damage. His central idea can be described as follows.

For the attainment of the steady state with respect to a certain polluting agency, for instance the emission of CO_2, it is necessary that the cleansing capacity for that agency equals the yearly emissions. The cleansing capacity in tons (Z) equals the density of the earthly biomass (d), in tons per square mile, present on the natural area of the earthly surface multiplied by the cleansing productivity in tons per ton biomass weight (z), multiplied by the natural area of the surface of the earth. This natural area equals total area (O) minus the indurated part. The indurated part equals the necessary infrastructure per head (i) multiplied by the world population B. The total cleansing capacity for CO_2 can now be written as follows:

(9) $$Z = z \cdot d \cdot (O - i \cdot B).$$

The yearly emission in tons (V) equals total population (B), multiplied by the GNP per head (p), multiplied by the emission factor (v) in tons per monetary unit GNP. The yearly emission can now be written as:

(10) $$V = v \cdot p \cdot B.$$

In order to reach the steady state the yearly emission has, of course, to equal the cleansing capacity:

(11) $$V = Z$$

$$v \cdot p \cdot B = z \cdot d \cdot (O - i \cdot B).$$

It is clear that in this model population is the most important variable. If the population grows too fast, it will be very difficult to reach the steady state. To achieve this, huge emission reductions per unit product are necessary. This can be illustrated with the following example. If time is included, then equation (11) can be written as follows (with A for natural surface and t for time):

(12) $$v_0 \cdot p_0 \cdot B_0 \cdot e^{(\bar{v}+\bar{p}+\bar{b})\cdot t} = z_0 \cdot d_0 \cdot A_0 \cdot e^{(\bar{z}+\bar{d}+\bar{a})\cdot t}$$

In equation (12) the bar indicates a growth rate. It can be deduced from equation (12):

(13) $$\bar{v} = \bar{z} + \bar{d} + \bar{a} - \bar{p} - \bar{b} - \frac{1}{t}\ln\frac{v_0 \cdot p_0 \cdot B_0}{z_0 \cdot d_0 \cdot A_0}.$$

From Table 1 it can be computed that, in a moderate scenario from 1975 till 2075, the world population will grow by 0.75% a year ($\bar{b} = 0.0075$). I have assumed further moderate values for $\bar{z}$, $\bar{d}$ and $\bar{a}$, for instance -0.1%, -0.05%, -0.05% respectively, and a zero growth in the output per head ($\bar{p} = 0$). I also assume that the emission-cleansing capacity ratio of the world equals 6 in the year 1990 and that a world wide steady state must be reached in the year 2050 (Zoeteman, 1989, pp. 330-336). These assumptions give a necessary emission reduction per unit output of about 3.9% each year. This means that, relative to 1990, by the year 2050 the emission per unit product must be reduced by over 90%. Even if it is assumed that the emission-cleansing capacity ratio equals 1 in 1990, an emission reduction per unit output of almost 1% each year would be necessary. This implies that by the year 2050, total reduction of the emission per unit output must equal 45% of the 1990 emission. This example shows that, if a physical steady state has to be reached within about sixty years, even moderate assumptions may make a huge reduction of the emission per unit product necessary in the next sixty years.

7. The importance of renewable resources

Both exhaustible as well as renewable resources are limited and human production reduces total stock of limited resources. Renewable resources have a limited renewal capacity, so that the change in the total stock of limited resources is the result of both human production and natural renewal. If natural renewal equals human expenditure of nature, then one condition for a physical steady state is fulfilled (the other is a constant stock-depletion ratio for exhaustible resources).

As the stock of non-renewable resources diminishes and the prices of these resources increase, the use of renewable resources becomes more important in an economic sense. However, the unlimited exploitation of these resources easily leads to overexploitation and exhaustion. Indeed, over-exploitation of renewable resources is as great a danger today as the exhaustion of non-renewable resources. Therefore it is important to investigate the possibilities of ensuring an efficient and lasting use of renewable resources (Heijman, 1988).

8. Natural production, human production and the optimum steady state

In laboratory culture models of succession, the development of the amount of biomass of an eco-system (n_t) in time (t) from the first stage onwards can be expressed in a so-called 'logistic curve' (Odum, 1975, p. 153). Such a curve is presented in Figure 3. In the first stages there is a regressive development of the ecosystem (in terms of biomass). After a certain point in time (t^*) the development of the volume of biomass becomes degressive. Finally the volume reaches its climax stage (n_c).

In such a model, net natural production[2] in a certain period of time (dn_t/dt) can be approximately described as a parabolic function of the existing total stock of biomass at the beginning of this period. This function is described with equation (14)[3]:

$$(14) \qquad \frac{dn_t}{dt} = \alpha \cdot (n_c - n_t) \cdot n_t .$$

In equation (14) α is a positive constant. The function is graphically presented in Figure 4.

2 The 'net natural production' of an ecosystem during a certain period is the difference between the gross natural production, *i.e.* the production by photosynthesis and the respiration of plants and animals, excluding respiration of man. The 'growth of nature' is the difference between net natural production and man's respiration, *i.e.* the human process of production and consumption.

3 The solution of this differential equation is:

$$n_t = \frac{n_c}{1 + \frac{n_c - n_0}{n_0} \cdot e^{-\alpha \cdot n_c \cdot t}} .$$

Further dn_t/dt is at the maximum for:

$$t^* = \frac{\ln\left(\frac{n_c - n_0}{n_0}\right)}{n_c \cdot \alpha} .$$

and:

$$n^* = \frac{1}{2} \cdot n_c .$$

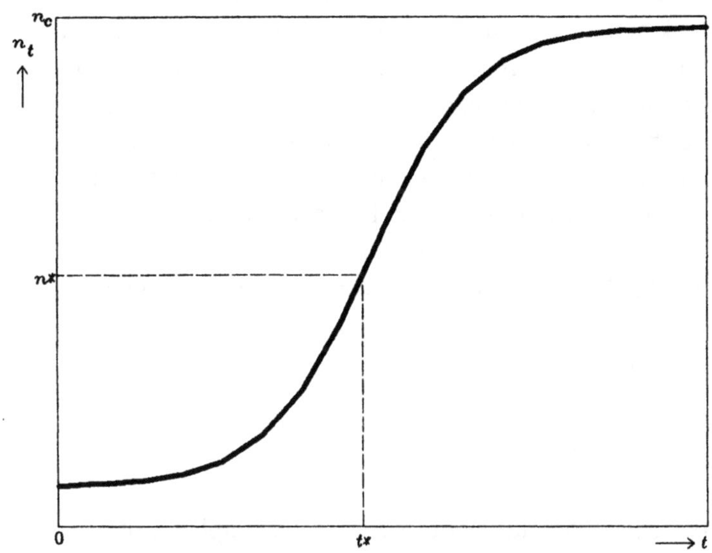

Figure 3: The development of nature in time in laboratory models.

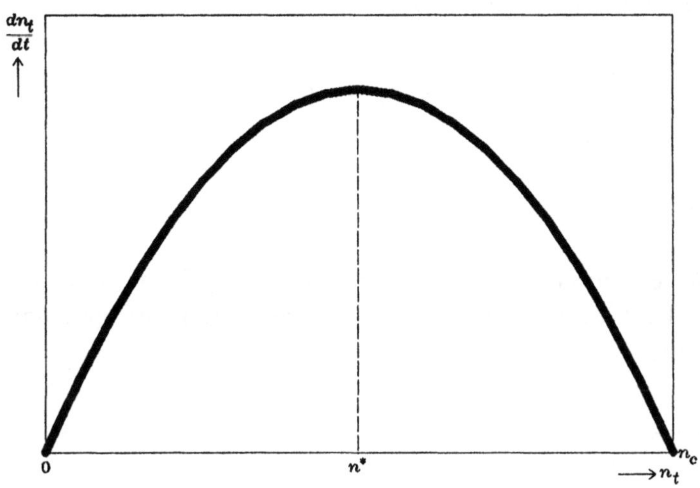

Figure 4: Net natural production as a function of the total volume of biomass.

The parabolic shape of the function can easily be explained. In the climax stage, net natural production equals zero. The same applies to a situation in which the total stock of nature equals zero. Net natural production is at a maximum when the stock of nature reaches the volume connected with the point of inflexion of the logistic curve. Net natural production is to be interpreted here as the increase of the volume of biomass. In laboratory models no account is taken of the use of nature originating from the human respiration. Indeed, the 'growth of nature' in the real world is defined as net natural production minus the volume of the human use of nature.

If net natural production equals human use of nature (g_t), a physical steady state exists, since the volume of biomass is then constant. This is reflected in equation (15):

$$(15) \qquad g_t = \alpha \cdot (n_c - n_t) \cdot n_t .$$

In this situation the growth of nature equals zero, which implies a physical steady state. The optimum steady state can be defined as the physical steady state in which human use of nature is at a maximum. This is when net natural production reaches the top of the parabolic function, which is at point n^* in Figure 4. This maximum implies that the first derivative of the human use of dn_t/dt with respect to n_t must be zero, so:

$$(16) \qquad \frac{d(\alpha \cdot (n_c - n_t) \cdot n_t)}{dn_t} = -2 \cdot \alpha \cdot n_t + \alpha \cdot n_c = 0$$

$$n^* = \frac{1}{2} \cdot n_c .$$

Equation (16) also explains the position of n^* in Figure 3. The outcome of equation (16) can be substituted in equation (15). This delivers the optimum human use of nature:

$$(17) \qquad g^* = 0.25 \cdot \alpha \cdot n_c^2 .$$

For human production per unit of time, *e.g.* a year, a certain amount of energy is necessary. The total human need for energy (g_t) equals the need of energy per unit of product (β) multiplied by total human production (y_t). This is shown with equation (18).

$$(18) \qquad g_t = \beta \cdot y_t$$

The optimum use of nature (g^*) of equation (17) substituted in equation (18) delivers the optimum human production (y^*)[4].

$$(19) \qquad y^* = 0.25 \cdot \frac{\alpha}{\beta} \cdot n_c^2$$

From equation (19) it follows that, without affecting total stock, human production can grow up to a maximum level determined by the regeneration speed of nature, the need of energy per unit of product and the volume of biomass in the climax stage.

4 As long as the optimum steady state has not been reached yet, the human use of nature must be less than natural production. In that case there will be a positive growth of nature if

$$\frac{dn_t}{dt} > g_t \qquad \text{for } n_t < n_c$$

Suppose, for instance:

$$g_t = \gamma \cdot \alpha \cdot (n_c - n_t) \cdot n_t \qquad 0 < \gamma < 1 \text{ for } n_t < n_c, \quad \gamma = 1 \text{ for } n_t = n_c.$$

From this it follows:

$$\frac{dn_t}{dt} = \alpha \cdot (n_c - n_t) \cdot n_t - \gamma \cdot \alpha \cdot (n_c - n_t) \cdot n_t = \alpha \cdot (1 - \gamma) \cdot (n_c - n_t) \cdot n_t.$$

Further it is assumed that the optimum steady state must have been reached within T years. So, by using note 3):

$$n_T = n^* = \frac{1}{2} \cdot n_c$$

$$T = \frac{\ln\left(\frac{n_c - n_0}{n_0}\right)}{n_c \cdot \alpha \cdot (1 - \gamma)}$$

$$\gamma = 1 - \frac{\ln\left(\frac{n_c - n_0}{n_0}\right)}{\alpha \cdot T \cdot n_c}.$$

It will be clear that the above solution is not the only possible one.

In this way human production does not affect future means of support in an irresponsible way, so that humanity may survive with enough power for as long as the sun shines (another 5 billion years on estimate). Equation (19) delivers a very strict prescription for human production. However, there are many kinds of (bio)technological renewals which may widen the ecological borders. These will be studied in the next sections.

9. The development of technology and the growth of human production

Without doubt it has been the technological developments which have caused the large-scale exhaustion of natural resources. However, it is also clear that technology is also an indispensable instrument in solving the ecological crisis which the world faces today (for a number of examples, see Brown *et al.*, 1990). In fact there is a distinction between 'nature-conserving' and 'nature-affecting' technological innovations.

In human history most technological renewals have meant a further assault on the stock of limited resources. When man first practised agriculture several thousands of years ago, he profoundly influenced the ecological system. Even more influential was the industrial revolution in the eighteenth, nineteenth and twentieth centuries. A great number of inventions and innovations made it possible to process large amounts of resources. Because of rapidly diminishing stocks of resources, a point has now been arrived where it is realized that technological renewals should have a nature-conserving rather than a nature-affecting character. In economic terms, nature has become a scarce commodity.

It is possible to distinguish between two types of technological change; inventions and innovations. An invention is a creative act of the human mind, an innovation the application in the production process of an invention. So every innovation must be preceded by an invention, but not every invention is followed by an innovation. Whether innovation follows an invention is the outcome of a complicated economic and political process. It might even be that the character of the inventions is directed by this same process. If this is the case, then public opinion and politics decide which direction technological evolution will take, towards nature-affecting inventions and innovations or towards nature-conserving inventions and innovations.

10. Nature-sparing and nature-creating technological renewals

This section concentrates on nature-conserving technological change. This change can be subdivided into 'nature-sparing' and 'nature-creating' technological changes. Nature-sparing technological renewals are aimed at using less energy per unit of human production. Mathematically this is represented by a reduction of parameter β in equation (6). This type of technological change can be demonstrated by several examples. The use of sun, wind and water as energy sources is one of them. Another is the invention of the fuel cell. With this cell chemical energy can be directly transformed into electric energy. In present-day power plants chemical energy is, out of sheer necessity, first degraded to heat which in turn is transformed by turbines into electric energy. This procedure causes a loss of energy of about 66 per cent of the total input of chemical energy. This loss could be reduced considerably, the intermediate stage of transformation of chemical energy into heat could be avoided, which would be possible by the use of fuel cells. Although the technical realization of this invention cannot be expected in the near future, this example offers an interesting outlook on nature-sparing technological renewals that one day may be possible (Fast, 1982).

The discovery of super conductivity at moderate temperatures of certain materials is another promising development in this field. In future, the loss of electric energy through the transport system might be eliminated by using materials which are even super conductive at normal temperatures. It has to be realized that these possible future innovations diminish the scarcity of the energy sources. It is even conceivable that a future invention might abolish the scarcity of a specific resource, which means that a zero rent for this resource remained.

The total amount of organic matter generated by plants each year is enormous. It is the equivalent of one hundred billion (10^{14}) tons of carbon. This natural production needs only 1 per cent of all sunlight shed on earth. *Nature-creating* technological development could try to retain a greater part of sunlight in plants and vegetables each year. Think, for example, of fast-growing trees. Nature-creating technological renewals can be expressed by an increase in parameter α in equation (19). It may also be possible to enlarge the possible volume of biomass in the climax stage by introducing new energy crops which can be grown in regions where climate and soil are less suitable for traditional crops. This type of biotechnological change can be represented by an increase of n_c in equation (19).

The need for nature-conserving technological renewals is obvious. How quickly technology will develop in the direction pointed to in this section is hard to predict because political decisions and public opinion play a major part in the process.

11. Economic growth and nature-conserving technological change

The aim of this section is to determine a sustainable growth rate of human production considering the possibilities of nature-conserving technological change. The starting point of this calculation is equation (19). Now, suppose that we start in period 0 and that the growth rate of production equals $\bar{y}$. Further it is assumed that in period 0 mankind lives in the optimum steady state. If no technical changes occur, there can be no economic growth if the optimum steady state is to be maintained.

Now nature-sparing and nature-creating innovations are assumed. This means that equation (19) can be rewritten as follows:

$$(20) \qquad y_0 \cdot e^{\bar{y} \cdot t} = 0.25 \cdot \frac{\left(n_{c,0} \cdot e^{\bar{n}_c \cdot t}\right)^2 \cdot (\alpha_0 \cdot e^{\bar{\alpha} \cdot t})}{(\beta_0 \cdot e^{\bar{\beta} \cdot t})}.$$

In equation (20) $\bar{\alpha}$ and $\bar{n}_c$ represent the nature-creating technological changes, while $\bar{\beta}$ represents the nature-sparing technological change. Equation (20) gives:

$$(21) \qquad \bar{y} = 2 \cdot \bar{n}_c + \bar{\alpha} - \bar{\beta}.$$

It can be concluded from equation (21) that human production can grow, maintaining the optimum steady state, if growth equals the difference between the nature-creating technological changes and the nature-sparing technological changes. Indeed, in case of nature-sparing technological innovations $\bar{\beta}$ will be negative, while in case of nature-creating technological innovations $\bar{\alpha}$ and $\bar{n}_c$ will be positive.

12. The necessity of technological change

Normally economists define a steady state the same as the concept *state of steady growth.* This means a state of the economy with a constant capital-output ratio, a constant rate of growth of output, consumption, wages *etc.* (Stiglitz, 1974, p. 125; Daly, 1980(a)). Because of limited resources some economists have reconsidered this definition. In this type of analysis a steady state is characterized by a constant population, a constant output *etc.*; in other words as Mill's stationary state. Tinbergen concluded that this state can be maintained by technical innovation increasing the productivity of the exhaustible resource. Stiglitz and Solow proved that this technical renewal is not a necessary condition if the exhaustible resource can be substituted by capital sufficiently. Another approach is the making use of the productivity of nature. In that case one focuses on the renewable resources instead of the exhaustible resources.

Since the stock of non-renewable resources is decreasing, the stock of renewable resources is becoming more important. From my computations it is clear that a steady state with the use of renewable resources is possible without the assumption of technological change. Only if one assumes a growing population combined with a constant or growing production per head technological change is necessary. This conclusion is the same in the case in which substitution between capital and an exhaustible resource was assumed. There one made use of the productivity of capital, instead of the productivity of nature.

If a constant population with a constant income per head is to be maintained, two conditions must be fulfilled. First the substitution possibilities of capital and the limited stock of exhaustible resources must be sufficient. Second, for renewable resources at least a physical steady state must be maintained, which means that there is a balance between natural production and human respiration. However, as has been shown in the first section, the world population is not constant, but is expected to grow. This implies directly that (bio)technical innovations are inavoidable to assure a sufficient level of income per capita. The overall conclusion must be that, even under the assumption of a growing population, the dismal forecasts of the Club of Rome need not materialize, provided that technological change sufficiently increases productivity. No sustainable growth without (bio)technological innovations.

Appendix: A constant consumption per head with a constant population by substitution of nature by capital

To prove Stiglitz' proposition, I use the following linearly homogenous Cobb-Douglas production function, with y for production, k for capital, and n for the flow of the exhaustible resource:

$$y = k^{\beta} \cdot n^{(1-\beta)}.$$

The production elasticities of capital and nature, β and $(1-\beta)$ respectively, also indicate the income distribution, which means that:

$$\upsilon \cdot k = \beta \cdot y,$$

$$p_n \cdot n = (1-\beta) \cdot y.$$

In these two equations υ stands for interest and p_n for the price of the resource (rent). The second equation can be written in growth rates as follows:

$$\overline{p}_n + \overline{n} = \overline{y}.$$

Since, according to the Hotelling rule, $\overline{p}_n$ equals υ and since a stationary economy is assumed, this equation can be rewritten as follows:

$$\upsilon = -\overline{n}.$$

The production function written in growth rates gives:

$$\overline{y} = \beta \cdot \overline{k} + (1-\beta) \cdot \overline{n}.$$

Knowing that $\overline{y}$ equals zero, the last two equations can be combined to form:

$$\overline{k} = \frac{(1-\beta) \cdot \upsilon}{\beta}.$$

The rate of interest (υ) multiplied by the the capital-output ratio κ gives the production elasticity of capital as:

$$\upsilon \cdot \kappa = \beta .$$

A combination of the last two equations gives:

$$\bar{k} = \frac{(1-\beta)}{\kappa} .$$

Because the growth rate of capital $(\bar{k})$ equals the marginal propensity to save divided by the capital-output ratio (σ / κ), the last equation can be rewritten as:

$$\sigma = 1 - \beta .$$

This implies that, if the production process can be modelled with a Cobb-Douglas production function a constant consumption per head with a constant population can be maintained so long as the marginal propensity to save equals the production elasticity of the exhaustible resource. Indeed, the marginal propensity to save must be lower than the production elasticity of capital, which implies that the production elasticity of capital must exceed the production elasticity of the resource (Stiglitz, 1974, pp. 129-130). See also Solow (1974, p. 43).

References

Anonymous, *World population: squeezing in the next five billion.* The Economist, January 20, 1990.

Arvill R., *Man and environment: crisis and the strategy of choice.* Penguin, Harmondsworth 1983 (1967).

Baumol W.J., On the possibility of continuing expansion of finite resources. *Kyklos* Vol. 38 (1985), pp. 282-297.

Boulding K.E., The economics of the coming spaceship Earth. In: W. A. Johnson and J. Hardesty (eds.), *Economic growth vs. the environment.* Wadsworth, Belmont (Cal.) 1971 (1966), pp. 58-68.

Brown L.R., C. Flavin and S. Postel, Schets van een duurzame wereld. In: Brown L.R. (ed.), Hoe is de wereld eraan toe? 1990. Translation of *State of the World 1990.* World Watch Institute, Norton, New York 1990.

Clark C.W. and R.E. Munn (eds), *Sustainable development of the biosphere.* Cambridge University Press, Cambridge 1986.
Daly H.E., Some common misunderstandings and further issues concerning a steady-state economy. Postscript in: Daly H.E. (ed.), *Economics, ecology, ethics: essays toward a steady state economy.* Freeman, San Francisco 1980a (1973).
Daly H.E., The steady state economy: toward a political economy of biophysical equilibrium and moral growth. In: Daly H.E. (ed.), *Economics, ecology, ethics: essays toward a steady state economy.* Freeman, San Francisco 1980b (1973).
Daly H.E., The world dynamics of economic growth: the economics of the steady state. *American Economic Review* Vol. 64 (1974), Nr 2, pp. 15-21.
Ehrlich P.R., A.H. Ehrlich and J.P. Holdren, Availability, entropy, and the laws of thermodynamics. In: Daly H.E. (ed.), *Economics, ecology, ethics: essays toward a steady state economy.* Freeman, San Francisco 1980a (1973).
Ehrlich P.R., and A.H. Ehrlich, Humanity at the crossroads. In: Daly H.E. (ed.), *Economics, ecology, ethics: essays toward a steady state economy.* Freeman, San Francisco 1980b (1973).
Ehrlich P.R., *De bevolkingsexplosie.* Amsterdam 1971. Translation from: Ehrlich P.R., *The population bomb.* Ballantine Books, New York 1968.
Ehrlich P.R., The limits to substitution: a meta-resource depletion and a new economic-ecological paradigm. *Ecological Economics,* Vol. 1 (1989), pp. 9-16.
Fast J.D., *Materie en leven.* Malmberg; Het Spectrum, Utrecht 1982 (1972)
Fisher I., *The nature of capital and income.* Kelley, New York 1965 (1906)
Georgescu-Roegen N., *The entropy law and the economic problem.* Harvard University Press, Cambridge (Mass.) 1971.
Georgescu-Roegen N., *The entropy law and the economic problem.* In: Daly H.E. (ed.), *Economics, ecology, ethics: essays toward a steady-state economy.* Freeman, San Francisco 1980 (1973).
Heijman W.J.M., The need for a steady state economy. In: J.J. Krabbe (ed.), Principles of Environmental Policy. *International Journal of Social Economics,* Vol. 15 (1988), Nr. 3/4, pp. 80-87.
Heilbroner R., Ecological Armageddon. In: Johnson W.A. and J. Hardesty, *Economic growth vs the environment.* Wadsworth, Belmont (Cal.), 1971 (1970).
Jevons W.S., *The theory of political economy.* MacMillan, London 1888 (1871).
Keynes J.M., Economic possibilities for our grandchildren. In: Johnson W.A. and J. Hardesty, *Economic growth vs the environment.* Wadsworth, Belmont (Cal.) 1971 (1931).
Klundert Th. van de and H. Peer, *Energie: een economisch perspectief.* Stenfert-Kroese, Leiden 1983.
Malthus T.R., *An essay on population.* Everyman's Library. London 1958 (1798).
Mandel E., *De economische theorie van het marxisme,* deel 1. Het wereldvenster, Bussum 1980 (1962).
Marrewijk C. van, *Endogenous population growth and the economy.* Research memorandum nr. 363, Institute of Economic Research, Faculty of Economics, University of Groningen, Groningen 1990.
Meadows D.L., D. Meadows, J. Randers and W. Behrens. *The limits to growth: a report from the club of Rome's project on the predicament of mankind.* Potomac, Washington 1972.
Mill J.S., *Principles of political economy,* edited with an introduction by W. Ashley (1909). Kelley, Clifton 1973 (1848).
Nordhaus W.D. and J. Tobin, Growth and natural resources. In: Dorfman R. and N.S. Dorfman, *Economics of the environment.* Norton, New York 1977 (1972).

Odum E.P., *Ecology*. Holt Rinehart and Winston, London 1975 (1963).
Pearl R., *The biology of population growth*. Knopf, New York 1925.
Peer H., An inquiry into the nature and causes of the wealth of planet Earth. Paper presented to the conference *Economics of the environment*, Center for Economic Research, September 17-19, Tilburg 1990.
Rijks Instituut Voor Milieuonderzoek (RIVM), *Zorgen voor morgen: nationale milieuverkenning 1985-2000*. Samsom, Alphen aan den Rijn 1988.
Siebert H., *Economics of the environment*. Springer, Berlin 1987 (1981).
Solow R.M., Intergenerational equity and exhaustible resources. *The Review of economic studies*. Symposium 1974.
Srinivasan T.N., *Population growth and food: an assessment of issues, models, and projections*. In: Lee R.D., W.B. Arthur, A.C. Kelley, G. Rodgers and T.N. Srinivasan (eds), *International studies in demography: population, food, and rural development*. Clarendon, Oxford 1988.
Stiglitz J., Growth with exhaustible natural resources: efficient and optimal growth paths. *Review of economic studies*. Symposium 1974.
Tinbergen J., De verdeling van hulpbronnen over toekomstige generaties. *ESB (Economisch Statistische Berichten)* Vol. 74 (1989), Nr. 3715, p. 677.
Verhulst P.F., Notice sur la loi que la population suit dans son accroissement. *Correspondance Mathématique et Physique* Vol. 10 (1838), pp. 113-121.
WCED (World Commission on Environment and Development), *Our common future*. Oxford University Press, Oxford 1987.
Welles J.G., The economy doesn't need more people. In: Johnson W.A. and J. Hardesty, *Economic growth vs the environment*. Wadsworth, Belmont (Cal.), 1971 (1970).
World Bank, *World development report 1989*. Oxford University press, New York 1989.
Zoeteman K., *Gaiasofie: anders kijken naar evolutie, ruimtelijke ordening en milieubeheer*. Ankh-Hermes, Deventer 1989.

Chapter 9

ENTROPY, SYNERGY AND ECONOMIC CHANGE

Siegfried Karsten*

In economics, as in many other social and physical sciences, man is confronted with complex systems, which can be researched from various perspectives. One may investigate the functions of individual parts or analyse a given structure as a whole. The science of economics exists in an inseparable symbiosis with the social and physical environment and *vice versa*. This fact makes any connecting links between them important.

The laws of thermodynamics and synergy not only broaden the perspective of quantitative processes of change but also, more importantly, those of a qualitative nature, complementing the dialectical methods of evaluation. They greatly aid in understanding the dynamics of economic processes and theories. In the words of Whitehead,

> there are two principles inherent in the very nature of things ... the spirit of change, and the spirit of conservation. There can be nothing real without both. Mere change without conservation is a passage from nothing to nothing. ... Mere conservation without change cannot conserve (Whitehead, 1959, p. 699).

This paper briefly discusses the first and second laws of thermodynamics, synergy, dialectics, the environmental and social effects on economic processes, and the qualitative changes influencing the evolution of economic thought.

* S.G. Karsten is Professor of Economics, West Georgia College, Carrollton.

1. Nature and theory

Economics as a science must have a general conception of nature and its manifestations. The economic process deals with the transformation of the environment, *i.e.*, of natural resources into consumable goods and services. In this context, economics provides the basis of civilization if not of life itself.

As Hans Immler pointed out, the ability of nature to produce is influenced by human action. A positive social conception of industry, growth, development, civilization, and human life necessitates the complementarity of human productivity and the productivity of nature. In other words, the evolution of human civilization depends upon the corresponding evolution of nature (Immler, 1989, pp. 65, 129).

However, as economics plays a definite role in shaping human culture and values, especially those of a material nature, economics in turn is influenced by the physical and social environment. For example, quantum theory led physicists to "adopt a much more subtle, holistic, and 'organic' view of nature" (Capra, 1983, p. 54; Karsten, 1990). The effect of this development has been that in modern physics the universe is

> viewed as a dynamic, inseparable whole which always includes the observer in an essential way. ... the traditional concepts of space and time, of isolated objects, and of cause and effect, lose their meaning (Capra, 1983, p. 81).

Furthermore, quantum theory implies that the socio-economic world "acts more like a single individual unit, in which even the 'intrinsic' nature of each part ... depends to some degree on its relationships to its surroundings (Briggs and Peat, 1984, p. 95).

It is the laws of thermodynamics which link economics to the processes of the physical environment. They provide a more profound perspective of the irreversibility of the basic economic problem: scarcity. Georgescu-Roegen took the position that thermodynamics is mainly a physics of economic value, that it forms the material basis of life, and is necessary for a thing to have value in use and in exchange, in terms of Aristotle's definition of value (Georgescu-Roegen, 1974, pp. 276-78).

The first law of thermodynamics deals with the conservation of matter and energy. In essence it states that all matter and energy is fixed, that it can neither be created nor destroyed; it can only be transformed. That is, the total quantity of matter and energy is in a continuously self-adjusting, mechanical, state of equilibrium, reflecting the Newtonian model of the universe.

The Newtonian paradigm looks upon economic and social change as being mechanical and repetitive, conditioned by fixed laws of nature and caused by elements from outside of the socioeconomic system (Hamilton, 1970, pp. 3-4). This mechanical, functional point of view was embraced by the classical and neoclassical schools of economic thought. They were preoccupied with the mechanics of self-interest, growth, and the maximization of utilities. Economic growth assured greater material abundance and a more ordered economic sphere. They considered "man as an autonomous being, acting in freedom and a kind of splendid isolation..." (Solo, 1975, p. 611). However, "... any system that involves a conservation principle (given means) and a maximization rule (optimal satisfaction) is a mechanical analogue" (Georgescu-Roegen, 1974, pp. 318-19).

The absolutist method of analysis asserts that the evolution of economic thought is brought about by an 'inner momentum' which is non-dialectical in nature. The emphasis is on empirical facts, disregarding future potentialities of economic theories. The absolutist position may, therefore, be more reflective of the Newtonian concept of change and the first law of thermodynamics rather than of evolutionary developments which are conditioned by qualitative factors.

The second law of thermodynamics, the entropy law, states that energy can only be transformed in one direction – from free (available or usable) to bound (unavailable or unusable) energy, or from a state of order to one of disorder. It reflects the laws of physics that heat flows from the hotter to the colder body. The entropy law posits that the amount of free energy constantly decreases and that of bound energy constantly increases, *i.e.*, "there is a *continuous* and *irrevocable* qualitative degradation of free into bound energy" (Georgescu-Roegen, 1974, pp. 5-6, 281; Rifkin, 1980). It is impossible to recycle energy. In other words, entropy is an index of the amount of energy which is no longer available for doing work (bound energy) in an isolated system, such as the planet Earth. As Immler asserted, the whole productive-reproductive processes in nature do not return to the same point from which they started but face an irreversible new situation after each production cycle (Immler, 1989, p. 43).

Georgescu-Roegen saw the entropy law as the most economic of all laws. The basic economic problem of scarcity can be interpreted as the economic struggle of entropy – all economic processes being entropic or qualitative in nature. Analyses of economic and entropic processes will, therefore, reveal the qualitative features of the development of economic processes and theories. They are influenced by the continuous emergence of novelties and qualitative changes (Georgescu-Roegen, 1974, pp. 3, 10-11. 321-25), effecting structural and institutional changes.

The entropy law is, in essence, reflective of the Darwinian concept of change, which holds that change is developmental and not mechanical, that it is continuous and cumulative, caused from within the system, resulting in economic, social, and political development. That is, any socioeconomic system, as supported by quantum theory, "moves, grows, and changes continually," *i.e.*, its "interconnections are dynamic and not static" (Capra, 1990, p. 192).

The differences between classical/neoclassical and institutional or evolutionary economics can be interpreted as being rooted in these two laws of thermodynamics, especially the entropy law. These differences, however, are the result of two *Weltanschauungen* based on the Newtonian paradigm and a theory of evolution which explains development in terms of mutations or of constantly changing forms. For example, institutional economics holds that economic progress does not end with capital formation, or the stationary state of the classical economists, but is conditioned by the continuous mutation of human behavior from one stage of development to another. As Veblen wrote,

> ... economic history ... is a cumulative process of adaptation of means to ends that cumulatively change as the process goes on, both the agent and the environment being at any point the outcome of the last process (Veblen, 1942, pp. 74-75).

Just as in quantum physics, economics and the economist are not separable but form one indivisible whole. Applying Heisenberg's observations about nature to economics: "... what we observe is not economics itself, but economics exposed to our method of questioning" (Heisenberg, 1963, p. 57). In other words, the economist not only observes the properties of an economic system or paradigm, but he also defines its properties. Hence, the economist functions as an 'active participator' and not merely as an 'impartial observer' whose very act of observing the system also changes the system (Peat, 1987, p. 37).

This implies, for example, that microeconomic evolution does not build up in steps to create a macroeconomic evolution, and *vice versa*. Each of them is connected with the other by complex feedback mechanisms involving economists as 'active participators'. Paraphrasing Briggs and Peat, "what we call the micro- and macroeconomic worlds are different theoretical abstractions of the same economic world: the enfolding and unfolding implicate-explicate socioeconomic order" (Briggs and Peat, 1984, p. 147).

2. Dialectics and synergy

The concept of synergy stands for the combined action or operation of the discrete parts of a structure such that the total effect of the structure is greater than the sum of the effects of its individual parts acting independently of each other. The fundamental question which arises is whether this concept lends itself as a tool of analysis of socioeconomic systems or theories.

Haken formulated that (Haken, 1981, pp. 17-22, 65-68), on the one hand, the individual parts of a structure are driven by an invisible hand to organize into larger structures, which on the other hand, it is the cooperation of the parts which in essence creates this 'invisible hand', to be referred to as the monitor, for want of a better term. The outcome of the synergetic process is that the monitor, created by the parts, also governs their functions or dominates them. This regulating function of the monitor corresponds to the sociological concept of objectification. For example, Kuhn's paradigms exhibit both monitoring and objectification functions. Adam Smith's 'invisible hand' or 'impartial spectator' is only too familiar as both an organizing and regulating principle. The evolution of socioeconomic structures entails the subjugation of subsystems into a dominant order regulating their functions according to prevalent norms. Thus, schools of thought such as Mercantilism, Physiocracy, classical political economy, Keynesian and Marxian economics, to mention a few, have affected group behaviour in that the members of the various groups accepted or subordinated themselves to the respective ideas and concepts.

What provides the dynamic force for change or evolution? The answer, according to Haken, is to be found in random events or shocks and necessity, caused by competition and, in my opinion, also by entropic processes. Hayek posited that equilibrium exists only relative to the knowledge which people acquire and any change in their knowledge brings about disequilibrium or movement to another state of equilibrium, a process depending on foresight and time. (Hayek, 1937, pp. 33-37) Random events and increasing scarcity bring about economic fluctuations which in turn may lead to a greater search for another paradigm, as evidenced by the present attempts to find an alternative to Keynesian economics.

Haken argued that synergetic processes, both in the natural environment as well as in socioeconomic systems, together with the forces of competition, stimulated through the collective efforts of scientists in search for new paradigms, generate open systems. (Haken, 1981, pp. 26-29, 89-92, 243-45). The interplay of man, organization, capital, and technology continuously creates new possibilities. According to Haken, disorder, as the result of entropic processes, is to be understood in the context of the number of opportunities which open up. Entropy, therefore, is indicative of the number of possibilities or opportunities which become available. That is, the entropy law, in the context of closed systems, may be of short-term validity. Glansdorff and Prigogine essentially took the same position (Glansdorff and Prigogine, 1971, pp. 287-89). In my opinion, entropic processes are dominant factors which bring about synergetic action.

Economic paradigms evolve, cease to be dominant, compete with each other, or combine to form new paradigms. In the search for new structures, new monitors (invisible hands) and their regulating functions appear on the scene. The outcome may be greater order and not disorder. Does classical political economy, with its static equilibrium, represent a paradigm of greater order than the Keynesian model? It is hardly reasonable to assume that the classical paradigm would have remained intact in the face of institutional, ecological, and political changes. One characteristic of the concept of synergy is that the equilibrium of a socioeconomic structure may be readily upset by changes in the surrounding environment. As a result, both science and society are engaged in a continuous dialogue or symbiosis to reformulate theories and goals in the light of changing conditions.

The evolutionary development of economic thought is due to the mutual interaction of past and present theories with the socioeconomic setting, which is a process that is continuous over time. The historian of economic thought continues to consider the unresolved practical and theoretical problems which are the driving forces of all developmental processes (Landgrebe, 1960,

p. 2). As Popper pointed out, "the growth of knowledge proceeds from old problems to new problems, by means of conjectures and refutations" (Popper, 1972, p. 258).[1]

Analysis and dialectics link the researcher to the phenomena with which he is concerned. The applicability of Hegelian dialectics in the analyses of the evolution of economic theories has been discussed in Karsten (1973). The driving force of the dialectical process is to close the gap between actuality and potentiality. Hegel thought that nothing that surrounds man is final in form; everything is subject to change and, therefore, an example of dialectical processes. (Hegel, 1964, pp. 190-92). The idea here is that anything, *i.e.*, as a thesis, whether subjective or objective in nature, contains or generates within itself a contradiction or reaction, the antithesis. This "contradiction never completely destroys what is contradicted but merely refashions it to suit new ends" (Ollman, 1971, 57). How can a thesis and its antithesis be applied to an idea or a theory at the same time? The answer is to be found in the process of 'becoming' which resolves the contradiction, leading to the third step in the triad, the synthesis, which both abolishes and preserves the thesis and antithesis and which represents the unity of the two (Hegel, 1964, pp. 22-23, 73, 94-98). The nature of dialectics is, therefore, the dynamics of change and deals with the understanding of the processes of development and evolution.

3. Entropy, economics and environment

The entropy law represents the major link which connects economics to the larger physical and social environment of which it is a part. "The human economy is a subsystem of the steady-state ecosystem", as Daly defined it (Daly, 1973(b), p. 153). This has important implications with regard to demand- and supply-side effects and production theory.

In the light of the laws of thermodynamics, aggregate demand is the driving force of higher entropy or of the degradation of matter and energy. To combat unemployment, excess demand inflation, and to raise the material standard of living more economic growth is required. However, higher levels of consumption and investment deplete resources, increase scarcity, which in

1 Popper agreed that ideas and theories evolve in dialectical contexts. He interpreted some of his own methodologies as "... improvements and rationalizations of Hegelian dialectical schema..." (p. 297). He objected to Hegel's notion that divine consciousness, working through man, assures that the evolution of ideas proceeds by man consciously positing hypotheses, testing, criticizing, and correcting them (p. 300).

turn translates into higher prices. Rifkin viewed inflation basically as an indicator of the entropy state of the economy (Rifkin, 1980, pp. 123-26). Boulding asserted that "price theory is an extension of general ecological theory into the ecology of commodities" (Boulding, 1976, p. 14). Immler essentially agreed with Boulding when he observed that there is a primary connection between nature, ethics, and value. Furthermore, he posited that the true ethics of human society manifests in its value and pricing systems (Immler, 1989, pp. 59, 226). Hence, socioeconomic problems arise because of the way economists and policy makers relate to nature, society, culture, and to the economy.

Immler (Immler, 1985; Karsten, 1987) further argued that the role and function of the natural environment, and its neglect, has been disregarded in the formulation of economic theories of value and their long-term consequences on contemporary socioeconomic theories and on society. In his opinion, nature can no longer be exploited without substantial costs to society. Hence, in order to understand and to resolve ecological problems, nature has to be considered as an economic factor, being allocated its proper remuneration to assure her regeneration of her productive powers.

A growing and expanding economy which results in more round-aboutness in the organization of production activities is also one which increases its total entropy, *i.e.*, the loss of free or usable into bound or unusable energy. In this context, the emphasis on technological change, productivity, or increasing returns to scale translate into increased energy flows, depletion of the stock of energy matter, a higher state of entropy (Chase, 1980, p. 55), which, in turn, may set in motion synergetic processes. As a result one experiences attempts to modify traditional economic theory with its emphasis on the maximization of production and consumption to one which minimizes them and which is oriented toward the maintenance of a constant stock of material wealth and population (Daly, 1973(b), p. 153).

Boulding looked at "economics as the study of the provisioning of the human race" and calls a "revision of the theory of production" to be in line with the evolution of the science. He advanced the idea that emphasis needs to be shifted to know-how, energy, and materials as the real factors of production instead of holding on to the traditional ones of labor and capital (Boulding, 1976, pp. 11-12). This appears to be in line with his "spaceman economy" in which

> the essential measure of the success of the economy is not production and consumption at all, but the nature, extent, quality, and complexity of the total capital stock, including in this the state of the human bodies and minds ... what we are primarily concerned with is stock maintenance... (Boulding, 1973, p. 127).

This implies that synergetic processes are set in motion, leading to the creation of new structures consisting of new combinations of the elements of existing structures. However, synergy is dynamic in nature and does not support a static socioeconomic order. As Hutchison put it:

> Institutions, expectations, and reactions, change historically and crucially. In particular, the ways in which expectations change and the forces shaping these processes ..., and the institutions which form it, shift significantly, to an extent which puts severe limitations on attempts at general macroeconomic theories (Hutchison, 1981, p. 235).

4. Development-creation of new processes

The division of labour, specialization and exchange are the crucial parameters in Adam Smith's model of the economy. Without explicitly stating it, Smith tied the production of commodities to the requisite production of processes or at least laid the groundwork for what Böhm-Bawerk later referred to as 'round-aboutness' in the methods of production. Economic investment lengthens the processes of production. It results in greater flow-throughs of matter and energy and exploitation of the environment, *i.e.*, in a higher state of entropy. As Rifkin described it, free energy is constantly transformed, exchanged, and discarded (Rifkin, 1980, p. 57), similar to new investment involving the discarding of existing capital. That is, "economic processes are produced just as commodities are" (Georgescu-Roegen, 1974, pp. 269, 275). Economic development is, therefore, synonymous with the creation of new processes, which implies not only quantitative but also qualitative change.

The law of entropy, through the degradation of matter and energy, induces changes in the value structure of a society and, therefore, synergetic processes. For example, Rifkin argued that when Western Europe was forced to move from an energy base of wood to one of coal, it brought about the fall of the medieval era and ushered in the industrial revolution, fundamentally changing not only the modes of production but also the entire way of life (Rifkin, 1980, pp. 68-77). In a similar vein, Toffler saw the development of new industries: electronics and computers, space, sea, and biological, to result in profound structural and functional changes in the socioeconomic as well as political environments (Toffler, 1981, pp. 131-54, 179-93). As Gurwitsch put it: "By his work, man transforms his socio-historical world, whose transformation then reverberates on man, transforming him (Gurwitsch, 1969, p. 49).

Without matter and energy, *i.e.*, without the law of entropy, economics has no relevance. However, the qualitative changes brought about by the entropy law cause constant and unpredictable changes in the relevant parameters which bring into play the forces of synergy. Therefore, the development of economic thought is the result of dialectical processes from one theory or school of thought to another, similar to economic growth being indicative of the movement from one stationary state to another one.

The history of modern economics, for example, may be thought of as having its origin in medieval Europe, with the doctrines of just price and usury. In the course of history important changes in the structure and function of the socioeconomic environment occurred, necessitating modifications of economic theories. This is evidenced by the various schools of thought: Mercantilism, Physiocracy, classical, neoclassical, institutional, Marxian, monetarist, and Keynesian. Each one of these developments can be viewed as being representative of cumulative evolutionary change from one stage to another, indicative of the mutation of behavior and production patterns.

These evolutionary processes shed light on why some schools of thought, theories or concepts succeed in replacing others. It also facilitates the understanding why different schools of thought, theories, or concepts continue to coexist in spite of competitive forces, *e.g.*, Marxian and neoclassical economics or the Keynesian and monetarist schools of thought. Their coexistence and collective functions may not only stabilize them internally but also set into motion forces which may affect their future development. In more recent times, environmental and energy crises along with the phenomenon of stagflation, which could be viewed as entropic in nature, mandate a continuing updating of economic theories and institutions to create more order out of existing states of disorder. In the words of Boulding: "The closed Earth of the future requires economic principles which are somewhat different from those of the open Earth of the past", (Boulding, 1973, p. 127) forcing the modification of the traditional assumption of unlimited resources.

5. Evolution and qualitative change

The question that arises is whether or not the concepts of entropy and synergy are complementary to other methodologies analysing the evolution of economic thought and theories. The entropy law implies qualitative change and development, the end product in a closed system being the total degradation of matter-energy, the total transformation of free into bound energy, and increasing challenges or possibilities. The two laws of thermodynamics indicate that all aspects of a socioeconomic nature tend to move by their own momentum, in turn forcing society and individuals to evolve. The question, of course, arises: Toward what end?

The concept of synergy indicates that the evolution is towards greater order and not disorder. Certainly, changed values, theories, and institutions will be the result. For example, Hutchison discussed the evolutionary process of development which leads from the German Historical School to Eucken's formulation of a social market economy with its concepts of order and justice (Hutchison, 1981, pp. 155-73). In Eucken's theory (Eucken, 1959, pp. 238-42; Jöhr, 1950, pp. 272-76) a sound legal and institutional framework is essential for a modern market economy. Man not only needs a concrete economic order, characterized by a flexible price mechanism and stability in policies, in which he can function but also a useful and just order which enables him to live a life of dignity, free of economic deprivation. "Thought which finds its expression in a true, non-speculative national economy is not antithetical to life, but serves to enlighten the life we live, which surrounds us and which was lived in the past" (Eucken, 1959, p. 242, my translation). It is Eucken's paradigm which formed the basis for West Germany's economy.

Daly's pyramid of stewardship may serve here as a starting point (Daly, 1973(a), pp. 8, 172-73). Free matter-energy, low entropy, forms the base of the pyramid. Technology gives rise to intermediate means (imputed value) which in turn bring about political economy, resulting in intermediate ends (hierarchy), leading to ethics, with the ultimate end being theology (or moral growth), which implies a greater if not perfect state of order. Similarly, the theological interpretation of synergy, semi-Pelagianism, involves the cooperation of divine grace and human activity. The whole process entails feedback; progress from the base to the *apex* is irreversible.

Daly's configuration of the process of evolution reveals great affinity to Hegelian dialectics. Hegel posited that through the mechanism of his triad consisting of thesis, antithesis, and synthesis, development or evolution is automatically brought about by an inner momentum inherent in all objects. The end result was the unification of man with the ultimate spirit.

Several scholars have embraced dialectical reasoning but rejected Hegel's method of analysis. For example, Georgescu-Roegen strongly argued that one can hardly evaluate qualitative changes without dialectical concepts (Georgescu-Roegen, 1979, pp. 322-24). However, he was reluctant to accept Hegel's synthesis that 'being is becoming' and posits that dialectical processes reveal themselves through the entropy law and the 'novelty by combination' (Georgescu-Roegen, 1974, pp. 12-14, 211).

Popper, though he admitted that Hegelian dialectics is applicable in a great number of analyses, also took issue with Hegel's dialectically self-changing conceptions or notions. Popper took the position that it is man's ability to reason and to challenge existing theories, attempting to falsify them, that is the pivotal force (Popper, 1972, 71, 297-300).

Lowe's 'instrumental analysis' defines the initial state, the goal to be achieved, and the pursuit of certain laws and rules to achieve that goal appear to be in line with Daly's pyramid (Lowe, 1976, pp. 12-16). The path of development is from one stipulated stationary state (goal) to another.

The major differences between these various methodological approaches from Hegelian dialectics are to be found in the question of what the fundamental constituent of the universe is, *i.e.*, the driving force of evolution – spirit, matter, or reason. All methodologies proceed by way of dialectical reasoning, in Popper's terminology, by conjectures, refutations, and critique.

6. Complementarity of methodologies

The development of economic ideas, thought, or theories without purpose is meaningless. This fact is essentially reflected in all methods of analyses. Since evolution of thought and theory is qualitative in nature, the concepts of entropy and synergy can be applied to complement analyses of the development of economic theories. In the words of Georgescu-Roegen: "The economic process, to be sure, is entropic in each of its fibers, but the paths along which it is woven are traced by the utility of man" (Georgescu-Roegen, 1974, p. 282).

Controversies and critiques in the science of economics do not arise primarily for their own sake but have their roots in the material conditions of life. Questions of values, goals and policies take on extra dimensions in an environment characterized by accelerating higher states of entropy, by either disorder or greater possibilities. In the final analysis, accumulation of capital or bound matter-energy is useless if man is unable to create new modes of production which relate to man's and society's changing needs and requirements.

The ultimate end or goal of an evolutionary process is, of course, a value question. Like John Stuart Mill, contemporary social scientists make strong arguments for the stationary state, in which human fulfillment and the enjoyment of life are not characterized by continued accumulation of material wealth but by intellectual and moral growth. One thing appears to be certain: our time horizon needs to be broadened to anticipate the welfare of future generations (Boulding, 1973, pp. 128-30).

Immler saw the solution in a fundamental change in the value structure of society, accepting nature as a factor of production entitled for just compensation as is the case for labor and capital. This would require, in essence, the transformation of the 'industrial consumer' who produces for the sake of production regardless of the effects on nature and the environment, to the 'ecological consumer' who produces with considering the long-run viability of nature (Immler, 1989, pp. 181-88, 273-99). At least in the past, however, such profound changes in value structures have tended to escape mankind.

In my opinion, the first and, especially, the second laws of thermodynamics (the entropy law), together with the concept of synergy, complement the dialectical method of analysis and thus facilitate the research of the evolution of economic theories. The laws of thermodynamics and the concept of synergy induce the researcher to analyse economic processes and theories from different perspectives, influencing theoretical developments.

The interesting task facing the economist is to identify developmental processes which are entropic and dialectical in nature. Historical developments in thought and theories may lend themselves more readily for analyses along the lines suggested by entropy, synergy, and dialectics. However, these concepts cannot be used to predict future developments. At best they can be employed to define alternative paths of development and to evaluate and to modify them on a continuing basis.

References

Boulding K.E., Economics as an evolutionary science. Paper presented at the Southwestern Social Science Meeting, Tempe, Arizona, April 30, 1976.

Boulding K.E., The economics of the coming spaceship Earth. In: H.E. Daly (ed.), *Toward a steady-state economy.* Freeman and Company, San Francisco 1973.

Briggs J. and F. D. Peat, *Looking glass universe.* Simon & Schuster, New York 1984.

Capra F., *The Tao of physics.* Shambhala, Boulder CO, 1983.

Chase R., Structural-functional dynamics in the analysis of socio-economic systems: II Adaptation of structural change processes to biological systems of human interaction. *American Journal of Economics and Sociology* Vol. 39 (1980), Nr 1, pp. 49-64.

Daly H.E., Introduction. In: H.E. Daly (ed.) *Toward a steady-state economy.* Freeman and Company, San Francisco, 1973(a).

Daly H.E., The steady-state economy. In: H.E. Daly (ed.), *Toward a steady-state economy.* Freeman and Company, San Francisco, 1973(b).

Eucken W., *Die Grundlagen der Nationalökonomie.* Springer-Verlag, Berlin, 1959.

Georgescu-Roegen N., *The entropy law and the economic process.* Harvard University Press, Cambridge, MA, 1974.

Georgescu-Roegen N., Methods in economic science, *Journal of Economic Issues* Vol. 13 (1979), Nr 2, pp. 317-328.

Glansdorff P. and I. Prigogine, *Thermodynamic theory of structure, stability and fluctuations.* John Wiley & Sons, Ltd., London, 1971.

Gurwitsch A., Social science and natural science. In: R.L. Heilbronner (ed.), *Economic means and ends.* Prentice-Hall, Englewood Cliff NJ, 1969.

Haken H., *Erfolgsgeheimnisse der Natur.* Deutsche Verlags-Anstalt, Stuttgart, 1981.

Hamilton D., *Evolutionary economics.* University of New Mexico Press, Albuquerque NM, 1970.

Hayek F.A. von, Economics and knowledge. *Economica* N.S. Vol. 4 (1937), pp. 33-54.

Hegel G.W.F., *Phänomenologie des Geistes.* Vol. 2 of *Sämtliche Werke.* Hermann Glockner (ed.), Friedrich Frommann Verlag, Stuttgart-Bad Cannstatt, 1964(a).

Hegel G.W.F., *System der Philosophie, erster Teil, Die Logik.* Vol. 8 of *Sämtliche Werke.* Hermann Glockner (ed.), Friedrich Frommann Verlag, Stuttgart-Bad Canstatt, 1964(b).

Heisenberg W., *Physics and philosophy.* George Allen & Unwin, London, 1963.

Hutchison T.W., *The politics and philosophy of economics.* New York University Press, New York, 1981.

Immler H., *Natur in der ökonomischen Theorie.* Westdeutscher Verlag, Opladen, Germany, 1985.

Immler H., *Vom Wert der Natur.* Westdeutscher Verlag, Opladen, Germany, 1989.

Jöhr W.A., Walter Euckens Lebenswerk. *Kyklos* Vol. 4 (1950), pp. 257-278.

Karsten S.G., Dialectics and the evolution of economic thought. *History of Political Economy* Vol. 5 (1973), Nr 2, pp. 399-419.

Karsten S.G., Nature in economic theories: the investigations of Hans Immler. *American Journal of Economics and Sociology* Vol. 46 (1987), Nr 1, pp. 61-70.

Karsten S.G., Quantum theory and social economics. *American Journal of Economics and Sociology* Vol. 49 (1990), Nr 4, pp. 385-399.

Landgrebe L., Das Problem der Dialektik. In: I. Fetscher (ed.), *Marxismusstudien*, Vol. 3 (1960), pp. 1-65.

Lowe A., *The path of economic growth.* Cambridge University Press, Cambridge, 1976.

Ollman B., *Alienation.* Cambridge University Press, Cambridge, 1971.

Peat F.D., *Synchronicity.* Bantam Books, New York, 1987.

Popper K.R., *Objective knowledge*. Oxford University Press, London, 1972.
Rifkin J., *Entropy*. Viking Press, New York, 1980.
Solo R.A., What is structuralism? *Journal of Economic Issues* Vol. 9 (1975), Nr 4, pp. 605-625.
Toffler A., *The third wave*. Bantam Books, New York, 1981.
Veblen T., *The place of science in modern civilization*. Viking Press, New York, 1942.
Whitehead A.N., Science and the modern world. In: J.L. Beatty and O.A. Johnson (eds), *Heritage of Western civilization*. Prentice-Hall, Englewood Cliffs, 1959.

Chapter 10

THE NEO-CLASSICAL AND STEADY STATE APPROACHES TO ENVIRONMENTAL ECONOMICS: a few methodological remarks

Roelof Jongeneel*

In this chapter I attempt to analyse the methodological foundations of environmental economics. Attention is paid to two important schools of thought: the neo-classical and the steady state analysis. The first school, which is the mainstream school of thought in contemporary (non-environmental) economic analysis, concentrates on the subjective welfare or utility theoretical approach, while the second pays particular attention to physical laws. The latter is also known as ecological economics. This essay attempts to gain a clearer insight into the methodological backgrounds or meta-economic structures of both schools. The term meta-economics which was used by Schumacher (1973) is defined here as the underlying assumptions of economic analysis. Underwood and King (1989) spoke of the 'set of first principles shaping theoretical development'. In particular, Gunnar Myrdal (1954) and Joan Robinson (1962) re-established the importance of these (metaphysical) first principles for the development and evolution of economic thought. They both argued that all analyses ultimately rest on ideologically conditioned subjective beliefs. Economists may approach the subject differently and come to different conclusions, depending on how they think about meta-economic and ideological principles.

The organization of the paper is as follows. First, I examine the meta-economic structures of both schools of thought. I then briefly discuss developments in the philosophy of science, in particular the

* R. A. Jongeneel is Lecturer in the Department of General Economics of Wageningen Agricultural University. The author would like to thank Professor E. Schuurman, Department of Philosophy, Delft Technical University and Wageningen Agricultural University, and Emeritus Professor B. Goudzwaard, Department of Economics, Amsterdam Free University, for their valuable comments on an earlier draft of this paper. The usual disclaimer applies.

structure-theoretical approach by H.Dooyeweerd, a Dutch philosopher. This is done to create a reference-framework for evaluating both environmental economics schools. Finally, I make several conclusive remarks.

1. Neo-classical environmental economics

To determine the meta-economics upon which modern economic analysis is based, it is helpful to begin with a brief sketch of the 'wonderful world of Adam Smith' (Heilbroner, 1953). In this world, the free pursuit of self-interest by the individual economic actors leads to an allocation of resources, which maximizes their own welfare and social welfare simultaneously. The atomistic buyers and sellers, engaged in an egoistic drive to improve their individual utilities and profits, are 'led by an invisible hand to promote an end which was no part of their intention' (Heilbroner, 1953). In pursuing his own interest, the individual frequently promotes the welfare of society more effectually than when he is really intending to promote it. Using the metaphor of the 'invisible hand', Smith in fact fell back on the underlying metaphysical theory that the operationalization of private self-interest creates not-intended favourable over-all results (van Manenschijn, 1979). Also, modern versions of economics share the ontological view of the classicals, in which it is assumed that acquisitiveness and the pursuit of self-interest (rational egoism) are fundamental tenets of human nature. Consequently, neo-classical economics is characterized by a strong orientation towards economic growth.

An important component of the operation of an economy is the concept of value. According to Smith, the value of a good is mainly determined by its costs of production. He had no answer to the so-called paradox of value, the difference between the exchange value of a good and its subjective use-value. The exchange value of fresh air is low, but it has a high subjective value; it is an essential prerequisite for life. The answer to this paradox was given by the marginalistic revolution (1870) in economics, when the concept of (marginal) utility was introduced to measure value. At the same time, the method of deductive logic and the use of mathematics were increasingly used as tools for economic analysis. Mathematical attractiveness and elegance was to play an important role in shaping economic theory. Jevons (1871), Menger (1871), Walras (1874) and many others integrated the principle of marginal utility into a consistent mathematically formulated economic theory. Value became dependent on the subjective preferences of individual economic agents, and this leads to the concept of relative scarcity. The means, which were assumed to have alternative uses, were scarcely relative to the 'given' ends. Also, the subject matter of economic science was modified. Economics was no longer limited to particular activities, such as real market transactions, but was rather seen as an aspect of all human conduct (Robbins,1932).

The third point that should be made is that of the principle of substitution. According to neo-classical economics, substitution between goods is a keyelement in economic analysis and it is assumed to be nearly always possible (see Solow, 1974). For resource economics, this idea was clearly expressed by Barnett and Morse (1963, 11):

> Nature imposes particular scarcities, not an inescapable general scarcity. Man is therefore able, and free, to choose among an indefinitely large number of alternatives. There is no reason to believe that these alternatives will eventually reduce to one that entails increasing costs - that it must sometime prove impossible to escape diminishing quantitative returns. Science, by making the resource base more homogeneous, erases the restrictions once thought to reside in the lack of homogeneity. In a neo-Ricardian world, it seems, the particular resources with which one starts increasingly become a matter of indifference.

As a consequence, scarcity is always relative; the degree of scarcity depending on the limited availability of means in relation to the ends, the (infinite) needs or wants. Modern price theory states that relative price changes provide the appropriate guide for optimum goods and resource allocation. Relative price movements induce a re-direction of resource use and commodity allocation. As is shown by general equilibrium theory and Paretian welfare economics, a competitive market economy regulates production and consumption in such a way that no other alternative allocation can lead to an increase of welfare. The basic moral is that a competitive market system will give efficient allocations.

In fact, things do not always work out so nicely, as I have already touched on. Firstly, Pigou (1932) with his internal criticism of the market paradigm showed that the existence of external diseconomies could cause differences between private and social interests. In the case of externalities, the marginal social costs involved in the use of some resources can exceed the marginal private costs. This leads to self-interested individuals choosing resource-use patterns antagonistic to social welfare. One of the central issues in neo-classical environmental economics is how to reduce these external diseconomies, and Pigou's formula of internalization is often recommended.

According to this theory, the failure of the market has to be corrected by the state through the imposition of taxes and subsidies. A second issue is that a number of environmental goods are in fact unpriced free goods (common-property resources) with a public good character (for a more detailed discussion see Baumol and Oates, 1988).

An important question is whether neo-classical economics can deal with non-renewable recources. Non-renewable resources can be extracted and used only once, and represent a form of non-reproducible capital. Hotelling (1931) showed that in case of finite supply of resources, the neo-classical paradigm could also give the answer. In fact, the problem for the resource owner is knowing when to extract the resource. Should he extract and sell the resource today at the current market price, or should he exploit it in the future? Hotelling showed that if the net value of the resource (total value minus extraction costs) grows at the same rate as the opportunity cost of capital, then resource owners are indifferent to the moment of extraction. If the net value of the resource grows at this rate, posterity will be compensated by a larger stock of productive capital.

Provided that the net price of the resource grows exponentially at the discount rate, the joint producer and consumer surplus will be maximized. So, operating through competitive markets, the 'invisible hand' is also able to deal with the intertemporal allocation of resources with a finite supply. The use of a resource, in this model, causes prices to rise over a period of time. This induces the introduction of resource substitutes, and also induces the development of resource-augmenting new technology (see Withagen, 1990, for a survey and more detailed discussion).

The neo-classical environmental economics approach can be summarized as being based on the principles of the individual pursuit of self-interest (rational egoism), subjective utility being the ultimate factor for determining value and the possibility of substitution. The attractiveness of mathematically formulated economic theories leads to a monistic method. If there is a market failure, a correction is then needed to assure that the price system reflects the real scarcity. In practice, the assessment of environmental damage into monetary terms poses considerable problems. Much research has gone into the development of valuation methods like hedonistic pricing methods and contingent valuation methods (for a detailed discussion see Johansson, 1987). In practice, 'revealed preference' concepts may lead to monetized valuations of environmental goods but, according to Nijkamp (1979) and Hueting (1990), it is difficult to find a sound basis for such computations because of the problem of aggregation of subjective preferences.

The policy recommendations resulting from neo-classical analysis mainly focus on repairing the price system. Imposition of a set of effluent charges, based on the marginal willingness-to-pay for a 'clean' environment, combined with laissez faire will be sufficient to produce a Pareto optimum pattern of resource allocation. The neo-classical school of economics is not, *a priori*, against affecting the environment, but it tries to refine the balance of pros and cons, or, in more economic language, the weight of costs and benefits.

2. Steady state economics

The school of steady state analysis, or ecological economics, emerged under the influence of people like Georgescu-Roegen (1971), Ayres and Kneese (1969), Boulding (1970), and Daly (1977). Its roots date back to the work of Mill. As Boulding argued, the economy can no longer be seen as an open system, as was traditionally so. In this traditional view, the attention of economists was mainly focused on the production and consumption processes, or more succinctly, the 'throughput'. Inputs were assumed to come from an inexhaustible stock and outputs were regarded as being accepted without difficulty by the environment. According to Boulding (1966), not only throughput, but the complete input-throughput-output process deserves attention. The economy is a closed system, or a spaceship-economy, as Boulding called it, which needs to be based on recycling processes.

The steady state school of thought takes its first meta-economic principle from the first and second law of thermodynamics and the law of conservation of matter (*cf* Underwood and King, 1989). Both the first law of thermodynamics and the law of conservation of matter state that energy-matter cannot be destroyed but only altered in form. This means that the total mass of inputs used in the production process is equal to the total mass of outputs and wastes produced (materials balance principle). The second law of thermodynamics, the 'entropy law', implies that energy undergoes a transformation from an ordered, unbound and highly usable state to a disordered, bound, and less usable state. The implication of these laws is that, the more a society relies on an increase in material flows to satisfy the increasing demands for produced goods, the greater the level of pollution and the disamenities associated with it will be. It also implies a greater reliance on the assimilative and regenerating capacity of the biosphere and a reduction of the productive potential of the biosphere in the future. The implications of these laws are twofold: they deal explicitly with the problem of pollution and they deal with absolute resource scarcity.

According to steady state theories, the influence of all production and consumption actions on the entropy of the universe and the future productive potential of the biosphere means that the field of economic inquiry has to be extended by integrating ecology and economics within one evolutionary paradigm. "The goal was to expand and revise the methodology of economic analysis in order to make it consistent with the knowledge gained in other areas of scientific inquiry." (Underwood and King, 1989). The economic problem can only be understood in terms of the dialectical interactions between the economic process and the assimilative capacity of the environment. Within this model, room is also left for the functioning of the market and price system, albeit a limited and constrained room. In some articles on the steady state the scope of economics is broadened much further and ethical and political elements are introduced into the analysis of the environmental problem (*cf* Daly, 1973).

Summarizing, steady state analysis can be described as being based on the laws of thermodynamics and the law of conservation of matter. Contrary to the neo-classicals, steady state economists conclude that relative price changes are not enough to generate a welfare maximizing environmental resource allocation. In their view, traditional economic analysis does not recognize the limitations caused by absolute scarcity and this is also true for the way in which our market economies are structured. Also, the policy recommendations of the steady state economists differ from those recommended by the neo-classicals. Generally speaking, it can be said that they focus much more on conservation of the environment than the neo-classical school does. They plead strongly for a restriction of the over-all level of economic activity and its growth, since the current ecological problems, including pollutants like CO_2, SO_2, and NO_x, indicate that the assimilative capacity of the biosphere has already been surpassed. Because of the limited quantity of physical stocks, economic growth should take place through growth in the non-physical sphere; growth of service and leisure. Limitations on production and economic growth causes the distribution issue to become more and more important in a steady state economy. The norms, derived from ecology, are ultimately decisive and should guide the economy away from a 'cowboy-economy', as Boulding called it, to durability and maintenance of its natural capital stocks and endowments (Daly, 1973).

3. Developments in philosophy of science

Before evaluating both schools of thought, I want to first pay some attention to the evolution of the philosophy of science, particularly to the significance of the structure-theoretical approach of the rather unknown Dutch philosopher Herman Dooyeweerd (1894-1975). In his approach to the structure of reality he made some interesting points that can be useful in evaluating these schools.

Contemporary philosophy of science is an area of lively research and, equally, of controversy. There is some agreement about questions to be asked, but little about what the answers should be. Contemporary philosophy can largely be seen as a reaction against the view of the logical positivists and the still influential view of Popper. These philosophies focus especially on the assessment of theories and the separation of science and non-science. This last point is known as the problem of demarcation. The positivists stressed the need of empirical verification of theories. In the 1930s, Popper argued that there is no such thing as confirmation; all generalizations remain no more than tentative conjectures, regardless of how often they are empirically accepted. On the demarcation problem, both the positivists and Popper accentuated the need for empirically testable theories and a 'critical attitude' on the part of the scientist. The first meant that scientific theories should be related to observables, and the second point implied that scientists have to accept a whole set of methodological rules, such as seeking out the harshest possible tests for theories and refuting, not manipulating, theories when test results are negative.

Current philosophy of science has chosen a different approach to dealing with the problems of theory. Theory choice is thought more important than theory assessment. Empirical tests are no longer seen as decisive in deciding to give up valuable theories. Rather, their role is more to enable scientists to choose the best theory from a group of alternatives. Here the work of Lakatos in particular should be mentioned. His philosophy of scientific research programmes has influenced many economists (Blaug, 1976). To a certain extent, Lakatos' philosophy concurs with that of Popper. Though less extreme about the rejection of theories, it agrees with Popper's basic point that the making of empty excuses to save 'clearly' rejected theories is a bad attitude, for then we are condemned to never being able to learn from experience. Lakatos was especially concerned with formulating the rules which have to be followed in modifying and comparing theories. When modifying a theory, *ad hoc* modifications have to be avoided. A modification means an improvement if, and only if, the theory develops new testable implications and if the modification is theoretically progressive, is not arbitrary, but is linked with the central paradigm. Although Lakatos' view provides some guidance in the choice of theories, it nowhere near exhausts all possibilities. As Hausman (1984) rightly stated, it is of little use trying to discover whether current economic theories can be relied on. Since existing theories are wanted to be applied, it is less important to know about how much progress is being made than about its degree of confirmation. Moreover, it remains a difficult task to evaluate research programmes on their progressiveness. Though knowledge about science has increased, generally speaking, at the present time contemporary philosophy of science is not yet able to provide hard and fast rules for comparing and assessing theories.

The rather negative outcome resulting from this brief sketch of the philosophy of science makes it difficult to evaluate the schools I have already described. In fact, this outcome leaves room for methodological pluralism. Some interesting points, however, can be made about the structure of reality. Therefore I want to take a quick look at the structure-theory, as developed by Dooyeweerd (1955). He separated reality into a number of (hierarchical) aspects, each characterized by its own 'significance core' and its own set of laws. In fact, his structure-theory supports the idea of economics as an aspect-science (*cf* Robbins, 1932). As well as an economic aspect, Dooyeweerd distinguished other aspects, including spatial, physical, biological, historical, sociological, juridical and ethical ones. Most sciences concentrate on one particular aspect of reality, or even a part of it.

It is beyond the scope of this paper to show all the aspects Dooyeweerd distinguished and why a certain hierarchical sequence has resulted. However, some additional and important remarks can be made. Firstly, it should be noted that, according to Dooyeweerd, since reality exists as a whole and not as separated and isolated aspects, the whole of reality is as important as the different aspects separately. The 'isolation' of the economic aspect or any other aspect is, in fact, an abstract mental operation (only an act of the human mind) and therefore has an artificial character. The isolation of the economic aspect forms a helpful starting point in economic analysis. However, it also implies a strong reduction of reality and therefore it can only be a first step. In following steps, the degree of abstraction has to be lowered to obtain a better approximation of reality and therefore the isolation of the economic aspect will never be the end of all wisdom, but rather the beginning.

Secondly, the existence of the various aspects justifies the several scientific disciplines, since:

> every modal aspect of temporal reality has its proper sphere of laws, irreducible to those of other modal aspects, and in this sense it is sovereign in its own orbit, because of its irreducible modality of meaning (Dooyeweerd, 1953, Vol. I, p.102).

According to this, economic discipline has its own rights, and has to provide insight into the typical economic laws and/or regularities.

Thirdly, it is not possible to say everything about the whole from the viewpoint of an aspect. This implies that the economic approach has its limitations, although it does provide a significant contribution. Fourthly, according to Dooyeweerd, every individual aspect, to a certain extent, simultaneously reflects all other aspects, but the reflected aspects are then characterized by the leading aspect. This means, for example, that within the economic aspect the spatial aspect also has to be taken into consideration. However, in that case, the space-concept is characterized by the leading economic aspect. Space then becomes 'economic' space in which the 'economic' distance is of more importance than the geographical distance. Note that economic analysis essentially differs from, for example, geographics, and that taking into account the spatial aspect in economics does not necessarily ask for a synthesis, in the sense of both sciences being swallowed up into each other. For a more detailed discussion I refer you to the almost inaccessible work by Dooyeweerd (1953).

The question now arises what the implications of the above sketched philosophy are. On the one hand, it means that economics is a legitimate science, which should not be confused or mixed up with other sciences. Economics is a science in its own right and provides a view from a unique and important perspective: scarcity. On the other hand, it also means that since it limits itself to the economic aspect only, economics cannot explain everything about reality. Economics, for example, cannot give a substitute in the form of a certain amount of dollars for the ethical valuation of human life. The value of life in monetary terms may provide some information about 'revealed preferences', but no one would conclude from this that he is free to kill his neighbour if he pays compensation in this amount of dollars to his neighbour's wife. In other words, the implicit value placed on human life which economists derive from 'revealed' behaviour should never be seen as an exchange value or ordinary price.

As well as the economic aspect, several others are relevant for a full analysis of the daily actions of the economic agents. For a full and balanced view the policy maker should try to make a final synthesis, taking into account the non-economic aspects. A favourable cost/benefit ratio does not necessarily justify the execution of a certain project or policy proposal. There may be advantages and disadvantages related to other aspects of the project that make it better not to execute it. A well-known example of this is the so-called efficiency-equity trade-off. From an efficiency point of view a project may be good, but the equity implications of the project may be so unfavourable that it makes the project unattractive from a political point of view.

A large number of daily actions and phenomena, however, are (mainly) qualified by the economic aspect. Markets and companies, for example, are typically economically qualified entities. In the same way buying, selling and investing are outstanding examples of the phenomena for which the economic explanation is the dominating one. This does not mean that other aspects are irrelevant, but for these phenomena, the economic aspect is the most important one and economics is the first science to provide an explanation for them. This does not imply that other non-economic (reflected) aspects may not be important. However, these reflected aspects are coloured by the leading economic aspect, although they may not be reduced to economics. In some economic theories, for example, the spatial aspect is not either explicitly dealt with, or is wholly neglected. This may be right since the spatial aspect does not always play a significant role in the economic explanation, though it always exists. Economists must take the reflected aspects into account, but in their own way. This is so in cases where the spatial aspect is important as, for example, in regional economics.

Summarizing, the Dooyeweerdian structure-theoretical approach emphasizes that economizing always takes place within a certain context. Economic life does not take place in isolation, but always presupposes that certain things are respected. For example, it nearly always presupposes that a number of juridical laws (in the sense of norms) are satisfied (think for example of the legal order). In principle it may be possible to analyse the economy of an anarchaic and chaotic society, but that would not be a very meaningful activity. Room for meaningful economic analysis is only created if a number of laws (norms) corresponding to the non-economic aspects are satisfied. In other words, there are threshold values and degrees of tolerance that must be accounted for in advance. Real economizing, therefore, is characterized by careful and responsible management or stewardship.

4. Evaluation

In this final section I further evaluate the meta-economic principles underlying both schools of thought, taking into account what I have already suggested about the philosophy of science. First, it can be said that the wonderful world of Smith and his modern followers is a highly idealized world. (This is also true for a spaceship-world, for a spaceship is the height of human achievement and mastering). The meta-economic principle of the 'invisible hand' has some real flaws. The pursuit of self-interest might and in many circumstances, will not automatically lead to good results, but will even generate bad ones. The economic depression of the 1920s and 1930s showed that a vicious circle of disaster is also one possibility. This led to Keynes' fundamental break with the old naturalistic paradigm.

According to the Dooyeweerdian framework, the neo-classical meta-economic principle of the invisible hand which causes only good is not a purely economic one. The implicit hypothesis that the pursuit of self-interest leads to the social good is principally an ethical (political) statement, which does not fall within the competence of economics. The 'high' explanatory power of the assumption of rational egoistic individuals in economic theory provides no reason for prescribing how people ought to behave. The orientation towards economic growth is therefore not something which is necessarily inherent to economics as a science. The same is, in fact, true for the preference for a steady state. This is also a non-economic value judgement, for there is no economic reason why a stationary state is in itself good.

The neo-classical theory of value is focused on relative scarcity and is not suited to capture the concepts of intrinsic or immanent value and absolute scarcity. This should not be seen as a disadvantage for, within an economic context, the meaning of the concept of absolute scarcity is not clear. Economics has to do with inter-human valuation which is relative by its very nature. Achterhuis (1989) argued that scarcity is nothing absolute, but rather socially and culturally determined. In his book he showed that this idea dated back to Hobbes and his followers, Locke and Rousseau. Economic value is essentially a relational concept.

It may be possible to speak of absolute scarcity but then absolute needs, such as basic needs for survival, first have to be introduced. The criteria needed for defining such needs, however, go beyond economics and are subject to other sciences.

The Dooyeweerdian philosophy draws attention to the fact that there are more concepts of value than those derived from economics. The economic value concept, which is always related to relative scarcity, differs from esthetical value, historical value or the (ethical) value of life. No simple relationship exists which relates all these differing value concepts into monetary terms. To deal with these non-economic, but nonetheless important and valued things, the corresponding non-economic sciences have first to provide the information, and the necessary laws and norms. Expressing environmental losses of, say, a polluting industry in monetary terms, and then suggesting that, if benefits exceed costs that the industry must be free to pollute, is a premature conclusion. To do so is equal to making the economic law of efficiency the final criterion, while, at the same time, not asking whether there are other norms which should also be respected.

Hotelling's proof, which showed that neo-classical analysis could deal with resources with a finite supply, does not guarantee that natural stocks will not be completely used or exploited. Furthermore, in his analysis, not much attention is paid to the role of uncertainty.

The meta-economic principle of substitution is a strong one, particularly in a world with a large 'lake' of scientific knowledge and technical possibilities. If the price of a particular resource rises to a very high level, there are nearly always a number of substitutes possible which will become economically relevant. This phenomena is likely to be underestimated in the steady state school of thought, though Barnett and Morse may have exaggerated it. Although substitution may be technically possible, a lot of practical difficulties are usually encountered in making such substitutional changes (*e.g.* for example nuclear power for fossil fuels).

Unfortunately, recent developments in the mainstream philosophy of science provide no clear rules for comparing theories and leave room for methodological pluralism. The dominance of neo-classical theory and agreement on method within this school, however, reflects that there are strong pressures for conformity within the discipline. The emphasis on using the correct method may hamper the incorporation of non-economic aspects, like the ecological aspects of economic behaviour and the introduction of new approaches, and may create a tendency to undervalue field knowledge and observations in neo-classical economics.

The steady state analysis of environmental and resource economics makes some important points. Firstly, it stresses the individual character of environmental analysis by introducing the concept of absolute scarcity and by also taking into account the non-economic ecological aspect of the problem. Just as Keynes did for labour, steady state economists mention a number of reasons aimed at justifying a special treatment of environmental problems in economic analysis. The neo-classical 'solution' to consider the laws of thermodynamics and conservation as just one more source of relative scarcity looks somewhat premature to steady state economists.

The second and related point steady state economists make is their questioning of the insular character of the neo-classical model. By this they mean that neo-classical analysis tends to concentrate too much on the isolated (abstract) economic aspect. As I have already remarked, this artificial isolation must largely be seen as a matter of convenience. Abstraction makes it possible to reduce the complex real world to a simplified system open to scientific analysis. All other aspects are assumed to be 'given' or constant (*ceteris paribus* clause). It has to be said that this method of abstraction is a necessary characteristic of all scientific analysis. It has its own place and has proved to be very useful and powerful in economic theorizing.

It should be noted that, historically, neo-classical economists have had a strong sense that, apart from explaining economic phenomena, their models have limited applicability. Marshall wrote in his 'Principles' that:

> Economic laws and reasoning in fact are merely a part of the material which Conscience and Common-sense have to turn into account in solving practical problems and in laying down rules which may be a guide in life (Marshall, 1925,iv).

Moreover, Knight (1956, 26), the founder of the Chicago school, wrote with regard to other non-economic approaches to economic phenomena that:

> All are needed to supply data and interpretation, to put content and definiteness into the valid but highly abstract "laws" of economic choice and market phenomena. Without such supplementation, economic laws have little value for prediction, since the essential factor of wants is not open to sense observation and any course of events that occurs can be fitted into the theoretical pattern.

The same conclusion was arrived at by Sir John Hicks (1979, 12):

> It is because the phenomena with which economics deals is so narrow that economists are continually butting their heads against its boundaries.

Nevertheless, supporters of the steady state argue correctly that relationships and interactions between the economic process and its environment (in its broadest sense) also deserve attention in economic analysis since there is really no isolated economic aspect. I believe this to be the most valuable contribution of ecological economists to economic science. In fact, I have also pointed this out in my earlier discussion on philosophical structure theory.

It has to be admitted that this point, made by economists like Boulding, Georgescu-Roegen and Daly, has for a long time been largely ignored by the neo-classical establishment of the economic community. As Ehrlich (1988, 10) stated:

> The majority of economists have never been taught that ecosystems provide humanity with an absolutely indispensable array of services, including maintenance of the gaseous quality of the atmosphere, amelioration of the climate, operation of the hydrolic cycle (including the control of floods and the provision of fresh water to agriculture, industry and homes) disposal of wastes, recycling of nutrients essential to agriculture and forestry, generation of soils, pollination of crops, provision of food from which humanity has already withdrawn the very basis of its civilization. While these services are "free", they would, of course, be infinitely costly to replace.

Mainstream neo-classical economics often implicitly assumed an infinite number of resources to be available and that, if necessary, a satisfactory substitute could always be found to replace any one of them.

It is no accident that both economics and ecology share the same Greek root, *oikos*. The common origin of their names makes clear that one cannot focus on society's housekeeping only and ignore nature's housekeeping. Just as both disciplines are intertwined in name and patterns of explanation and mathematical models used (Norgaard, 1989), so they are in their fields of analysis. Keeping nature's house in order is a prerequisite for a sustainable economy. Fortunately, it is increasingly recognized by modern neo-classical environmental economics (*e.g.* the survey article of Fisher and Peterson, 1976) that arguing correctly from economic theory entails digging into the specifics of each case or the 'nitty gritty' of environmental systems. This asks for a 'new' neo-classical synthesis which will incorporate ecological aspects in economic analysis without, however, economics and ecology swallowing each other up. Environmental economics must pay attention to the ecological aspects of economic behaviour, but in its own way. In addition, it would be fruitful if environmental economics, though up to now a mere subdiscipline within economics, were to have more influence on mainstream economic thinking. This would probably make the economic profession 'sensitive' to other weaknesses or neglected aspects in its methodology.

Some ecological economists, in particular Richard Norgaard (1989), in line with the developments in modern philosophy of science have been stressing the need for a new paradigm which will be a mixture of economics and ecology, and which will leave room for methodologies to multiply. This corresponds with the many approaches to understanding within ecology. I believe that arguments for such a hodgepodge of diverse methodologies are not very convincing. There should be a certain agreement on method in science and if it is felt necessary to use more diverse methodologies, there should be a meta-theory which guarantees their internal consistency and indicates when and why a certain methodology should be applied to solve a particular problem. Up to now, insights provided by the methodological intersection of economics and ecology have been limited (Norgaard, 1989, 51).

Steady state scientists, in their function as economists, are wrong in choosing the laws of thermodynamics and the law of the conservation of matter as their basic principles. There may exist relationships within an economy that are 'analogous' to physical laws, but that does not justify the direct application of physical laws into economics. If these analogous relationships exist and are important for the problems analysed, then they should be explicitly introduced into economic analysis. However, economists must do this in their own way since the laws of thermodynamics, as pure physical laws, are not directly relevant to economics. On the contrary, directly introducing them into economics is misleading. It is not the materials balance principle as such that matters, but rather the inter-human valuation of the total mass of inputs in relation to the total mass of outputs. While the material balance principle will necessarily hold, the economic balance may be distorted.

It should be noted that these remarks are not aimed at denying that there may be some ecological norms that must be respected in advance if economic theorizing is to be a really meaningful activity. As I have already admitted, there will be such norms and not only ecological ones but also others like social and ethical ones. Moreover, I have not said that the laws of thermodynamics have no economic aspect. They do, but they are primarily characterized by the physical aspect. However, steady state economists are mistaken in thinking that taking non-economic aspects into consideration will make it necessary to deny the leading role of the scarcity aspect in economics. Among all the questions that can be asked, there will always be the question of (social) efficiency which economics will have to answer.

The foregoing arguments lead to the conclusion that economics plays an essential role in solving the environmental problems of society, since reality has an economic aspect and since there is always the efficiency question which has to be answered. As soon as environment becomes scarce, economics can provide a valuable contribution from a unique point of view.

In their economic analysis, economists should also pay attention to the wholes of reality, and not only to one artificially isolated aspect. However, economics has to remain economics and when dealing with other aspects it must do it in its own way. This means that economics in its analysis will mainly focus on the economic implications, even when it takes other aspects into consideration.

Fortunately, economic research practice is 'stronger' than the sometimes narrow neo-classical economic doctrine. Modern environmental economic research usually incorporates relevant non-economic aspects, such as technical diffusion-processes, into its analysis. However, a clear, balanced and systematic view on the position of economics within the whole of reality is often lacking, and not only among economists. Hopefully this essay may provide a positive contribution to that issue.

References

Achterhuis H., *Het rijk van de schaarste; van Thomas Hobbes tot Michael Foucault.* Ambo, Baarn 1988.

Ayres R.U. and A.V. Kneese, Production, consumption and externalities. *American Economic Review* Vol. 59 (1969) pp.282-97.

Baumol W.J. and W.E. Oates, *The theory of environmental policy*, (second edition). Cambridge University Press, Cambridge 1988.

Barnett J. and C. Morse, *Scarcity and growth: the economics of natural resource availability.* Johns Hopkins University Press, Baltimore 1963.

Blaug M., Paradigms versus research programmes in the history of economics. In: D.M. Hausman (ed.).

Boulding K.E., The economics of the coming spaceship Earth. In H.Daly (ed.) (1973).

Daly H.E. (ed.), *Economics, ecology, ethics: essays towards a steady state economy.* Freeman, San Francisco Calif. 1973.

Daly H.E., *Steady state economics.* Freeman, San Francisco Calif., 1977.

Dooyeweerd H., *A new critique of theoretical thought*, 3 vol.. Philadelphia, Presbyterian and Reformed Publ. Co., Philadelphia 1953.

Ehrlich P.R., The limits to substitution: meta-resource depletion and a new economic-ecological paradigm. *Ecological Economics* Vol. 1 (1989) pp.9-16.

Fisher A.C. and F.M. Peterson, The environment in economics: a survey. *Journal of Economic Literature* Vol. XVI (1976) pp.1-33.

Georgescu-Roegen N., *The entropy law and the economic process.* Harvard University Press, Cambridge Mass., 1971.

Hausman D.M. (ed.), *The philosophy of economics: an anthology.* Cambridge University Press, Cambridge, 1984.

Heilbroner R.L., *The worldly philosophers.* Simon & Schuster Inc., New York, 1953

Hicks J., *Causality in economics.* Basic Books, New York, 1979.

Hotelling H., The economics of exhaustible resources. *Journal of Political Economy* Vol. 39 (1931) pp.137-75.

Hueting R., Correcting of national income for environmental losses: a practical solution for a theoretical dilemma. Paper prepared for the Conference on Ecological Economics. Washington, D.C., May 21-23, 1990.

Jevons S.J., *The theory of political economy.* Penguin, Baltimore, 1970.

Johansson P-O., *The economic theory and measurement of environmental benefits.* Cambridge University Press, Cambridge, 1987.

Knight F.H., *On the history and method of economics: selected essays.* University of Chicago Press, Chicago, Ill., 1956.

Latour B. and S. Woolga, *Laboratory life: the construction of scientific facts.* Princeton University Press, Princeton, 1986.

Manenschijn G. van, *Moraal en eigenbelang bij Thomas Hobbes en Adam Smith.* Rodopi, Amsterdam, 1979.

Menger C., *Principles of economics.* Free Press, New York, 1953.

Myrdal G., *The political element in the development of economic theory.* Harvard University Press, Cambridge, Mass., 1954.

Nijkamp P., *Naar een prijzenswaardig milieu?!* Van Gorcum, Assen, 1979.

Norgaard R.B., The case for methodological pluralism. *Ecological Economics* Vol. 1 (1989) pp.37-57.

Pigou A.C., *The economics of welfare.* MacMillan, London, 1932.

Robbins L., *An essay on the nature and significance of economic science.* Macmillan, London, 1932.

Robinson J., *Economic philosophy.* Aldine, Chicago Ill., 1962.

Schumacher E.F., *Small is beautiful: a study of economics as if people mattered.* Blond Briggs, London, 1973.

Solow R.M., The economics of resources and the resources of economics. *American Economic Review* Vol. 64 (1974) pp.1-14.

Underwood D.A. and P.G. King, On the ideological foundations of environmental economics. *Ecological Economics* Vol. 1 (1989) pp.315-34.

Walras L., *Elements of pure economics* (translation). Irwin, Homewood Ill., 1954.

Withagen C., Topics in resource economics. In: F van der Ploeg (ed.), *Advanced Lectures in Quantitative Economics*, Academic Press, London, 1990.

INDEX

Economy & Environment

1. F. Archibugi and P. Nijkamp (eds.): *Economy and Ecology: Towards Sustainable Development.* 1989 ISBN 0-7923-0477-2
2. J. Bojö, K.-G. Mäler and L. Unemo: *Environment and Development: An Economic Approach.* 1990 ISBN 0-7923-0802-6
3. J. B. Opschoor and D. W. Pearce (eds.): *Persistent Pollutants: Economics and Policy.* 1991 ISBN 0-7923-1168-X
4. D.J. Kraan and R. J. in 't Veld (eds.): *Environmental Protection: Public or Private Choice.* 1991 ISBN 0-7923-1333-X
5. J.J. Krabbe and W.J.M. Heijman (eds.): *National Income and Nature: Externalities, Growth and Steady State.* 1992 ISBN 0-7923-1529-4

KLUWER ACADEMIC PUBLISHERS – DORDRECHT / BOSTON / LONDON

MIX
Papier aus verantwortungsvollen Quellen
Paper from responsible sources
FSC® C105338

If you have any concerns about our products,
you can contact us on
ProductSafety@springernature.com

In case Publisher is established outside the EU,
the EU authorized representative is:
Springer Nature Customer Service Center GmbH
Europaplatz 3, 69115 Heidelberg, Germany

Printed by Libri Plureos GmbH
in Hamburg, Germany